WITHDRAWN

D1393198

£20.0
741.
Sl

700000 35218

ILLUSTRATION NOW!

VOLUME 2

JULIUS WIEDEMANN

ILLUSTRATION NOW!

VOLUME 2

TASCHEN

HONG KONG KÖLN LONDON LOS ANGELES MADRID PARIS TOKYO

CONTENTS   SOMMAIRE   INHALT

ON THE STATE OF THE ART (AND CRAFT) AND FUTURE OF ILLUSTRATION NOW

A dialogue between Steven Heller and Christoph Niemann

HELLER Illustration has changed so much since I was first introduced to it as a kid in the fifties, when it was primarily comprised of realistic and literally rendered tableaux of passages in text or products. The invasion of other media, like photography and video, has made that type of narrative illustration superfluous, but not entirely extinct. It was, however, largely replaced by more cerebral, symbolic and allegoric imagery that represented abstract concepts and psychological concerns. You are a veteran newbie, illustrating for a decade now, how have you experienced change? Has it been conceptual, technological, or both?

NIEMANN All the technological possibilities that computers brought to the table have certainly revolutionized the field. As a 10 year old I desperately searched for a way to fill my ink outlines with flat bright colors. I do consider Adobe Photoshop and Illustrator straightforward answers to my adolescent prayers. Nonetheless, other than for some more or less interesting visual vocabularies that have emerged, the computer hasn't changed the thinking or quality of illustrations much (and I want to remind all these old bitter illustrators who keep whining about how computers have ruined illustrations, that generations of artists have proved perfectly capable of doing dreadful work just with pencils, and watercolor).

HELLER You're right (take that bitter-ones!), but there has been a change in philosophical attitude at least, and what an illustration is supposed to do has also changed. The old illustrators were primarily doing editorial and advertising. Today the range of multimedia platforms is huge, from animation to toys to information graphics, etc.

NIEMANN The more significant change in illustration that I have witnessed is this: There seem to be a lot of new styles that emerge, but very few that disappear or completely fall out of fashion. There are so many "hip" styles that happily coexist —hard-edged computer generated images, the painterly California school, the odd little-doodle-with-a-funny-line-of-copy art— every "new" thing that emerges is now added to the canon of accepted styles, rather than replacing one with another. Similarly, I find that even the recent appetite for very elaborate baroque renderings has not made what I see as colder or more abstract conceptual approaches obsolete. Everything is doable and acceptable.

HELLER In the "good ole days" styles emerged (as if by magic, but really by one or two original form-givers), lasted for a relatively long time, and then vanished (or became passé). But I believe that began to change with the start of Push Pin Studios in 1955. Founders Seymour Chwast and Milton Glaser reintroduced once "old fashioned" styles, like Victorian, Art Nouveau, and Art Deco. And by mixing and matching the characteristics of these styles with their otherwise unique visual conceits they produced styles that were contemporary; being able to switch from one hybrid to another allowed Push Pin to stay fresh while at the same time referencing history. Today's illustrators wear their respective styles like an overcoat, and unless major changes in fashion occur overnight, they tend to keep that coat for many seasons, while adding accessories that keep it up-to-date. I don't mean to reduce all style to outerwear, because often style is the message, but I do think in this eclectic age, style is not as important as it was when an illustrator was known almost exclusively for their style. Why do you think the canon of modes and styles is continually expanding rather than contracting, and do you believe illustration is, in fact, overly stylized today?

NIEMANN Obviously the huge number of media outlets has led to an increased diversity of styles. There are a stunning number of cutting edge fashion/lifestyle magazines out there that provide an impressive stage for very experimental and diverse illustration. I think it is easier these days to expose your art to a wide audience without going through the large illustration venues (like *The New York Times, The New Yorker*, etc). As far as the importance of style goes, I don't think it has become any less important. The majority of illustrators still do have very recognizable personal styles, and this seems to be the way illustration is taught at schools. I would say that 80% of all illustration assignments go entirely for style. Most assignments for music, fashion and lifestyle don't require smart ideas, but a strong sensibility for visualizing trends and emotions. And as far as advertising illustration goes, I would guess that in 99 of 100 jobs the illustrator executes an idea that was given by the ad agency. What I find interesting is how in a lot of cases my taste as an illustration creator is different from what I like as an illustration consumer.

HELLER Ah! That brings up the nebulous, subjective yet soporific issue of taste. That's also the 8000 pound gorilla in the room. So much of what is deemed good, and therefore becomes popular, is rooted in tasty style. I have certain preferences rooted in certain passions or prejudices that have more to do Pavlovian responses than intelligence. I love Wayne Thiebaud's luscious paintings of cakes and pastries – I'd buy his art in a minute – but I find his approach difficult to translate as illustration. So, like you, my taste as an art director and admirer govern my interest in art (almost anything) to illustration (fairly specific). How would you describe the difference between creator and consumer? Is there something called "objectively good illustration?"

NIEMANN OK. I guess it's time to bring out the strained metaphors. Jennifer Lopez probably makes five million bucks a year with the shape of her behind. But it's not her behind that earns the money; it's the behind in the context of music, fashion and perfume that gets the job done. I know it's a rather unglamorous approach to illustration (and design), but I think illustration is good when it gets the job done (sell toothpaste, draw interest to a story or just make people laugh). I am pretty sure that if I would pick my favorite drawing ever and put it on a cover of the latest JLo album, it would tank badly. On the other hand, it might be pretty hard to convince the editors of the *New York Times Op-Ed* page that Mrs. Lopez's behind doing ANYTHING would appropriately illustrate an article discussing supply-side economics (then again, the readers of the Times may disagree...). My ultimate goal as an illustrator is to draw a black square on a white background, which will make people laugh thunderously, just because in this particular context it is the perfect, witty and ultimate solution.

HELLER That's a very heady dialectic. But illustration must function in context. Art needn't be so contextual. So let's talk about the nitty-gritty about art. How do you define it? There is so much crossover between what's done on the page and in the gallery. Is this forced? Is this inevitable? As an illustrator then, what kind of artist are you?

NIEMANN That's exactly where it becomes difficult. Very generally speaking art doesn't have to "work" at all. As you said, an illustration has to function. A drawing for an article about the "Best Mutual Fund picks for 2009" has to somehow make the reader interested in mutual funds picks for 2009. The Mona Lisa just has to sit in the Louvre, smile and make people think whatever they want. But a lot of the stories that are illustrated don't have such an obvious topic. A lot of what you see in magazines and ads is simply visual entertainment (and there's nothing wrong with that). Once the only goal of an illustration is to visually entertain, the boundaries to art become very blurry. I spend a lot of time in galleries and art shows and I often think, "Oh you stupid artist, this is a lame joke that has been done a thousand times in illustrations, only much better executed". But if you're an illustrator, and you want to play the art market, you have to be aware that you're up against Picasso, Hockney and Kippenberger. Good luck! But it's really not a matter of "quality". Certain images work best when they are looked at by ten million people on the cover of a magazine on one particular day, and then they're gone. Other images would be too bland, weird or obscure to communicate anything in such a short time to so many people.

HELLER Yes, some images are best when seen relatively small and surrounded by text. I can always tell – because it grates on me – when a so-called illustrator is trying to be a so-called fine artist. The work does not perfectly fit the space or function on the page. This is not to say that illustrations should be done to exact reproduction size – Ralph Steadman and Marshall Arisman draw and paint on an unmanageably large size, so they have to be photographed to fit into a scanner – and now illustrators are doing most everything on computer in Photoshop

> "IT IS EASIER THESE DAYS TO EXPOS[E]
> YOUR ART TO A WIDE AUDIENCE
> WITHOUT GOING THROUGH
> THE LARGE ILLUSTRATION VENUES.

or Illustrator, so original size is not even an issue. But what I'm saying is the illustrator must understand the context, the fine artist needn't have any concern for the audience whatsoever. It's the job of the *audience* to decipher and appreciate (or not) the artist's work. The other way around is usually true for illustration. Conversely it is incumbent on the illustrator to provide understandable cues. Again, this is not always cut and dry. Saul Steinberg, for instance, challenged his audience to play his perceptual game – indeed to decode his illustrations, lest they don't understand them. In fact, his illustrations were not routinely tied to texts at all. They were freestanding images placed in editorial – mass media – contexts.

"THE ILLUSTRATOR MUST UNDERSTAND THE CONTEXT, THE FINE ARTIST NEEDN'T HAVE ANY CONCERN FOR THE AUDIENCE WHATSOEVER."

NIEMANN For me Steinberg is the greatest, smartest and most inventive illustrator ever. But ultimately it is the reproductions of his art that make him so outstanding. The value of the famous "View from Ninth Avenue" (the cover of the *The New Yorker* that has been reproduced and copied so often) is that it was printed as a cover, and that it struck a chord with millions of readers. The physical drawing itself pales in comparison. Of course Steinberg is a wonderful artist, but I just don't think his work would have had half as much impact if he had shown in galleries and museums instead of working for the *The New Yorker*. I recently saw new paintings by Christopher Wool — big, arrogant, smudgy grey canvasses. I can't imagine how they could possible communicate anything to anybody as a reproduction. But they were so incredibly beautiful that I could imagine living with one of them as the only thing on my walls for the next 20 years, and I would trade them in for any Steinberg original in a heartbeat.

HELLER I'm not sure I would do the same. I'd covet a Steinberg original, as I covet a signed color print I own by George Grosz. But you nailed the major difference between fine art and illustration (at least one of them): monumentality. The other is durability. Few illustrations are monumental, and most are not meant to endure the test of time. Your own work, which is always clever, and often brilliantly so, is no match for, say, Walton Ford in terms of its sheer ambition. While this is arguable apples and oranges – what you do is not intended to be monumental and Ford's paintings are – as an illustrator your tendency is to solve the problem at hand – you work in a state of transient immediacy. The fine artist is not restricted by time or place. This is why I think quite a few illustrators like Brad Holland, Seymour Chwast, Sue Coe and Marshall Arisman, and even graphic designers like Paula Scher (with her amazing hand-lettered maps of the world) have, perhaps as respites from the rigors of their daily work, gone BIG! This is not to say in each case the results are not BIG illustrations (some are), but the physical size, and the visionary ambition, is greater than any common illustration. Which leads me to ask if you as an illustrator feel that illustration in general, is basically an intellectually small art form?

NIEMANN Paul Rand said "art is not an intention, good work is an intention, art happens when you're lucky". The moment you consciously try to make big art, you're in trouble. Maybe in 300 years some benign spot illustration I did in 1998 will be hailed as the new "Starry Night"? Tom Bachtell's loose ink portraits in the *The New Yorker* are small, but I think the variations of Bush's eyebrows alone (how many are there now, 500?) add up to a truly monumental and visionary artwork. It's just administered in small, weekly chunks. I love Paula Scher's paintings, but I wouldn't want to say that they are intellectually "smaller" than, for example, her posters for the public theater.

"IT'S THE JOB OF THE AUDIENCE TO DECIPHER AND APPRECIATE (OR NOT) THE ARTIST'S WORK."

HELLER Do you have aspirations to be a gallery artist?

NIEMANN If I tried to enter the art market (and maybe one day I will), I am afraid that my motive would not be that I have *the* visual answer the world has been waiting for, but that my true reasons would be to a) seek fame that the illustration world can't offer b) show them stupid artists that I can do it too or c) make a couple of quick millions.

HELLER Motives for entering the art world are many, but what are the motives for entering the illustration world? Could there be a reason beyond that of hard currency or swooning fans? As I look at the work in *Illustration Now* I wonder whether any of these images, as smart and beautiful as some may be, stand up to the scrutiny of "what is art?" But they do stand up to "what is illustration?" By this I want to know if the standards are higher or lower for illustration than for fine art. Can the illustrator get away with more or less? I believe that illustration can be difficult because navigating through the clichés of illustration is harder than navigating through clichés of fine art. Do fine artists have more latitude to experiment? Do you experiment or are you locked into the prison of your success?

NIEMANN I take illustration very, very seriously. I do experiment. I try to extend my vocabulary and question my approach constantly. Quite often I experience something close to physical pain when I try to solve a problem. And what for? Both as a consumer and as a creator of illustration I simply think it is the most exciting visual field out there. Not because it is easy to produce or to digest, but because it is the most immediate visual interpretation of the world I live in. Here's another analogy: Art is Johann Sebastian Bach, and illustration is Glenn Gould. Bach wrote music that is by all accounts genius, but what I am even more interested in is the interpretation of that music. When Gould plays the Goldberg variations, once fast and energetic, and once slow and almost melancholic, you think you are listening to different compositions. Who is the greater "artist"? I can't say, but as far as visuals go I personally enjoy being a performer instead of a creator. As an illustrator I feel I live in a visual candy store that consists of ancient and modern art, pop culture, folk art, advertising, comics, religious iconography, simply EVERYTHING. Illustration takes all these wonderful images and reinterprets, rearranges, reinvents and sometimes makes fun of them.

"I TRY TO EXTEND MY VOCABULARY AND QUESTION MY APPROACH CONSTANTLY."

HELLER Great analogy! But I think you are a little too Pollyanna (or Shirley Temple). Certainly, if the interpreter takes the interpretation to new heights then new art, made on the shoulders of other art (or artists), is the result. But illustration is not always Glenn Gould; sometimes it's MUSAK – a neutered version, reduced to pure imitation of the original art form. I agree that illustration is a rich amalgam of culture (that's exactly what I love about it) and illustrators soak it all up, yet I'd argue that too much of what you call rearrangement is actually appropriation and not reinvention. How many times have you seen surrealism just used as Dali or Magritte would have used it? How often does primitivism rear its head as an illustrational style? I don't want to be overly critical, but I want to believe that illustration offers more than regurgitation of formerly *avant-garde* techniques.

NIEMANN Of course there is a ton of shallow crap out there. But I find that neither surprising nor disturbing. A lot of what's happening in this art world is shallow and superficial. If illustration mirrors the world we live in, it *has* to be as stupid (or smart) as its subjects. When I do a lightweight idea for a magazine, it will at least only live a couple of hours, maybe give somebody a little laugh and then go where it belongs: in the garbage. How many spaced out flying cows of Chagall did I have to endure in my life? Or take Jawlensky, a fine artist indeed, but how many of these idiotic twenty second paintings of faces has he produced (whenever I see them, I get reminded of art class and imagine the teacher go: "Alexej, you have to put a little bit more effort into this"). You want me to keep going? What about the never-ending supply of cute kids in the Constable village paintings? El Greco, anyone? And then we haven't even entered the real dungeons of what people put above their sofas these days (Kinkade & Co.). If you compare the entire field of illustration with Van Gogh, Max Beckmann and Gerhard Richter, of course we're dead meat.

HELLER Okay meat-boy, with that in mind, what do you think are the truly novel, unique, inventive, indeed transcendent approaches that are practiced today? And don't feel shy about naming names.

NIEMANN I think Maira Kalman's visual diaries on *The New York Times* website are outstanding, also Tina Berning's drawings or Genevieve Gauckler's little characters. Maybe they all consider themselves artists, but I don't care.

HELLER Well, it's time for that inevitable question about the future of illustration. This book is called *Illustration Now*, but most of the now work is a few years old. Do you worry about what's next?

NIEMANN When I was at art school my teacher Heinz Edelmann told us the following about the future of illustration: "If aliens landed on planet earth tomorrow and taught you what graphic design looks like 20 years from now, it won't help you a bit, because nobody would get it. All that matters is what design looks like today and maybe a year from now". Hence, "illustration now" is all that really counts. Let's say aliens did in fact land on earth tomorrow, and showed us how to turn rocks into gold and live forever in harmony. That would probably be the immediate end to business magazines and political journalism — and with that, spot illustrations on mortgage rates, tax increases, intolerance and war. How could I possibly make a living? Should I start thinking about ideas about living on other planets today because I think it will be a relevant topic in 2020?

HELLER Given the current state of earth right now, other planets sound appealing. But wouldn't that be a great opportunity to make the illustration world a little different, or maybe everything would be radically different? What are the radical (or seismic) shifts in illustration?

NIEMANN Maybe what will come next will look "radically next" in retrospect. But I doubt that anybody will get up one morning and come up with the next new thing that revolutionizes illustration. The big challenge for me (and my competitors) is to stay fresh and understand what's happening out there in order to react to it in an interesting, relevant way. When you are a scientist, there are a number of big open questions out there: a cure for AIDS, energy efficiency, etc. Maybe you can sit in your basement, think really, really hard, and come up with the big trick that will change the world. There's no such thing for illustra-

"EVEN IF SOMEBODY AS GOOD AS NORMAN ROCKWELL WOULD COME AROUND AGAIN, I DON'T KNOW IF HE OR SHE COULD TURN SUCH SKILL IN A COMPARABLE CAREER."

tors. Design, art and illustration are about interaction with your audience. Since the audience changes constantly, the challenges change as well. Five years ago I thought it would all be about animation in the near future. Of course there is a lot of animation out there today, but who could have guessed that huge surge in luscious paintings or (at least technically) fairly conservative graphic novels? The one prediction I would dare make is that it won't be possible to base a lifelong career in illustration on one or two tricks (be it a style, a particular kind of humor or even something like a "voice", no matter how successful you are at any given time). Even if somebody as good as Norman Rockwell would come around again, I don't know if he or she could turn such skill in a comparable career. Illustration will blend even more into art, design, literature, advertising and journalism and will become even more fast paced. My personal role model (even if it is somebody about five sizes too large) is Milton Glaser. He is an impeccable draftsman and designer and has always had perfect ideas. But the reason he has been able to have such a long and incredibly successful career is that he is a true communications visionary.

HELLER What I want to see in the future is more independent art on a mass level, for a large public. The graphic novel phenomenon is a good start. But I believe that somewhere down the pike, especially with generations raised on YouTube and other video media, the visual artist – the illustrator – will have even more relevance and impact. Picture literacy will be studied in school in the same way we've learned readin' writin' and rithmetic. Learning the codes and symbols of art will be as important as learning to parse a poem. If you were working towards this future, what would you do?

AS AN ART DIRECTOR I LOOK AT N ILLUSTRATOR'S IMAGE-MAKING S AN EXTENSION OF MY OWN EELINGS AND THOUGHTS."

NIEMANN Illustration for me is still about a single sender, and multiple (ideally thousands or even millions of) receivers. The whole Web 2.0 phenomenon is about millions of senders that are simultaneously receivers. I don't know how much longer I'll get away with producing work that is so one-directional. I am a great fan of Ze Frank. He is not an illustrator, he's a web performer, but I think what he is doing on his website is the most accurate glimpse I have of what the future might look like: he is an incredibly smart, witty and entertaining guy. He throws out these really funny ideas and let's his audience "interfere" with his creations. It's all about interactivity (he had a three minute daily video cast, and for one episode he had is audience write a script, that was then acted out), but at the end of the day, he is still the "designer". It is still his brilliant way of playing with language, images, codes, etc., that makes people interested in his work.

HELLER Interactivity is great, but what about integrity of the product – or image? Don't too many cooks spoil the broth? Won't committees, so to speak, drain the life out of originality? Are artists willing to let their art be manipulated and reinterpreted? I think that has the makings of a real nightmare because images will be communalized.

NIEMANN It's very easy to become gloomy, when you imagine that audiences will be so fractionalized that it becomes impossible to create something that hits a chord with a large number of people. But I think, for the foreseeable future, folks still want to be entertained, and Ze's website is a beautiful example of how that can be done. Ultimately it was, is and will be about creating work that connects you with your readers. You have to be genuinely interested in how your audience thinks. So maybe I will have to go out there and get me some new fans through a MySpace page.

HELLER I realize that MySpace and YouTube and FaceBook have simply scratched the surface of what will come in the next few years. But in closing I want to address a fundamental concern, which is the art and craft of image-making. Most illustrators, indeed most plastic artists in general, started as doodlers making marks on paper that somehow reflect internal turmoil or emotion of some kind. The talented (or tenacious) ones were somehow able to harness this rawness into style and manner, as well as conceptual methods that serve a mass communicative function. As an art director I look at an illustrator's image-making as an extension of my own feelings and thoughts. I take it very personally. Of course, I will "interfere" insofar as I can help make it better (or worse, as the case may be), but I fear that if illustration turns into this formless state that you describe, it will no longer have the artistic power it has had. By way of concluding tell me what good all this technology will bring to the art of picture-making, and how will illustration retain its value in the process?

NIEMANN There are people out there that have spent the last thirty years drooling over Robert Crumb's cross-hatching. They may be insane, but I can absolutely sympathize! Apart from all intellectual communication involved in illustration, it is of course the joy of seeing a complex expression or gesture reduced to a couple of simple ink strokes that is the most immediate appeal. And as every illustrator knows (at least the mere mortals among us), you pretty much have to waste your entire youth drawing all those fighting monsters, spaceships and explosions to achieve even remotely convincing results. Craft can be refined at school, and I certainly have learned *a lot* from a number of very, very intelligent and benevolent people. But ultimately, illustration is not a profession you pick after talking to your student career counselor. There is no god-given right to make a living drawing strange pictures, but I am confident, that there will always be plenty of weirdoes like myself who will keep trying nonetheless.

STEVEN HELLER
Co-Chair MFA Designer as Author Program
at the School of Visual Arts, New York

CHRISTOPH NIEMANN
Illustrator
www.christophniemann.com

"PICTURE LITERACY WILL BE STUDIED IN SCHOOL IN THE SAME WAY WE'VE LEARNED READIN' WRITIN' AND RITHMETIC. LEARNING THE CODES AND SYMBOLS OF ART WILL BE AS IMPORTAN' AS LEARNING TO PARSE A POEM."

LE PRÉSENT ET LE FUTUR DE L'ART (ET DES MÉTIERS) DE L'ILLUSTRATION

Un dialogue entre Steven Heller et Christoph Niemann

HELLER L'illustration a complètement changé depuis que j'ai découvert ce monde lorsque j'étais enfant dans les années cinquante, alors qu'elle consistait principalement à faire une traduction graphique réaliste et littérale de passages de textes ou de produits. L'invasion d'autres supports tels que la photographie ou la vidéo a rendu superflu ce type d'illustration narrative, mais ne l'a pas fait complètement disparaître. Il a cependant été en grande partie remplacé par des images plus cérébrales, plus symboliques et allégoriques, qui représentaient des concepts abstraits et des préoccupations psychologiques. Vous êtes un nouveau venu vétéran, vous faites de l'illustration depuis une dizaine d'années maintenant. Quelle a été votre expérience du changement ? A-t-il été conceptuel, technologique, ou les deux ?

NIEMANN Toutes les possibilités technologiques que les ordinateurs ont apportées ont sans aucun doute révolutionné le domaine. Lorsque j'avais dix ans, je cherchais désespérément un moyen de remplir mes contours à l'encre d'aplats unis de couleurs vives. Maintenant, je considère qu'Adobe Photoshop et Illustrator sont les réponses à mes prières d'adolescent. Cependant, à part quelques vocabulaires visuels plus ou moins intéressants qui sont apparus, l'informatique n'a pas beaucoup changé la philosophie ou la qualité des illustrations (et je veux rappeler à tous les illustrateurs aigris qui n'arrêtent pas de dire que les ordinateurs ont ruiné les illustrations, que des générations entières d'artistes ont prouvé que l'on peut très bien faire un travail atroce rien qu'avec des crayons et de l'aquarelle).

HELLER Vous avez raison (prenez ça, les aigris !), mais il y a quand même eu un changement dans l'attitude philosophique, et ce qu'on attend des illustrations a également changé. Les illustrateurs d'antan travaillaient essentiellement dans l'édition et dans la publicité. Aujourd'hui, la gamme de plateformes multimédias est immense, de l'animation aux jouets en passant par le graphisme d'information, etc.

NIEMANN Le changement le plus significatif que j'aie pu voir dans l'illustration, c'est qu'il semble que de nombreux styles nouveaux apparaissent, mais très peu disparaissent ou se démodent complètement. Un grand nombre de styles « en vogue » cohabitent dans la joie et la bonne humeur (les images hyper définies générées par ordinateur, l'école californienne picturale, les gribouillis accompagnés d'une ligne de texte humoristique). Chaque nouveauté s'ajoute au canon des styles acceptés, plutôt que de remplacer les anciens. De la même façon, je trouve que même le récent intérêt pour les rendus très baroques et élaborés n'a pas fait oublier des approches conceptuelles que je considère plus froides ou plus abstraites. Tout est faisable et acceptable.

HELLER Au « bon vieux temps », les styles apparaissaient (comme par magie, mais en fait à partir d'un ou deux instigateurs originaux), duraient un temps relativement long, puis disparaissaient (ou se démodaient). Mais je pense que cela a commencé à changer avec la création de Push Pin Studios en 1955. Les fondateurs, Seymour Chwast et Milton Glaser, ont relancé des styles « démodés », comme le style victorien, l'Art nouveau ou l'Art déco. En mélangeant et en assortissant les caractéristiques de ces styles avec leurs concepts visuels originaux, ils ont produit des styles contemporains. En passant d'un hybride à l'autre, Push Pin a réussi à rester original tout en faisant référence à l'histoire. Les illustrateurs d'aujourd'hui portent leurs styles respectifs comme on porte un pardessus, et à moins que des changements importants ne se produisent d'un jour à l'autre dans la mode, ils tendent à garder ce pardessus durant de nombreuses saisons, et y ajoutent des accessoires pour rester au goût du jour. Je ne veux pas réduire le style à quelque chose de superficiel, parce que souvent le style lui-même est le message, mais je pense qu'à notre époque caractérisée par l'éclectisme, le style n'est pas aussi important qu'il l'était lorsqu'un illustrateur était connu presque exclusivement pour son style. Pourquoi pensez-vous que le canon des modes et des styles s'agrandit continuellement plutôt que de se contracter, et pensez-vous qu'aujourd'hui l'illustration est en fait trop stylisée ?

NIEMANN Il est évident que le nombre immense de supports média a conduit à une diversité croissante des styles. On trouve un nombre impressionnant de magazines d'avant-garde sur la mode et les styles de vie qui sont une plateforme impressionnante pour des illustrations très expérimentales et diverses. Je pense qu'il est plus facile aujourd'hui d'exposer son art pour un vaste public sans passer par les voies royales de l'illustration (comme *The New York Times*, *The New Yorker*, etc.). En ce qui concerne l'importance du style, je ne pense pas qu'elle soit moindre aujourd'hui. La plupart des illustrateurs ont encore des styles personnels très reconnaissables, et il semble que l'illustration soit enseignée de cette manière dans les écoles. Je dirais que 80 % de tous les projets d'illustration sont entièrement axés sur le style. La plupart des projets dans les domaines de la musique, de la mode et des styles de vie ne requièrent pas des idées brillantes, mais une grande sensibilité pour visualiser les tendances et les émotions. Et en ce qui concerne l'illustration publicitaire, je dirais que dans 99 projets sur 100 l'illustrateur exécute une idée qui lui a été donnée par l'agence de publicité. Ce que je trouve intéressant, c'est que dans de nombreux cas mes goûts en tant que créateur d'illustrations diffèrent de ce que j'aime en tant que consommateur d'illustrations.

HELLER Ah, cela nous amène à la question nébuleuse, subjective et néanmoins soporifique du goût. C'est aussi un sujet que l'on ne peut évidemment pas passer sous silence. Une grande partie de ce que l'on considère comme bon, et donc qui devient populaire, prend ses racines dans un style au goût sûr. J'ai certaines préférences qui viennent de certaines passions ou de certains préjugés, qui ont plus à voir avec des réactions pavloviennes qu'avec l'intelligence. J'adore les tableaux somptueux de gâteaux et de pâtisseries de Wayne Thiebaud, je les achèterais sans hésiter, mais je trouve que son approche est difficile à transposer dans l'illustration. Tout comme vous, mes goûts en tant que directeur artistique et amateur d'art gouvernent l'intérêt que je porte à l'art (presque tout) et à l'illustration (plus spécifique). Comment décririez-vous la différence entre créateur et consommateur ? Peut-on parler d'une « illustration objectivement bonne » ?

« JE PENSE QU'IL EST PLUS FACILE AUJOURD'HUI D'EXPOSER SON ART POUR UN VASTE PUBLIC SANS PASSER PAR LES VOIES ROYALES DE L'ILLUSTRATION. »

NIEMANN OK. Je pense qu'il est temps de ressortir les bonnes vieilles métaphores. Jennifer Lopez gagne probablement cinq millions de dollars par an simplement grâce à la forme de son derrière. Mais ce n'est pas son derrière qui gagne l'argent, c'est le derrière dans le contexte de la musique, de la mode et du parfum qui fait tout le boulot. Je sais que c'est une approche pas très glamour de l'illustration (et du design), mais je pense qu'une illustration est bonne lorsqu'elle est efficace (vendre du dentifrice, attirer l'attention sur une histoire ou simplement faire rire). Je suis à peu près sûr que si je prenais mon dessin préféré et que je le mettais sur la couverture du dernier album de JLo, ce serait un fiasco total. D'autre part, il serait assez difficile de convaincre les rédacteurs des pages éditoriales du *New York Times* que le derrière de Mme Lopez, sous quelque angle que ce soit, pourrait illustrer de façon satisfaisante un article sur l'économie de l'offre (et pourtant, les lecteurs du *Times* seraient peut-être enchantés..). En fin de compte, mon objectif en tant qu'illustrateur est d'arriver à dessiner un carré noir sur fond blanc qui fera rire les gens à s'en tenir les côtes, tout simplement parce que, dans son contexte, ce sera une solution parfaite, pleine d'esprit et impossible à améliorer.

HELLER C'est une dialectique implacable. Mais l'illustration doit fonctionner dans son contexte, alors que l'art, pas forcément. Alors parlons de la réalité concrète de l'art. Comment le définissez-vous ? Il y a tant de croisements entre ce que l'on fait sur une page et pour une galerie. Est-ce forcé ? Est-ce inévitable ? En tant qu'illustrateur, quel genre d'artiste êtes-vous ?

NIEMANN C'est exactement là que les choses se compliquent. D'une manière très générale, l'art n'a pas besoin de « marcher » du tout. Comme vous l'avez dit, une illustration doit fonctionner. Un dessin pour un article sur les « Meilleurs fonds communs de placement pour 2009 » doit arriver à intéresser le lecteur aux fonds de placement pour 2009. Mona Lisa peut se contenter d'être au Louvre, de sourire et d'évoquer aux spectateurs ce qu'ils ont envie de penser. Mais dans l'océan de documents illustrés, beaucoup n'ont pas un sujet aussi évident que les fonds de placement. Une grande part de ce que vous voyez dans les magazines et dans les publicités est du pur divertissement visuel (et il n'y a rien de mal à ça). Lorsque l'objectif de l'illustration est de servir de divertissement visuel, les frontières avec l'art deviennent très floues. Je passe beaucoup de temps dans les galeries et les expositions artistiques, et je pense souvent « ah, stupide artiste, cette astuce boiteuse a déjà servi à des milliers d'illustrations, là elle est tout simplement mieux exécutée ». Mais si vous êtes un illustrateur, et que vous voulez vous frotter au marché de l'art, il faut savoir que vous vous mesurez à Picasso, à Hockney et à Kippenberger. Bonne chance ! Mais ce n'est vraiment pas une question de « qualité ». Certaines images fonctionnent mieux lorsqu'elles sont vues par dix millions de personnes en couverture d'un magazine un certain jour, puis qu'elles disparaissent. D'autres images seraient trop fades, trop bizarres ou trop obscures pour communiquer quoi que ce soit en aussi peu de temps et pour un public aussi nombreux.

« L'ILLUSTRATEUR DOIT COMPRENDRE LE CONTEXTE, ALORS QUE L'ARTISTE N'A PAS À SE SOUCIER DU TOUT DU PUBLIC. »

HELLER Oui, certaines images fonctionnent mieux en petit format, entourées de texte. Je remarque toujours (parce que ça me fait grincer) lorsqu'un soi-disant illustrateur essaie d'être un soi-disant artiste. Son travail ne s'adapte pas parfaitement à son espace ou à sa fonction dans la page. Cela ne veut pas dire que les illustrations devraient être faites au format exact de reproduction (Ralph Steadman et Marshall Arisman dessinent et peignent à une échelle incroyablement grande, et il faut photographier leurs œuvres pour les passer au scanner), et maintenant les illustrateurs font presque tout sur ordinateur, sous Photoshop ou Illustrator, alors la question de la taille originale ne se pose même pas. Mais ce que je veux dire, c'est que l'illustrateur doit comprendre le contexte, alors que l'artiste n'a pas à se soucier du tout du public. C'est le *public* qui doit déchiffrer et apprécier (ou non) le travail de l'artiste. Pour l'illustration, c'est généralement le contraire. Inversement, il revient à l'illustrateur de fournir des repères compréhensibles. Mais là encore, toute règle à des exceptions. Saul Steinberg, par exemple, a mis son public au défi de jouer *son* jeu de la perception, et en fait de décoder ses illustrations, au risque que le public ne les comprenne pas. En fait, ses illustrations n'étaient généralement même pas reliées à un texte. Il s'agissait d'images indépendantes placées dans des contextes rédactionnels, dans des médias de masse.

NIEMANN Pour moi, Steinberg est le plus grand, le plus intelligent et le plus inventif de tous les illustrateurs. Mais en fin de compte, ce sont les reproductions de ses œuvres qui le rendent aussi exceptionnel. La valeur de la célèbre *Vue depuis la 9e avenue* (la couverture du *New Yorker* qui a été si souvent reproduite et copiée) vient du fait qu'elle a été imprimée sous forme de couverture, et qu'elle a fait vibrer une corde chez des millions de lecteurs. Le dessin physique en lui-même est insignifiant en comparaison. Bien sûr, Steinberg est un magnifique artiste, mais je ne pense pas que son travail aurait eu la moitié de l'impact qu'il a eu s'il avait exposé dans des galeries ou des musées au lieu de travailler pour le *New Yorker*. Récemment, j'ai vu des tableaux de Christopher Wool — de grandes toiles arrogantes salies de gris. Je n'arrive pas à imaginer comment elles pourraient communiquer quoi que ce soit à qui que ce soit sous forme de reproductions. Mais elles étaient si incroyablement belles que je m'imaginais facilement vivre vingt ans avec l'une d'entre elles comme seule décoration sur mes murs, et je n'hésiterais pas à troquer un original de Steinberg pour elles.

HELLER Je ne crois pas que je ferais la même chose. Si j'avais un original de Steinberg je le garderais jalousement, tout comme je garde jalousement le tirage couleur signé par George Grosz que je possède. Mais vous avez mis le doigt sur la principale différence entre les beaux-arts et l'illustration (ou du moins sur l'une d'entre elles) : la monumentalité. La durabilité en est une autre. Peu d'illustrations sont monumentales, et la plupart ne sont pas censées résister à l'épreuve du temps. Votre propre travail, qui est toujours intelligent, et souvent très brillant, ne fait pourtant pas le poids face à, par exemple, Walton Ford, en termes d'ambition pure. Mais il faut comparer ce qui est comparable, et ce que vous faites n'est pas censé être monumental, alors que les tableaux de Ford le sont. En tant qu'illustrateur vous avez tendance à résoudre un problème posé, vous travaillez dans un état d'immédiateté transitoire. L'artiste ne connaît de limites ni temporelles ni spatiales. D'après moi, c'est pour cela qu'un certain nombre d'illustrateurs, comme Brad Holland, Seymour Chwast, Sue Coe et Marshall Arisman, et même des graphistes, comme Paula Scher (avec ses magnifiques cartes du monde recouvertes de mots écrits à la main), pour se reposer de la rigueur de leur travail quotidien, ont voulu voir les choses en GRAND ! Cela ne veut pas dire que dans chaque cas les résultats ne sont pas de GRANDES illustrations (il y en a), mais les dimensions physiques et l'ambition visionnaire sont plus grandes que pour une illustration courante. Ce qui m'amène à vous demander si, vous en tant qu'illustrateur, et l'illustration en général, représentez en fin de compte une forme d'art intellectuellement inférieure ?

NIEMANN Paul Rand a dit : « L'art n'est pas une intention, un bon travail est une intention. L'art arrive lorsque l'on a de la chance. » À partir du moment où l'on essaie consciemment de faire du grand art, on est mal parti. Peut-être que dans 300 ans l'une de mes petites illustrations d'article réalisées en 1998 sera considérée comme la nouvelle *Nuit étoilée* ? Les portraits à l'encre de Tom Batchell dans le *New Yorker* sont de petites dimensions, mais je pense qu'à elles seules, les variations sur les sourcils de Bush (combien y en a-t-il maintenant ? 500 ?) sont une œuvre d'art véritablement monumentale et visionnaire. Simplement, cette œuvre est administrée en petits morceaux hebdomadaires. J'adore les tableaux de Paula Scher, mais je ne dirais pas qu'ils sont intellectuellement « inférieurs » à, par exemple, ses affiches pour le théâtre public.

HELLER Aspirez-vous à être un artiste de galerie ?

NIEMANN Si j'essayais d'entrer sur le marché de l'art (et peut-être que j'essaierai un jour), je ne crois pas que ce serait parce que j'aurais trouvé *la* réponse visuelle que le monde attendait. Ma véritable motivation serait de a) rechercher une reconnaissance que le monde de l'illustration ne peut pas offrir, b) montrer à ces imbéciles d'artistes que je peux le faire moi aussi ou c) gagner quelques millions rapidement.

HELLER Il y a beaucoup de raisons pour vouloir entrer dans le monde de l'art, mais quelles sont les raisons pour entrer dans le monde de l'illustration ? Y a-t-il une raison autre que l'argent ? Ou faire se pâmer les fans ? Lorsque je regarde les œuvres dans *Illustration Now* je me demande si certaines de ces images, aussi intelligentes et belles que certaines puissent être, supporteraient la réponse à la question « qu'est-ce que l'art ? ». Mais elles supportent tout à fait la réponse à la question « qu'est-ce que l'illustration ? ». Ce que je cherche à savoir, c'est si les critères sont plus ou moins stricts pour l'illustration que pour les beaux-arts. L'illustrateur peut-il se permettre plus ou moins de choses ? Je pense que l'illustration peut être difficile parce qu'il est plus délicat de naviguer entre les clichés de l'illustration que de naviguer entre les clichés des beaux-arts. Est-ce que les artistes ont plus de marge de manœuvre pour faire des expériences ? Faites-vous des expériences, ou êtes-vous enfermé dans la prison de votre succès ?

NIEMANN Je prends l'illustration très, très au sérieux. Je fais des expériences. J'essaie d'enrichir mon vocabulaire et je remets constamment mon approche en question. Lorsque j'essaie de résoudre un problème, je ressens assez souvent quelque chose qui ressemble à de la douleur physique. Et pourquoi ? En tant que consommateur et en tant que créateur d'illustrations je pense simplement que c'est le domaine visuel le plus captivant qui soit. Non pas parce qu'il est

> « J'ESSAIE D'ENRICHIR MON VOCABULAIRE ET JE REMETS CONSTAMMENT MON APPROCHE EN QUESTION. »

facile à produire ou à digérer, mais parce que c'est l'interprétation visuelle la plus immédiate du monde dans lequel je vis. Voici une autre analogie : l'art c'est Johann Sebastian Bach, et l'illustration c'est Glenn Gould. Bach a composé de la musique géniale à tous points de vue, mais ce qui m'intéresse encore plus, c'est l'interprétation de cette musique. Lorsque Gould joue les variations de Goldberg, une première fois avec vivacité et énergie, puis une deuxième fois avec lenteur et mélancolie, on a l'impression d'entendre deux compositions différentes. Qui est le plus grand « artiste » ? Je ne saurais pas le dire, mais en ce qui concerne l'art visuel, personnellement je préfère être un interprète plutôt qu'un créateur. En tant qu'illustrateur j'ai l'impression de vivre dans un magasin de bonbons visuels : l'art ancien et moderne, la culture pop, l'art populaire, la publicité, la bande dessinée, l'iconographie religieuse, en un mot, TOUT. L'illustration prend toutes ces merveilleuses images et les réinterprète, les réarrange, les réinvente et parfois se moque d'elles.

HELLER Superbe analogie. Mais je pense que vous êtes un peu trop naïf. Certes, si l'interprète emmène l'interprétation vers de nouvelles hauteurs, alors le résultat est une nouvelle œuvre d'art, créée grâce à une autre œuvre d'art (ou à d'autres artistes). Mais l'illustration n'est pas toujours du Glenn Gould, parfois c'est de la musique d'ascenseur, une version neutralisée, réduite à la pure imitation de la forme artistique originale. Il est vrai que l'illustration est un riche amalgame de cultures (c'est justement ce que j'aime dans l'illustration), et les illustrateurs absorbent cette diversité, pourtant je dirais que trop de réarrangement, comme vous dites, est en fait de l'appropriation et non de la réinvention. Combien de fois avez-vous vu du surréalisme exactement à la manière de Dalí ou de Magritte ? Combien de fois le primitivisme pointe-t-il son nez derrière un style illustratif ? Je ne voudrais pas être trop critique, mais je veux croire que l'illustration offre plus que la simple régurgitation de techniques qui ont autrefois été d'avant-garde.

NIEMANN Bien sûr, on voit des tas d'illustrations médiocres et superficielles. Mais ça ne me surprend pas, et ça ne me dérange pas non plus. Une grande partie de ce que l'on voit dans le monde de l'art est médiocre et superficiel. Si l'illustration est un miroir du monde dans lequel nous vivons, elle *doit* être aussi stupide (ou intelligente) que les sujets qu'elle dépeint. Lorsque je travaille sur une idée légère pour un magazine, elle vivra au moins une ou deux heures, fera peut-être sourire quelqu'un, puis ira là où elle doit aller : à la poubelle. Combien de vaches volantes sous LSD de Chagall ai-je dû endurer au cours de ma vie ? Ou bien prenez Jawlensky. C'est un très bon artiste, mais combien de ces stupides portraits faits en vingt secondes a-t-il produits (quand je les vois, ça me rappelle les cours de dessin, et j'imagine le prof disant « Alexej, il faut faire un peu plus d'efforts »). Vous voulez que je continue ? Que dire de ces foules interminables d'enfants adorables dans les scènes villageoises de Constable ? Et le Greco, ça vous dit quelque chose ? Et encore, nous ne sommes même pas entrés dans les sables mouvants de ce que les gens mettent sur leurs murs aujourd'hui (Kinkade et compagnie). Si vous comparez l'ensemble du domaine de l'illustration à Van Gogh, Max Beckmann et Gerhard Richter, évidemment, on n'a aucune chance.

HELLER Ok, alors en gardant cela à l'esprit, parmi les approches contemporaines, d'après vous lesquelles sont véritablement nouvelles, originales, inventives, et en fin de compte transcendantales ? Et n'ayez pas peur de donner des noms.

NIEMANN Je pense que les journaux intimes visuels de Maira Kalman sur le site Internet du *New York Times* sont exceptionnels, ainsi que les dessins de Tina Berning ou les petits personnages de Geneviève Gauckler. Peut-être qu'elles se considèrent toutes comme des artistes, mais je m'en fiche.

HELLER Bien, il est temps de poser la question inévitable de l'avenir de l'illustration. Ce livre est intitulé *Illustration Now*, mais la plupart des œuvres de maintenant ont déjà quelques années. Est-ce que la suite vous préoccupe ?

NIEMANN Lorsque j'étais à l'école d'art, mon professeur Heinz Edelmann nous a dit, à propos du futur de l'illustration : « Si des extraterrestres atterrissaient sur la Terre demain et vous disaient à quoi ressemblera le graphisme dans 20 ans, ça ne vous aiderait pas, car personne ne comprendrait. Tout ce qui compte, c'est à quoi le graphisme ressemble aujourd'hui, et peut-être à quoi il ressemblera l'année prochaine. » Donc, « illustration now » est tout ce qui compte. Disons que des extraterrestres atterrissent effectivement sur Terre demain, et nous montrent comment transformer la pierre en or et vivre dans une harmonie éternelle. Ce serait probablement la fin immédiate des magazines économiques et du journalisme politique (et donc des illustrations sur les taux de prêt hypothécaire, sur l'augmentation des impôts, sur l'intolérance et sur la guerre). Comment gagnerais-je ma vie ? Devrais-je commencer à réfléchir dès aujourd'hui à des idées sur la vie sur les autres planètes parce que je pense que ce sera un sujet d'actualité en 2020 ?

HELLER Étant donné l'état de la Terre actuellement, la vie sur les autres planètes est une idée séduisante. Mais ne serait-ce pas une formidable occasion de changer un peu le monde de l'illustration ? Ou peut-être que tout serait radicalement différent. Quelles sont les tendances radicales (ou sismiques) dans l'illustration ?

MÊME SI QUELQU'UN D'AUSSI BON
UE NORMAN ROCKWELL SE MANIFESTAIT,
NE SAIS PAS SI CETTE PERSONNE
OURRAIT CONSTRUIRE UNE CARRIÈRE
OMPARABLE SUR UN TEL TALENT. »

NIEMANN Peut-être que ce qui va suivre sera considéré comme un « changement radical » plus tard, rétrospectivement. Mais je doute que quiconque se lève subitement un matin avec une idée qui révolutionnera le monde de l'illustration. Pour moi, le grand défi (et celui de mes concurrents) est de garder une certaine fraîcheur et de comprendre ce qui se passe dans le monde afin d'y réagir de façon intéressante et pertinente. Pour les scientifiques, il y a un certain nombre de grandes questions à résoudre. Le traitement du sida, les économies d'énergie, etc. Peut-être qu'un scientifique peut s'enfermer dans sa cave et se mettre à réfléchir vraiment intensément, puis inventer quelque chose qui changera le monde. Mais ça ne marche pas comme ça pour les illustrateurs. Le design, l'art et l'illustration sont faits d'interactions avec le public. Comme le public change constamment, les défis changent également. Il y a cinq ans, je pensais que l'avenir serait complètement axé sur l'animation. Bien sûr aujourd'hui on voit beaucoup d'animations, mais qui aurait pu prévoir la grande remontée des tableaux somptueux ou des romans graphiques plutôt conservateurs (du moins techniquement) ? La seule prévision que je me risquerais à faire, c'est qu'il sera impossible de baser toute une carrière sur un ou deux éléments (que ce soit un style, un certain type d'humour ou même quelque chose comme une « voix », quel que soit le succès que vous puissiez rencontrer à un moment ou à un autre). Même si quelqu'un d'aussi bon que Norman Rockwell se manifestait, je ne sais pas si cette personne pourrait construire une carrière comparable sur un tel talent. L'illustration va se confondre de plus en plus avec l'art, le design, la littérature, la publicité et le journalisme, et prendra un rythme encore plus effréné. Mon modèle personnel (même si je ne lui arrive pas à la cheville), est Milton Glaser. C'est un dessinateur et un designer impeccable, et il a toujours eu des idées parfaites. Mais la raison pour laquelle il a pu avoir une carrière aussi longue et un succès aussi immense, c'est que c'est un véritable visionnaire de la communication.

HELLER Ce que je veux voir davantage à l'avenir, c'est plus d'art indépendant à un niveau global, pour le grand public. Le phénomène des romans graphiques est un bon début. Mais je pense que plus tard, surtout avec les générations élevées devant YouTube et les autres médias vidéo, les artistes visuels (les illustrateurs) auront encore plus d'importance et d'impact. Le décryptage des images sera enseigné à l'école, tout comme nous avons appris à lire, à écrire et à compter. L'apprentissage des codes et des symboles de l'art sera aussi important que d'apprendre à décortiquer un poème. Si vous travailliez à la préparation de ce futur, que feriez-vous ?

NIEMANN Pour moi, l'illustration est encore une affaire où il y a un seul émetteur, et de multiples récepteurs (dans l'idéal, des milliers ou même des millions). Tout ce phénomène du Web 2.0 est une affaire où il y a des millions d'émetteurs qui sont en même temps récepteurs. Je ne sais pas pendant combien de temps encore je pourrai continuer à produire un travail aussi unidirectionnel. Je suis un grand fan de Ze Frank. Ce n'est pas un illustrateur, c'est un intervenant artistique sur Internet, mais je pense que ce qu'il fait sur son site est l'aperçu le plus révélateur de ce à quoi l'avenir pourrait ressembler. C'est un type incroyablement intelligent, spirituel et amusant. Il lance un tas d'idées vraiment marrantes et laisse son public « interférer » avec ses créations. Il s'agit avant tout d'interactivité (il avait une émission vidéo quotidienne d'une minute, et pour un épisode, il a demandé à son public d'écrire le scénario, puis l'a joué), mais au bout du compte, c'est quand même lui le « créateur ». C'est quand même l'intelligence avec laquelle il joue avec le langage, les images, les codes, etc. qui fait que les gens s'intéressent à son travail.

HELLER L'interactivité c'est très bien, mais qu'en est-il de l'intégrité du produit (ou de l'image) ? Trop de cuisiniers ne gâchent-ils pas la sauce ? Est-ce que les comités, pour ainsi dire, ne risquent pas de trop diluer l'originalité ? Est-ce que les artistes sont disposés à voir leur art manipulé et réinterprété ? Je pense que cela a tout des prémisses d'un cauchemar, parce que les images seront communautarisées.

NIEMANN Il est très facile de devenir lugubre, lorsqu'on imagine que le public sera tellement fractionné qu'il deviendra impossible de créer quelque chose capable de toucher une corde sensible chez un grand nombre de personnes. Mais je pense que, pour l'avenir prévisible, les gens voudront encore être divertis, et le site Internet de Ze Frank est un magnifique exemple de la façon de le faire. En fin de compte il s'est toujours agi, et il s'agira toujours, de créer quelque chose qui vous relie à vos lecteurs. Il faut être véritablement intéressé par la manière dont votre public pense. Alors peut-être qu'il faudra que j'aille me chercher de nouveaux fans par le biais d'une page dans MySpace.

HELLER Je sais bien que MySpace, YouTube et FaceBook ne sont que des avant-goûts de ce qui arrivera dans les prochaines années. Mais pour conclure, j'aimerais parler d'un sujet fondamental : l'art de la création d'images. La plupart des illustrateurs, et d'ailleurs la plupart des artistes plasticiens en général, ont commencé par être des gribouilleurs dont les taches sur le papier reflétaient d'une manière ou d'une autre une émotion intérieure. Ceux qui avaient du talent (ou de la ténacité) ont d'une manière ou d'une autre réussi à canaliser cette primitivité et à en tirer un style et un savoir-faire, ainsi que des méthodes conceptuelles qui remplissent une fonction de communication de masse. En tant que directeur artistique, je vois le processus de création d'image des illustrateurs comme une extension de mes propres sentiments et pensées. Je le prends très personnellement. Bien sûr, je vais « interférer » dans la mesure où je peux aider à améliorer cette image (ou à la dégrader, le cas échéant), mais j'ai peur que si l'illustration parvient à cet état informe dont vous parlez, elle n'aura plus le pouvoir artistique qu'elle avait. En manière de conclusion, dites-moi ce que toute cette technologie va apporter de bien à l'art de la création d'images, et comment l'illustration réussira-t-elle à conserver sa valeur ?

NIEMANN Il y a des gens qui ont passé les trente dernières années à s'extasier sur la technique de hachures croisées de Robert Crumb. Ils sont peut-être fous, mais je les comprends très bien ! À part toute la communication intellectuelle qui joue dans l'illustration, c'est bien sûr la joie de voir une expression ou un geste complexe réduits à quelques simples traits d'encre qui fait l'attrait le plus immédiat de l'illustration. Et comme tous les illustrateurs le savent bien (ou du moins ceux d'entre nous qui sont de simples mortels), il faut en gros passer toute sa jeunesse à dessiner des monstres, des vaisseaux spatiaux et des explosions pour arriver à un résultat à peu près convaincant. On peut affiner la technique à l'école, et j'ai sans aucun doute appris *beaucoup* auprès de plusieurs personnes très très intelligentes et bien disposées à mon égard. Mais en fin de compte, l'illustration n'est pas un métier que l'on choisit en parlant avec un conseiller d'orientation. Personne ne naît avec un droit divin à gagner sa vie en dessinant des images bizarres, mais je suis sûr qu'il y aura toujours des tas de cinglés comme moi qui continueront d'essayer quoi qu'il arrive.

STEVEN HELLER
Coprésident du *MFA Designer as Author Program*
de la *School of Visual Arts*, New York

CHRISTOPH NIEMANN
Illustrateur
www.christophniemann.com

ZUR GEGENWÄRTIGEN LAGE UND ZUKUNFT DER ILLUSTRATION (ALS KUNST UND HANDWERK)

Ein Gespräch zwischen Steven Heller und Christoph Niemann

HELLER Die Illustration hat sich sehr verändert, seit ich als Kind in den 50er Jahren zum ersten Mal damit in Berührung kam. Damals ging es um realistische Darstellungen, die Texte veranschaulichen sollten. Die Invasion von anderen Medien wie Fotografie und Video hat diese Art von narrativer Illustration überflüssig gemacht, wenn sie auch noch nicht völlig ausgestorben ist. Sie wurde aber weitgehend durch eine intellektuellere, eher symbolische und allegorische Bilderwelt ersetzt, die abstrakte Vorstellungen und psychologische Aspekte darstellt. Du bist ja schon ein „alter" Newbie, illustrierst jetzt seit 10 Jahren. Wie hast du den Wandel erlebt? War er eher konzeptionell, eher technisch oder beides?

NIEMANN Die technischen Möglichkeiten, die durch Computer eröffnet wurden, haben den Bereich auf jeden Fall revolutioniert. Als 10-Jähriger suchte ich verzweifelt nach einer Möglichkeit, meine Tusche-Umrisszeichnungen mit matten kräftigen Farben zu füllen. Adobe Photoshop und Illustrator sind die direkten Antworten auf meine jugendlichen Gebete. Doch obwohl der Computer einige mehr oder weniger interessante visuelle Vokabulare hervorgebracht hat, haben sich die Denkweisen oder die Qualität von Illustrationen nicht wesentlich verändert (und an dieser Stelle möchte ich alle alten verbitterten Illustratoren, die ständig darüber jammern, dass Illustrationen durch Computer ruiniert wurden, daran erinnern, dass ganze Generationen von Künstlern durchaus in der Lage waren, nur mit Stiften und Wasserfarben absolut schreckliches Zeug zu produzieren).

HELLER Du hast recht (hört her, ihr Verbitterten!), aber zumindest die philosophische Einstellung hat sich doch geändert und auch die Vorstellung davon, was eine Illustration leisten soll. Die alten Illustratoren waren mit redaktionellen Texten und Werbung befasst. Heute ist das Spektrum an Multimedia-Bereichen riesig, von Animationen über Spiele bis hin zu Informationsgrafiken etc.

NIEMANN Ich glaube, entscheidender ist folgende Veränderung: Es tauchen viele neue Stile auf, aber nur sehr wenige davon verschwinden wieder oder kommen völlig aus der Mode. Es gibt so viele angesagte Stile, die friedlich nebeneinander bestehen – nüchterne Computerbilder, der malerische kalifornische Stil, die Kleines-Gekritzel-mit-komischer-Textzeile-Illustration – jede „neue" Richtung wird zum Kanon der akzeptierten Stile hinzugefügt, anstatt einen Stil durch einen anderen zu ersetzen. Ich stelle zum Beispiel fest, dass die neue Vorliebe für einen sehr barocken ausschweifenden Zeichenstil keineswegs das, was ich als einen kälteren oder abstrakteren Ansatz bezeichnen würde, verdrängt hat. Alles ist machbar und akzeptabel.

HELLER In den „guten alten Zeiten" tauchten Stile auf (anscheinend von Zauberhand, aber in Wahrheit von ein oder zwei originellen Köpfen erschaffen), hielten sich relativ lange und verschwanden schließlich in der Versenkung (oder kamen aus der Mode). Das änderte sich mit Gründung der Push Pin Studios 1955. Die Gründer Seymour Chwast und Milton Glaser führten „altmodische" Stile wie den viktorianischen Stil, Jugendstil und Art déco wieder ein. Durch Vermischen und neues Zusammensetzen der Charakteristika dieser Stile entstanden zeitgenössische Bildsprachen. Push Pin wechselte von einem Hybriden zum anderen und blieb dadurch gleichzeitig frisch und historisch verwurzelt. Illustratoren tragen heutzutage ihre jeweiligen Zeichenstile wie einen Mantel und wenn nicht über Nacht extreme modische Richtungswechsel eintreten, behalten sie den Mantel jahrelang und fügen nur aktuelle Accessoires hinzu, um auf der Höhe der Zeit zu bleiben. Ich möchte Stil nicht auf Bekleidung, also auf etwas Äußerliches reduzieren, weil Stil häufig die Botschaft ist. Aber ich glaube schon, dass in diesem eklektizistischen Zeitalter Stil nicht so wichtig ist wie früher, als Illustratoren fast ausschließlich für ihren Stil bekannt waren. Warum, denkst du, weitet sich der Kanon an Moden und Stilen ständig aus, anstatt sich zu verkleinern? Und glaubst du, dass Illustration heutzutage überstilisiert ist?

NIEMANN Sicherlich hat die enorme Menge an medialen Möglichkeiten zu einer größeren Stilvielfalt geführt. Es gibt unglaublich viele innovative Mode- und Lifestyle-Magazine, die als Plattform für sehr experimentelle Illustrationen unterschiedlichster Art dienen. Heutzutage ist es, glaube ich, leichter, seine Kunst einem breiten Publikum zu präsentieren, ohne dabei die etablierten Anlaufstellen (wie *The New York Times*, *The New Yorker* etc.) anzusteuern. Ich glaube aber nicht, dass Stil weniger wichtig geworden ist. Die meisten Illustratoren haben immer noch persönliche Zeichenstile mit hohem Wiedererkennungswert und so scheint Illustration auch unterrichtet zu werden. Ich würde sagen, 80% aller Illustrationsaufträge richten sich nach dem Stil. Bei den meisten Aufträgen aus den Bereichen Musik, Mode und Lifestyle geht es nicht um gute Ideen, sondern um die Fähigkeit, Trends und Emotionen zu visualisieren. Im Bereich der Werbeillustration würde ich schätzen, dass bei 99 von 100 Aufträgen der Illustrator eine Idee ausführt, die von der Werbeagentur entwickelt wurde. Was ich interessant finde, ist, dass in vielen Fällen mein Geschmack als Schöpfer von Illustrationen abweicht von dem, was mir als Konsumenten von Illustrationen gefällt.

HELLER Aha, da sind wir bei der verschwommenen, subjektiven und ausgiebig erörterten Frage des Geschmacks, die immer irgendwann auftaucht. Vieles von dem, was als gut gilt und deshalb populär wird, ist einfach instinktiv ansprechend. Ich habe einige Vorlieben, die auf bestimmten Gelüsten oder Vorurteilen beruhen und die mehr mit Pawlow'schen Reflexen zu tun haben als mit Intelligenz. Ich liebe zum Beispiel Wayne Thiebauds appetitanregende Gemälde von Kuchen und Süßigkeiten – ich würde sofort etwas von ihm kaufen –, aber ich finde es schwierig, seinen Ansatz allgemein

> „HEUTZUTAGE IST ES LEICHTER, SEINE KUNST EINEM BREITEN PUBLIKUM ZU PRÄSENTIEREN, OHNE DABEI DIE ETABLIERTEN ANLAUFSTELLEN ANZUSTEUERN.

auf die Illustration zu übertragen. Wie bei dir bestimmt auch mein Geschmack als Artdirector und Bewunderer mein Interesse an Kunst (alles Mögliche) und Illustrationen (ziemlich spezifisch). Wie würdest du den Unterschied zwischen Schöpfer und Konsument definieren? Gibt es so etwas wie eine „objektiv gute Illustration"?

NIEMANN O.k., Zeit, die überstrapazierten Metaphern rauszuholen. Jennifer Lopez verdient wahrscheinlich fünf Millionen Dollar mit ihrem Hintern. Aber es ist nicht der Hintern an sich, der so viel einbringt; es ist der Hintern im Kontext von Musik, Mode und Parfüm, der den Erfolg ausmacht. Ich weiß, dass das ein ziemlich bodenständiger Zugang zu Illustration (und Design) ist, aber ich bin der Meinung, dass eine Illustration dann gut ist, wenn sie erfolgreich ist (das heißt, Zahnpasta verkauft, Interesse an einer Geschichte weckt oder einfach Leute zum Lachen bringt). Ich bin mir ziemlich sicher, dass meine absolute Lieblingsillustration auf dem Cover des neuesten JLo-Albums nicht besonders erfolgreich wäre. Andererseits wäre es wahrscheinlich schwierig, die Redakteure der Kommentarseite der *New York Times* davon zu überzeugen, dass der Hintern von Frau Lopez jemals – auch wenn er eine Wirkung hat – eine angemessene Bebilderung eines Artikels über angebotsorientierte Wirtschaftspolitik wäre (die Leser der *Times* mögen da widersprechen ...). Mein ultimatives Ziel als Illustrator ist es, ein schwarzes Quadrat auf einen weißen Hintergrund zu malen und die Leute damit zum Lachen zu bringen, weil es in diesem bestimmten Kontext einfach die perfekte und zugleich komische visuelle Lösung ist.

HELLER Das ist ja eine verwegene Dialektik. Aber Illustration muss im Kontext funktionieren. Kunst hingegen muss es nicht. Lass uns also über Kunst reden. Wie definierst du sie? Es gibt so viele Überschneidungen zwischen dem, was auf dem Blatt entsteht, und dem, was in Galerien ausgestellt wird. Ist das forciert? Ist es unausweichlich? Was bist du als Illustrator für ein Künstler?

NIEMANN Genau da wird es schwierig. Generell gesprochen muss Kunst überhaupt nicht „funktionieren". Eine Illustration schon, wie du zu Recht sagst. Eine Zeichnung für einen Artikel über „Die besten Investmentfonds für 2009" muss den Leser irgendwie für Investmentfonds begeistern. Mona Lisa hingegen muss nur im Louvre hängen, lächeln und die Leute denken lassen, was sie wollen. Aber viele illustrierte Geschichten haben kein so spezifisches Thema. Vieles, was man in Zeitschriften und in der Werbung sieht, ist einfach visuelles Entertainment (und daran ist nichts verkehrt). Sobald es Ziel einer Illustration ist, visuell zu unterhalten, verwischen sich die Grenzen zur Kunst. Ich verbringe viel Zeit in Galerien und Ausstellungen und denke dabei oft: „Du blöder Künstler, das ist doch ein alter Witz, der schon tausend Mal in Illustrationen gemacht wurde, nur besser ausgeführt." Aber wenn du als Illustrator auf dem Kunstmarkt mitspielen willst, muss dir klar sein, dass du mit

Picasso, Hockney und Kippenberger konkurrierst. Viel Glück! Aber es geht nicht wirklich um „Qualität". Manche Bilder wirken am besten, wenn sie an einem bestimmten Tag von zehn Millionen Menschen auf einem Zeitschriftencover gesehen werden, und danach sind sie weg. Andere Bilder sind aber zu schlicht oder zu seltsam oder zu komplex, um in so kurzer Zeit etwas an so viele Menschen zu vermitteln.

HELLER Ja, manche Bilder wirken dann am besten, wenn sie klein und von Text umflossen sind. Ich kann immer erkennen – weil es mich wurmt –, wenn ein sogenannter Illustrator versucht, ein sogenannter Maler zu sein. Das Bild passt dann im Hinblick auf Größe und Funktion nicht genau in die Seite. Damit will ich nicht sagen, dass Illustrationen in dem genauen Abbildungsformat erstellt werden sollten – Ralph Steadman und Marshall Arisman zeichnen und malen in so unhandlich großen Formaten, dass die Bilder abfotografiert werden müssen, um auf einen Scanner zu passen – und heutzutage wird ja sowieso fast alles auf dem Computer in Photoshop oder Illustrator gemacht, sodass die Originalgröße kein Thema mehr ist. Was ich aber sagen will ist, dass der Illustrator den Kontext verstehen muss, während der bildende Künstler sich in keinster Weise um den Betrachter zu kümmern braucht. Es ist Aufgabe des Betrachters, das Werk des Künstlers zu interpretieren und zu würdigen (oder auch nicht). Für Illustrationen gilt meist das Gegenteil: Der Illustrator muss verständliche Hinweise geben. Auch hierbei gibt es natürlich Ausnahmen. Saul Steinberg zum Beispiel forderte sein Publikum zu einem visuellen Spiel heraus; sie sollten seine Illustrationen dechiffrieren. Diese waren oft überhaupt nicht an Texte gebunden, sondern wurden frei stehend innerhalb von redaktionellen Kontexten platziert.

„ES IST AUFGABE DES BETRACHTERS, DAS WERK DES KÜNSTLERS ZU INTERPRETIEREN UND ZU WÜRDIGEN (ODER AUCH NICHT)."

NIEMANN Für mich ist Steinberg der größte, klügste und innovativste Illustrator aller Zeiten. Aber letztendlich sind es die Reproduktionen seiner Bilder, die ihn so erfolgreich machen. Der Wert des berühmten „View from Ninth Avenue" (das Cover des *The New Yorker*, das so oft reproduziert und kopiert worden ist) liegt darin, dass es als Cover abgedruckt wurde und Millionen von Lesern ansprach. Die eigentliche Originalzeichnung verblasst dagegen. Natürlich ist Steinberg ein wunderbarer Künstler, aber ich glaube nicht, dass seine Arbeiten eine solche Wirkung gehabt hätten, wenn sie in Galerien und Museen gezeigt anstatt im *The New Yorker* abgedruckt worden wären. Vor Kurzem sah ich neue Gemälde von Christopher Wool – große, arrogante, schmutzig-graue Leinwände. Ich kann mir beim besten Willen nicht vorstellen, wie die als Druck irgendetwas kommunizieren könnten. Aber sie waren so unglaublich schön, dass ich durchaus gewillt wäre, für die nächsten 20 Jahre mit einem davon als einzige Wanddekoration zu leben. Und ich würde sofort ein Steinberg-Original dafür hergeben.

HELLER Ich bin mir nicht sicher, ob ich das auch täte. Ich würde ein Steinberg-Original schätzen, so wie ich einen handsignierten Farbdruck von George Grosz schätze, den ich besitze. Aber du sprichst da einen wesentlichen Unterschied zwischen bildender Kunst und Illustration an: Monumentalität. Ein anderer ist Langlebigkeit. Nur wenige Illustrationen sind monumental und darauf angelegt, die Zeiten zu überdauern. Deine eigenen Arbeiten, die immer clever sind, oft auf eine brillante Art, können im Hinblick auf pure Ambition zum Beispiel nicht mit den Werken von Walton Ford mithalten. Natürlich vergleicht man da Äpfel mit Birnen – deine Bilder wollen im Gegensatz zu denen von Ford ja gar nicht monumental sein – aber als Illustrator neigst du dazu, das gerade anstehende Problem zu lösen – du arbeitest in einem Zustand kurzlebiger Dringlichkeit. Der bildende Künstler hingegen ist nicht räumlich oder zeitlich eingeschränkt. Ich glaube, aus diesem Grund – als Erholung von den engen Auflagen ihrer täglichen Arbeit – sind einige Illustratoren wie Brad Holland, Seymour Chwast, Sue Coe und Marshall Arisman und sogar Grafikdesigner wie Paula Scher (mit ihren erstaunlichen handbeschrifteten Weltkarten) GROSS geworden. Das soll nicht heißen, dass dabei keine GROSSEN Illustrationen entstanden sind (in manchen Fällen schon), aber die physische Größe und der visionäre Ehrgeiz dieser großen Werke sind größer als bei einer normalen Illustration. Was mich zu der Frage führt, ob Illustration im Wesentlichen eine intellektuell kleine Kunstform ist.

NIEMANN Von Paul Rand stammt der Ausspruch: „Kunst entsteht nicht vorsätzlich. Gute Arbeit leistet man vorsätzlich, Kunst entsteht, wenn man Glück hat." Wer bewusst versucht, große Kunst zu schaffen, hat ein Problem. Vielleicht wird in 300 Jahren eine harmlose Illustration, die ich 1998 zeichnete, als die neue „Sternennacht" gefeiert werden. Tom Bachtells lockere Tuscheporträts im *The New Yorker* sind klein, aber allein die verschiedenen Variationen von Bushs Augenbrauen (wie viele gibt es inzwischen? 500?) ergeben ein wahrhaft monumentales und visionäres Kunstwerk. Es wird eben nur in kleinen wöchentlichen Häppchen serviert. Ich liebe die Gemälde von Paula Scher, würde aber nicht sagen wollen, dass sie intellektuell „kleiner" sind als zum Beispiel ihre Theaterplakate.

HELLER Möchtest du ein Galeriekünstler werden?

NIEMANN Wenn ich den Kunstmarkt betreten wollte (und eines Tages tue ich das vielleicht), wäre mein Motiv wohl nicht, dass ich *die* visuelle Antwort habe, auf die die Welt gewartet hat. Ich fürchte, die Gründe wären eher a) so berühmt zu werden, wie es mir als Illustrator nicht gelingen kann, b) diesen dummen Künstlern zu zeigen, dass ich genauso gut bin, oder c) schnell ein paar Millionen zu verdienen.

HELLER Es gibt viele Gründe, in die Kunstwelt einzutreten. Aber warum tritt man in die Welt der Illustration ein? Könnte es einen Grund geben jenseits von harter Währung – oder kreischenden Fans? Wenn ich die Arbeiten in *Illustration Now* betrachte, frage ich mich, ob diese Bilder – so intelligent und schön einige auch sein mögen – einer genauen Prüfung unter der Fragestellung „Was ist Kunst?" standhalten könnten. Aber können sie denn überhaupt der Fragestellung „Was ist Illustration?" standhalten? Im Grunde will ich wissen, ob es für Illustrationen höhere oder niedrigere Maßstäbe gibt als für Kunst. Wird Illustratoren mehr oder weniger nachgesehen? Ich glaube, dass Illustrieren schwieriger sein kann, weil es schwerer ist, die Klischees der Illustration zu umschiffen als die der Kunst. Haben bildende Künstler mehr Freiheit zu experimentieren? Experimentierst du oder bis du im Käfig deines Erfolgs gefangen?

NIEMANN Ich nehme das Illustrieren sehr, sehr ernst. Und ja, ich experimentiere. Ich versuche, mein Vokabular zu erweitern, und stelle meinen Ansatz permanent infrage. Oft erlebe ich fast so etwas wie physischen Schmerz, wenn ich versuche, ein Problem zu lösen. Und wofür das alles? Ich halte den Bereich der Illustration sowohl als Konsument als auch als Schöpfer für den aufregendsten visuellen Bereich, den es zurzeit gibt. Nicht, weil Illustrationen leicht zu produzieren oder zu konsumieren sind, sondern weil sie die unmittelbarste visuelle Interpretation der Welt, in der ich lebe, darstellen. Eine andere Analogie: Johann Sebastian Bach ist Kunst und Glenn Gould ist Illustration. Bach schrieb geniale Musik, aber ich interessiere mich noch mehr für die Interpretation dieser Musik. Wenn Gould die Goldberg-Variationen einmal schnell und energisch und ein andermal langsam und fast melancholisch spielt, scheinen es zwei unterschiedliche Kompositionen zu sein. Wer von beiden ist der größere „Künstler"? Das kann ich nicht beantworten, aber im Hinblick auf visuelle Kunst bin ich lieber ein ausführender als ein schaffender Künstler. Als Illustrator lebe ich in einem visuellen Süßwarenladen, der alte und moderne Kunst, Popkultur, Folk Art, Werbung, Comics, religiöse Ikonografie, einfach ALLES auf Lager hat. Die Illustration verwendet all diese wunderbaren Bilder, reinterpretiert und arrangiert sie, erfindet sie neu und macht sich manchmal über sie lustig.

> „ICH VERSUCHE, MEIN VOKABULAR ZU ERWEITERN, UND STELLE MEINEN ANSATZ PERMANENT INFRAGE."

HELLER Tolle Analogie. Aber ich denke, du siehst das etwas zu rosig. Wenn der Interpret das Werk zu neuen Gipfeln führt, dann entsteht neue Kunst auf den Schultern der alten Kunst (oder des Künstlers). Aber Illustration ist nicht immer Glenn Gould. Manchmal ist sie auch MUSAK – eine kastrierte Version, die die ursprüngliche Kunstform nur imitiert. Ich stimme dir zu, dass Illustration eine bunte Mischung an Kulturen umfasst (das liebe ich ja so daran) und dass Illustratoren diese Kulturen aufsaugen. Allerdings würde ich behaupten, dass zu viel von dem, was du Neuerfindung nennst, in Wahrheit nur eine unkreative Aneignung ist. Wie oft wird Surrealismus genau so eingesetzt, wie Dalí oder Magritte es taten? Wie oft erscheint Primitivismus als Illustrationsstil? Ich möchte nicht überkritisch sein, aber ich würde gerne glauben, dass Illustrationen mehr zu bieten haben als ein Wiederkäuen von ehemals avantgardistischen Stilen.

NIEMANN Natürlich gibt es viel oberflächlichen Mist, aber das finde ich weder überraschend noch beunruhigend. Vieles in der Kunstwelt ist nun mal hohl und oberflächlich. Wenn die Illustration die Welt widerspiegelt, in der wir leben, *muss* sie so dumm (oder klug) sein wie ihre Subjekte. Wenn ich eine belanglose Idee für eine Zeitschrift illustriere, lebt die Zeichnung wenigstens nur ein paar Stunden, entlockt vielleicht jemandem ein Schmunzeln und wandert dann dahin, wo sie hingehört: in den Müll. Aber wie viele verrückte fliegende Kühe von Chagall musste ich schon ertragen? Oder nehmen wir Jawlensky. Ein wirklich guter Künstler, aber wie viele von diesen idiotischen 20-Sekunden-Gesichtern hat er produziert? (Immer, wenn ich eins davon sehe, stelle ich mir vor wie sein Kunstlehrer zu ihm sagt: „Alexei, du musst dir etwas mehr Mühe geben.") Soll ich weitermachen? Was ist mit dem unerschöpflichen Kontingent an niedlichen Kindern in den Dorfgemälden von Constable? El Greco? Und damit befinden wir uns noch nicht mal in der Nähe der Abgründe dessen, was Leute sich heutzutage übers Sofa hängen (Kinkade & Co.). Vergleicht man das gesamte Feld der Illustration jedoch mit Van Gogh, Max Beckmann und Gerhard Richter, dann sind wir natürlich schnell weg vom Fenster.

HELLER O.k., o.k. Mit diesem Statement im Hinterkopf: Wo sind deiner Meinung nach heute die wahrhaft neuen, einzigartigen, innovativen, ja sogar transzendenten Ansätze? Und nur keine Scheu beim Nennen von Namen.

NIEMANN Ich halte Maira Kalmans visuelle Tagebücher auf der Website der *New York Times* für überragend. Auch die Zeichnungen von Tina Berning oder Geneviève Gaucklers kleine Figuren. Vielleicht sehen sie sich alle als Künstler, aber das ist mir egal.

HELLER Damit kommen wir zur unvermeidbaren Frage nach der Zukunft der Illustration. Dieses Buch heißt *Illustration Now*, aber die meisten Arbeiten sind schon ein paar Jahre alt. Machst du dir Sorgen darüber, was als Nächstes kommt?

NIEMANN Auf der Kunstschule sagte unser Lehrer Heinz Edelmann dazu Folgendes: „Wenn morgen hier Außerirdische landen würden und euch beibrächten, wie Grafikdesign in 20 Jahren aussieht, würde euch das nichts nützen, weil niemand es verstehen würde. Es zählt nur, wie Design heute und vielleicht in einem Jahr aussieht." Nur „Illustration Now" gilt also. Wenn Außerirdische wirklich morgen hier landen und uns zeigen würden, wie man Steine in Gold verwandelt und für immer in Frieden lebt, würde das wohl das Ende von Wirtschaftsmagazinen und politischem Journalismus bedeuten – und damit auch das Ende von Illustrationen zu Hypothekenraten, Steuererhöhungen, Intoleranz und Krieg. Wovon würde ich dann leben? Aber soll ich anfangen, darüber nachzudenken, ob andere Planeten bewohnbar sind, nur weil ich weiß, dass dies im Jahr 2020 relevant wird?

HELLER In Anbetracht des gegenwärtigen Zustands der Erde ist der Gedanke an andere Planeten durchaus verlockend. Aber wäre das nicht eine hervorragende Gelegenheit, um die Welt der Illustration zumindest etwas zu verändern? Oder vielleicht wäre alles radikal anders. Was sind radikale (oder seismische) Verschiebungen im Bereich Illustration?

> OGAR WENN ES NOCH EINMAL
> MANDEN WIE NORMAN
> OCKWELL GÄBE, WEISS ICH
> CHT, OB ER SEIN TALENT IN EINE
> NGEMESSENE KARRIERE
> MWANDELN KÖNNTE."

NIEMANN Vielleicht wird das, was als Nächstes kommt, im Rückblick „radikal" aussehen. Aber ich glaube nicht, dass irgendjemand eines Morgens aufwacht und das Genre der Illustration revolutioniert. Für mich (und meine Mitstreiter) besteht die Herausforderung darin, frisch zu bleiben und zu verstehen, was da draußen passiert, um in einer interessanten und relevanten Weise zu reagieren. Für einen Wissenschaftler gibt es eine Reihe von großen offenen Fragen: Wie heilt man Aids, wie erzielt man Energieeffizienz etc. Vielleicht kann man daheim in seinem Keller sitzen und grübeln und dann den großen Clou entdecken, der die Welt verändert. Aber für Illustratoren gibt es so etwas nicht. Bei Design, Kunst und Illustration geht es um Interaktion mit dem Publikum. Und da das Publikum sich ständig wandelt, verändern sich auch die Anforderungen. Vor fünf Jahren dachte ich, es würde sich bald alles nur noch um Animation drehen. Natürlich gibt es heute viel Animationskunst, aber wer hätte ahnen können, dass opulente Gemälde oder (zumindest technisch gesehen) recht konservative Graphic Novels einen solchen Aufschwung erleben würden. Das Einzige, was ich mich vorauszusagen wage, ist, dass man eine ganze berufliche Laufbahn nicht mehr nur mit ein oder zwei erfolgreichen Tricks wird bestreiten können (ob das nun ein Stil, eine besondere Art von Humor oder so etwas wie eine „Stimme" ist). Sogar wenn es noch einmal jemanden wie Norman Rockwell gäbe, weiß ich nicht, ob er sein Talent in eine angemessene Karriere umwandeln könnte. Die Grenzen der Illustration zu Kunst, Design, Literatur, Werbung und Journalismus werden noch fließender sein als jetzt. Und alles wird noch schnelllebiger sein. Mein persönliches Vorbild (auch wenn die Schuhe mir etwa fünf Nummern zu groß sind) ist Milton Glaser. Er ist ein hervorragender Zeichner und Designer und hatte immer perfekte Ideen. Aber seine lange und unglaublich erfolgreiche Laufbahn verdankt er der Tatsache, dass er ein Kommunikationsvisionär ist.

HELLER Ich möchte in der Zukunft mehr unabhängige Kunst mit großer Breitenwirkung sehen. Die Graphic Novel ist ein vielversprechender Anfang. Aber in Anbetracht dessen, dass Generationen mit YouTube und anderen Videomedien aufwachsen, glaube ich, dass der visuelle Künstler – der Illustrator – in Zukunft noch mehr Bedeutung und Einfluss haben wird. Bildsprache wird in der Schule dann denselben Stellenwert haben wie Lesen, Schreiben und Rechnen. Die Codes und Symbole der Kunst zu entziffern, wird genauso wichtig sein wie eine Gedichtinterpretation. Wenn du auf eine solche Zukunft hinarbeiten wolltest, was würdest du tun?

NIEMANN Illustration bedeutet für mich immer noch, dass ein einzelner Sender an viele (idealerweise Tausende oder Millionen) Empfänger ausstrahlt. Ich weiß aber nicht, wie lange man mir noch solche Einbahnstraßen-Werke abkauft. Ich bin ein großer Fan von Ze Frank. Er ist kein Illustrator, sondern ein Webkünstler, aber was er auf seiner Website macht, lässt mich erahnen, wie die Zukunft vielleicht aussehen könnte. Er ist unglaublich clever, geistreich und unterhaltsam. Er spuckt diese wirklich lustigen Ideen aus und lässt das Publikum dann aktiv daran teilnehmen. Es geht um Interaktivität (so produzierte er zum Beispiel eine tägliche dreiminütige Videosendung und eine Folge ließ er vom Publikum schreiben), aber unterm Strich ist er immer noch der „Designer". Es ist seine brillante Art, mit Sprache, Bildern, Codes etc. zu spielen, die die Menschen interessiert.

HELLER Interaktivität ist schön, aber was ist mit der Integrität des Produktes – oder des Bildes? Verderben nicht zu viele Köche den Brei? Sind „Gremien" nicht der Tod der Originalität? Sind Künstler bereit, ihre Werke manipulieren und neu interpretieren zu lassen? Ich finde die Vorstellung, dass Bilder kommunalisiert werden, albtraumhaft.

NIEMANN Man wird leicht trübselig bei der Vorstellung, dass das Publikum bald so aufgespalten ist, dass es unmöglich sein wird, etwas zu schaffen, was eine große Anzahl von Menschen berührt. Aber in der näheren Zukunft werden Menschen immer noch unterhalten werden wollen, glaube ich, und Ze Franks Website ist ein schönes Beispiel dafür, wie das funktionieren kann. Letztendlich geht es jetzt und in Zukunft darum, mit dem Leser in Verbindung zu treten. Du musst dich ernsthaft dafür interessieren, wie dein Publikum denkt. Vielleicht muss ich mir durch eine MySpace-Seite ein paar neue Fans beschaffen.

HELLER Mir ist klar, dass MySpace, YouTube und FaceBook nur an der Oberfläche dessen kratzen, was in den nächsten Jahren auf uns zukommt. Zum Schluss möchte ich noch ein Thema ansprechen, das mir sehr wichtig ist: die Kunst und das Handwerk der Bildproduktion. Die meisten Illustratoren, ja sogar die meisten Bildhauer, haben mit einem Gekritzel auf Papier angefangen, das irgendwie innere Unruhe oder Emotionen ausdrückt. Die Talentierten (oder Hartnäckigen) unter ihnen waren aber in der Lage, diese Rohheit des Ausdrucks zu einem Stil zu formen und als Mittel der Massenkommunikation einzusetzen. Als Artdirector betrachte ich die Bildersprache eines Illustrators als Ausdruck meiner eigenen Gefühle und Gedanken. Ich nehme das sehr persönlich. Natürlich mische ich mich ein, wenn ich meine, etwas verbessern (oder je nach Fall verschlechtern) zu können. Aber ich fürchte, dass Illustration, wenn sie wirklich diesen formlosen Zustand einnimmt, den du beschreibst, ihre künstlerische Kraft verliert. Verrate mir also zu guter Letzt, was diese ganze Technologie der Kunst des Bildermachens bringt und wie die Illustration dabei ihren Wert behalten kann.

> „BILDSPRACHE WIRD IN DER SCHULE DANN DENSELBEN STELLENWERT HABEN WIE LESEN, SCHREIBEN UND RECHNEN."

NIEMANN Manche Leute haben die letzten 30 Jahre damit verbracht, Robert Crumbs Schraffurstil zu verehren. Sie sind vielleicht verrückt, aber ich kann sie verstehen! Neben aller intellektuellen Kommunikation, die eine Illustration ausmacht, ist es einfach ein Vergnügen, wenn ein komplexer Gesichtsausdruck oder eine Geste auf ein paar einfache Tuschestriche reduziert werden. Und jeder Illustrator (zumindest die Sterblichen unter uns) weiß schließlich, dass du so ziemlich deine ganze Jugend mit dem Zeichnen von Monstern, Raumschiffen und Explosionen verschwenden musst, um auch nur entfernt überzeugende Resultate zu bekommen. Das künstlerische Handwerk kann auf Schulen verfeinert werden – und ich habe wirklich sehr viel von einigen sehr, sehr klugen und wohlwollenden Menschen gelernt. Aber letztlich wählt man die Illustration nicht als Beruf aus, nachdem man beim Berufsberater war. Es existiert kein gottgegebenes Recht darauf, mit dem Zeichnen von seltsamen Bildern seinen Lebensunterhalt zu verdienen. Aber ich bin zuversichtlich, dass es trotzdem immer genug schräge Typen wie mich geben wird, die es versuchen.

STEVEN HELLER
Co-Chair MFA Designer as Author Program
an der School of Visual Arts, New York

CHRISTOPH NIEMANN
Illustrator
www.christophniemann.com

„KUNST ENTSTEHT NICHT VORSÄTZLICH.
GUTE ARBEIT LEISTET MAN VORSÄTZLICH,
KUNST ENTSTEHT, WENN MAN GLÜCK HAT."
— PAUL RAND

"ART IS NOT AN INTENTION,
GOOD WORK IS AN INTENTION,
ART HAPPENS WHEN YOU'RE LUCKY."
— **PAUL RAND**

« L'ART N'EST PAS UNE INTENTION,
UN BON TRAVAIL EST UNE INTENTION.
L'ART ARRIVE LORSQUE L'ON A DE LA CHANCE. »
— **PAUL RAND**

CHRISSIE ABBOTT

NAME Chrissie Abbott
WEBSITE www.chrissieabbott.co.uk
LOCATION London, United Kingdom

AGENT YCN <www.ycnonline.com>
TOOLS Pen, pencil, paint, found images, scanner, Adobe Photoshop, Adobe Illustrator

CLIENTS The Barbican, The New York Times, Orange, Dazed & Confused, Lowlife, The Story Store

"I am not trying to change the world;
I just want to make things nice to look at."

« Je n'essaie pas de changer le monde, je veux simplement que les choses soient agréables à regarder. »

„Ich versuche nicht, die Welt zu verändern; ich möchte nur, dass Dinge schön aussehen."

3

1

2

1 Hunt + Gather
2 Hello, 2007
3 Bird Hair, 2007, Zip

MONIKA AICHELE

NAME Monika Aichele
WEBSITE www.monikaaichele.com
LOCATION 1 Berlin, Germany
LOCATION 2 New York, NY, USA

TOOLS Ink, acrylic, collage, digital media
CLIENTS The New York Times, Sueddeutsche Zeitung, The Guardian, Die Zeit, Doubleday, Bloomsbury, Penguin

AWARDS American Illustration, 3x3 ProShow, Society of Publication Designers, 100 Best Posters (Germany)

"To me, illustration is about discovering something new every day."

« L'illustration consiste pour moi à découvrir chaque jour quelque chose de nouveau. »

„Illustration bedeutet für mich, jeden Tag etwas Neues zu entdecken."

1 Summertime, 2006, personal work
2 "Don't Worry. Mama loves you anyway", 2006, personal work
3 Greenhorn, 2006, personal work

Nº
1

Greenhorn

A. RICHARD ALLEN

NAME A. Richard Allen
WEBSITE www.arichardallen.com
LOCATION Bournemouth, United Kingdom
TOOLS Brush, ink, paper, acrylic paint, pencil,
...rd, Adobe Photoshop

CLIENTS The Guardian, New Statesman,
The Times, The Financial Times, The Telegraph,
The Independent, Macmillan, BBC Worldwide,
Haymarket, The New York Times, Greenpeace

AWARDS Association of Illustrators
United Kingdom

1

1 12 Drummers, 2006, The Guardian
2 Hell's Angels, 2006, personal work

"My approach to illustration has shifted a little recently: I'm slowly emerging from a bunker where I'd been holed
...p, obsessively honing my style, blinking into the light of a million stimuli I'd ignored. I am appreciating more
...nd more being curious, flexible and spontaneous in my work. This may sound like a vapid testimony from a
...lf-help book but I do find that being receptive and not thinking of myself as a fixed, autonomous entity keeps
...e creative process absorbing."

« Dernièrement, mon approche de l'illustration a légèrement changé : je sors peu à peu d'un abri dans lequel je m'étais terré pour polir
...on style avec obsession, et je cligne des yeux à la lumière d'un million de stimuli que j'avais ignorés. Il me plait de plus en plus
...aborder mon travail avec curiosité, flexibilité et spontanéité. Tout cela sonnera comme un témoignage insipide tiré d'un ouvrage
...autoassistance, mais je pense que le fait d'être réceptif et de ne pas me voir comme une entité rigide et autonome rend le processus
...création captivant. »

...Mein Zugang zu Illustration hat sich in letzter Zeit etwas verändert. Ich krieche langsam aus einem Bunker hervor, in dem ich mich
...rschanzt hatte, um obsessiv an meinem Stil zu feilen, und blicke in das Licht von Millionen Anregungen, die ich bisher ignoriert hatte.
...n werde immer neugieriger, flexibler und spontaner in meiner Arbeit. Das klingt vielleicht wie eine hohle Phrase aus einem
...bsthilfebuch, aber ich stelle tatsächlich fest, dass der Schaffensprozess interessant bleibt, wenn ich offen bin und mich nicht als
...tgelegte autonome Einheit ansehe."

AREA3

NAME Area3
WEBSITE www.area3.net
LOCATION Barcelona, Spain

TOOLS Pencil, Adobe Illustrator, Adobe Freehand, Adobe Photoshop, Adobe Flash, 3D Studio Max, photos, mixed media

CLIENTS PlayStation, Nissan, Museu d'Art Contemporani de Barcelona, La Biennale di Venezia, Fossil, Comme des Garçons, Sonar
AWARDS OFFF, LAUS, Iman, Masters of the Groove, Premios Daniel Gil

2

1 Be area3, 2007, Beefeater Magazine
2 Unzziping Codes, 2004, Embassy of Spain in Seoul
3 Exhibitions for Forum Barcelona 2004

3

As in any other creative project, we work in a team in order to have different points of view when we analyze the project and define the main concept, the contents and the storyboard. We then research the images we need and look for examples that aesthetically fit the work. We like to reflect our surroundings with imagination and humor, try new things, experimenting and playing."

Comme pour n'importe quel autre projet créatif, nous travaillons en équipe afin de mettre divers points de vue en commun lorsque nous analysons les projets et que nous définissons le concept clé, le contenu et le story-board. Ensuite, nous recherchons les images dont nous avons besoin et des exemples adaptés au travail sur le plan esthétique. Nous aimons représenter ce qui nous entoure avec imagination et humour, essayer de nouvelles choses, faire des expériences et nous amuser. »

So wie bei jedem anderen kreativen Projekt auch, arbeiten wir im Team, um verschiedene Standpunkte zu haben, wenn wir das Projekt analysieren und das Hauptkonzept, die Inhalte und die Storyboard definieren. Dann recherchieren wir die Bilder, die wir brauchen, und suchen Beispiele, die ästhetisch zum Projekt passen. Wir reflektieren unsere Umgebung mit Fantasie und Humor, probieren neue Dinge aus, experimentieren, spielen."

MARSHALL ARISMAN

NAME Marshall Arisman
WEBSITE www.marshallarisman.com
LOCATION New York, NY, USA

TOOLS Oil, canvas, ragboard
CLIENTS Time Magazine, The Nation, Playboy, The New York Times, Esquire, Rolling Stone, The Progressive

AWARDS Society of Publication Designers, Society of Illustrators (Hamilton King Award), Communication Arts, AIGA, American Illustration

1 Last Tribe, 1990, Vison Press
2 Gary Gillmore, 1979, Playboy Magazine
3 Curse of Violence, 1982, Time Magazine

2

3

"I believe that personal vision can be printed on a page or hung on a gallery wall. Whatever form the image takes, it is, in the end, good or bad art."

« Je pense qu'une vision personnelle peut être imprimée sur une page ou accrochée dans une galerie. Sous quelque forme que ce soit, une image n'est au bout du compte rien d'autre que du bon ou du mauvais art. »

„Ich glaube, dass eine persönliche Vision sowohl auf eine Seite gedruckt als auch auf eine Galeriewand aufgehängt werden kann. Dabei entsteht gute oder schlechte Kunst, egal, welche Form das Bild annimmt."

ARNO

NAME Arn0
WEBSITE www.arn0.com
LOCATION Paris, France

AGENT 1 Debut Art, London, <www.debutart.com>
AGENT 2 Agent 002, Paris, <www.agent002.com>
TOOLS Adobe Photoshop

CLIENTS Coca-Cola, MTV, Penguin, Sony
PlayStation, Transworld, Berlin Philarmonic,
TONI&GUY, Men's Health, FHM, Loaded, Maxim,
The Sunday Times

1 Back to Love, 2006, Hedkandi, Ministry of Sound
2 Nu Cool, 2006, Hedkandi, Ministry of Sound
3 A Flowering Tree, 2006, Berlin Philarmonic Orchestra

3

2

Illustration. Not a melodic word like 'butter' or 'shampoo'. I try to avoid four syllable words as much as I can. Especially now that 'illustration' stands for 'clarification' or 'explanation'. Who needs that? I much prefer the original meaning: 'illumination'... I'd rather identify myself in keeping with the light metaphor: warm, uplifting, something everybody should get to create a sweet and mellow atmosphere in the bedroom. But that's just me..."

Illustration. Le terme n'est pas aussi chantant que ‹ beurre › ou ‹ shampooing ›. J'évite dans la mesure du possible les mots de quatre syllabes, surtout maintenant qu'‹ illustration › s'emploie pour ‹ clarification › ou ‹ explication ›. Qui peut bien vouloir de ça ? Je préfère de loin le sens premier d'‹ illumination › et me retrouve davantage dans la métaphore lumineuse : chaleur, gaieté, quelque chose dont tout le monde devrait disposer pour créer une atmosphère douce et veloutée dans sa chambre. Mais ce n'est que mon opinion... »

Illustration. Kein melodisches Wort wie ‚Butter' oder ‚Shampoo'. Ich versuche so weit wie möglich viersilbige Wörter zu vermeiden. Vor allem jetzt, wo ‚Illustration' für ‚Klarifikation' oder ‚Explikation' steht. Das braucht doch niemand. Ich bevorzuge die ursprüngliche Bedeutung: ‚Illumination'. Ich identifiziere mich lieber mit der Lichtmetapher: warm, erhebend, etwas, was jeder haben sollte, um eine lieblich-sanfte Stimmung im Schlafzimmer zu erzeugen. Aber das ist nur meine Meinung ..."

LISEL ASHLOCK

NAME Lisel Ashlock
WEBSITE www.liseljane.com
LOCATION New York, NY, USA
AGENT Heflinreps <www.heflinreps.com>

TOOLS Acrylic, wood panel
CLIENTS The New York Times Style Magazine,
3x3, Spin, CosmoGIRL!, Chicago Magazine,
Sephora, Abercrombie & Fitch

AWARDS American Illustration,
Communication Arts

1

2

3

1 Girl on Horse, 2006, personal work
2 Portrait of Patty Hearst, 2005, promotional
3 Boy on Deer, 2005, commission

"Lisel's illustration work has been described as being expressive and semi-surreal, while still maintaining a tangible quality. Being the daughter of a photographer, she strives to bring a clear breath of reality to her paintings, while never ignoring humanity's perplexing but subtle ambiguities."

« Les illustrations de Lisel ont été décrites comme expressives et moitié surréalistes, tout en conservant une qualité tangible. Fille de photographe, elle s'efforce de doter ses peintures d'une dose de réalisme, sans jamais oublier les ambiguïtés complexes et subtiles de l'humanité. »

„Lisels Arbeiten gelten als expressiv und semi-surreal, doch gleichzeitig konkret. Als Tochter eines Fotografen will sie den frischen Hauch der Realität in ihre Bilder einlassen, dabei aber niemals die verwirrenden, doch subtilen Zweideutigkeiten des menschlichen Daseins ignorieren."

4 Upstate in September, 2007, personal work
5 Portrait of Nico, 2005, promotional

6 Arcade Fire, 2007, Spin Magazine
7 Portrait of Sofia Coppola, 2004, promotional
8 Portrait of Norman Porter, 2006, Chicago Magazine

STEFANIE AUGUSTINE

NAME Stefanie Augustine
WEBSITE www.stefanieaugustine.com
LOCATION Providence, RI, USA
TOOLS Acrylic, collage, paper

CLIENTS The New York Times, Utne Reader, Food & Wine, Seventeen, Consumer Reports, The North American Review

AWARDS Art Directors Club, Communication Arts, Print, Society of Publication Designers

1

2

1 Math, 2006, personal work
2 Portrait of Prince William, 2007, personal work
3 A Heated Debate, 2004, personal work

My illustrations are entirely handmade, with painted images over layers of paper and fabric. I like to take inspiration from the emotional angle of an assignment, and try to select imagery that will reinforce the tone of the article."

Mes illustrations sont entièrement faites à la main, avec des images peintes sur des couches de papier et de tissu. J'aime me laisser inspirer par l'angle émotionnel d'une commande et j'essaie de sélectionner les images qui souligneront le ton de l'article. »

Meine Illustrationen sind komplett von Hand gemalt. Sie bestehen aus Bildern, die über Papierschichten und Stoff gemalt wurden. Ich greife gerne den emotionalen Aspekt eines Auftrags auf und versuche, Bilder auszuwählen, die den Ton des Artikels verstärken."

JASHAR AWAN

NAME Jashar Awan
WEBSITE www.jasharawan.com
LOCATION Brooklyn, NY, USA
TOOLS Pen, ink, Adobe Photoshop

CLIENTS The New Yorker, The New York Times, Dark Horse Comics, American Medical News, Vibe, The Stranger, The Progressive

AWARDS Society of Publication Designers, American Illustration, Society of Illustrators, 3x3

1 Balkan Beatbox, 2006, The New Yorker
2 Lemony Snicket's A Series of Unfortunate Events, 2004, The New Yorker

1

"Each of my drawings begins as a blind contour. Not intentionally imposing a style allows for a confident, candid line. In this way, the drawing features the hand's natural tendencies, similar to penmanship. The spontaneous nature of this method keeps the illustration creatively satisfying from sketch to finish."

« Je commence tous mes dessins par un contour aveugle. Le fait de ne m'imposer aucun style me permet d'avoir un tracé assuré et franc. De cette façon, le dessin obéit aux mouvements naturels de la main, un peu comme avec la calligraphie. Grâce à la spontanéité de cette méthode, le niveau de créativité de l'illustration est satisfaisant du début à la fin. »

„Alle meine Zeichnungen fangen als blinde Umrisszeichnungen an. Der Strich ist selbstbewusst und unvoreingenommen, weil ich mir nicht von vorneherein einen bestimmten Stil auferlege. Die Zeichnung gibt die natürliche Neigung der Hand wieder, ähnlich wie Kalligrafie. Das Spontane an dieser Methode macht den Prozess des Illustrierens von der Skizze bis zur Vollendung gleichbleibend befriedigend."

BARD

NAME Bard
WEBSITE www.hellobard.com
LOCATION 1 Oslo, Norway

LOCATION 2 London, United Kingdom
TOOLS Adobe Illustrator, Adobe Photoshop,
Adobe After Effects, Adobe Flash, pen, paper

CLIENTS Disney TVA, Red Magic Style, IdN/WIWP,
Play Imaginative, Radioactive, Telenor, Dinamo

"A magic popping mix of playful characters, absurd humor and bright colors, stirred together in a cauldron warmed by a soul on fire! It's Pop Art gone so very horribly wrong!"

« Un assortiment magique et détonant de personnages espiègles, d'humour absurde et de couleurs vives, le tout mélangé dans un chaudron chauffé par une âme en feu ! Du pop art qui a terriblement mal tourné ! »

„Eine magisch-knallige Mischung aus verspielten Figuren, absurdem Humor und grellen Farben, verrührt in einem Hexenkessel, der angewärmt wird von einer Seele in Flammen! Es ist eine völlig verkorkste Version von Pop Art!"

2

3

1-2 Netherworld, 2006, Disney TVA
3 Skull Cat, 2006, Stupid Devil
4 Skull Monkey, 2006, Stupid Devil

4

GEORGE BATES

NAME George Bates
WEBSITE www.georgebatesstudio.com
LOCATION Brooklyn, NY, USA
TOOLS Brush, ink, mixed media, Adobe Illustrator, Adobe Photoshop

CLIENTS American Express, Burton Snowboards, Comedy Central, Electra Entertainment, MTV, The New Yorker, The New York Times, Nick@Nite, Nickelodeon, The Wall Street Journal, Noggin, Sony Music, Vibe

AWARDS American Illustration, Art Directors Club Young Guns, Broadcast Design Association, Society of Publication Designers

2

1 Gidget, 2003, Surf Culture / David Carson
2 Respect Poster, 2006, Outhouse Communications

Guiding Star: '...making something singularly explicit through the pleasurable stimulation of consciousness.' – Susan Sontag"

Principe directeur : ‹ ...rendre quelque chose singulièrement explicite grâce à une stimulation agréable de la conscience. › – Susan Sontag »

Leitspruch: ‚... etwas zu verdeutlichen durch die angenehme Stimulation des Bewusstseins.' – Susan Sontag"

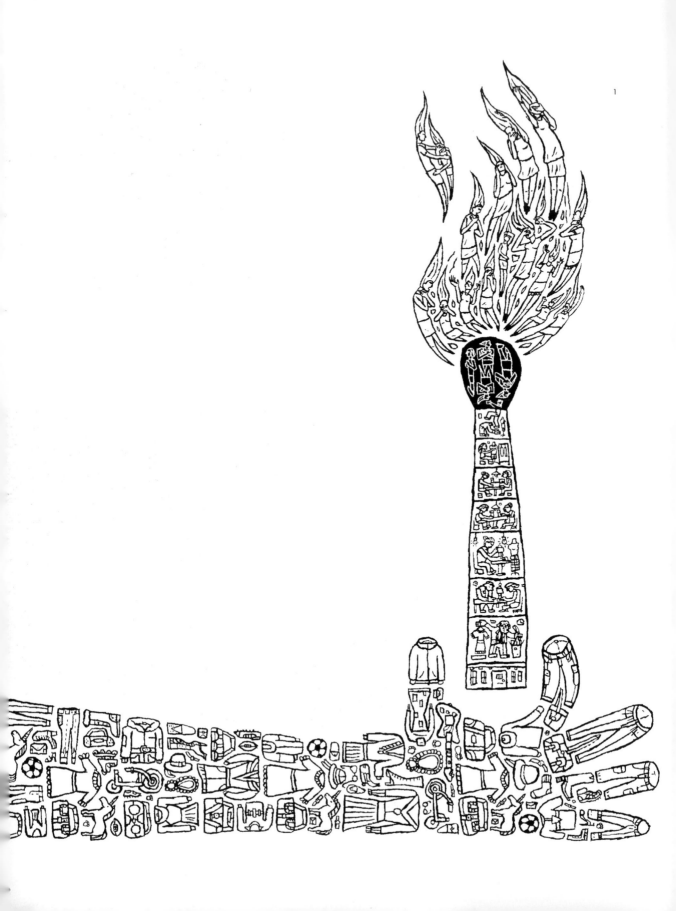

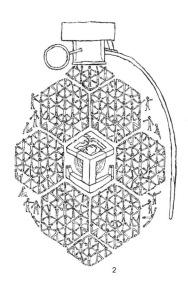

2

3

4

5

1 The Factories of Lost Children, 2006,
2 Blowing up an Assumption, 2005, The New York Times
3 Why Insist on the Surrender of Ratko Mladic?, 2006, The New York Times
4 Big Surf, cover #2, Big Magazine / David Carson
5 Big Surf, cover #1, Big Magazine / David Carson

MONTSE BERNAL

NAME Montse Bernal
LOCATION Barcelona, Spain
AGENT 1 Kate Larkworthy Artist Representation, New York, <www.larkworthy.com>

AGENT 2 Zegma, Madrid, <www.zegma.com>
TOOLS Mixed media, pen, pencil, paper, Adobe Photoshop, oil, canvas

CLIENTS BMW, Nike, Beefeater, Evian, Revlon, Wella, Camper, Marie Claire, Elle France, Nylon, Paste, The Guardian, The Times

1 Sunset, 2006, personal work
2 Icon, 2006, promotional
3 Neko, 2006, personal work

"I illustrate because I draw, because I draw, because I draw. I draw because it's the best I can do, because it's what I do best, because I have drawn since I was a little kid. I draw slowly. I draw with pencils. I draw in color. I draw black and white. I draw because I like the company of that face. I draw and do portraits. I draw someone and rediscover the person, then I draw all night long. And I draw the whole next day. Draw. Draw. Draw because I breathe. Breathe because I draw."

« J'illustre parce que je dessine, parce que je dessine, parce que je dessine. Je dessine parce que c'est le mieux que je puisse faire, parce que c'est ce que je sais faire de mieux, parce que je dessine depuis que je suis toute petite. Je dessine lentement. Je dessine avec des crayons. Je dessine en couleur. Je dessine en noir et blanc. Je dessine parce que j'aime la compagnie de ce visage. Je dessine et je fais des portraits. Je dessine quelqu'un et je redécouvre la personne, puis je dessine toute la nuit. Et je dessine aussi tout le jour suivant. Dessiner. Dessiner. Dessiner parce que je respire. Respirer parce que je dessine. »

„Ich illustriere, weil ich zeichne, weil ich zeichne, weil ich zeichne. Ich zeichne, weil ich darin gut bin, weil ich das am besten kann, weil ich zeichne, seit ich klein bin. Ich zeichne langsam. Ich zeichne mit Stiften. Ich zeichne in Farbe. Ich zeichne in schwarz-weiß. Ich zeichne, weil ich gern in Gesellschaft eines bestimmten Gesichts bin. Ich zeichne und mache Porträts. Ich zeichne jemanden und entdecke die Person neu. Dann zeichne ich die ganze Nacht. Und den ganzen nächsten Tag. Zeichnen. Zeichnen. Zeichnen, weil ich atme. Atmen, weil ich zeichne."

TINA BERNING

NAME Tina Berning
WEBSITE www.tinaberning.de
LOCATION Berlin, Germany
AGENT 1 CWC International, New York,
<www.cwc-i.com>

AGENT 2 CWC, Tokyo, <www.cwctokyo.com>
AGENT 3 2Agenten, Berlin, <www.2agenten.com>
TOOLS Mixed media

CLIENTS Vogue, The New York Times Magazine,
Vanity Fair, Cosmopolitan, Mercedes-Benz
AWARDS Art Directors Club (Germany),
Clio Awards, The One Show, American Illustration,
Communication Arts

1 Deurbanisation, 2005, Shrinking Cities Catalog
2 Bless Less, 2006, Licht2, Die Krieger des Lichts
3 What Men Are Able To, 2005, SZ-Magazin, Germany

2

1

3

"'No nipples, no guns, no cigarettes' was part of a briefing I once received from an American client. I was amused at first, but it later became a motto. Not that I don't show nipples or dissociate from cigarettes, I am just not interested in the monotonic triad of provocation. Drawing is more."

« ‹ Pas de mamelons, pas d'armes, pas de cigarettes › : ce sont les instructions que j'ai une fois reçues d'un client américain. Au début, ça m'a amusée, puis c'est devenu une devise. Non pas que je n'exhibe jamais de mamelons ou que je sois anti-tabac, mais la triade monotone de la provocation ne m'intéresse tout simplement pas. Le dessin va bien au-delà. »

„‚Keine Brustwarzen, keine Waffen, keine Zigaretten' hieß es mal im Briefing eines amerikanischen Kunden. Zuerst war ich nur amüsiert, aber später wurde es zu einem Motto. Nicht, dass ich keine Brustwarzen zeige oder mich von Zigaretten distanziere – ich bin nur nicht an dieser monotonen Triade der Provokation interessiert. Zeichnen ist mehr."

TIM BISKUP

NAME Tim Biskup
WEBSITE www.timbiskup.com

LOCATION La Canada, CA, USA
TOOLS Acrylic, gouache, paper, canvas, wood

"Most of my work is personal and/or allegorical.
I occasionally do illustration work, but focus mainly
on the fine art world, showing in galleries and museums."

« Mon travail est en grande partie personnel et/ou allégorique. Parfois, je fais de l'illustration,
mais la priorité reste les œuvres d'art exposées dans les galeries et les musées. »

„Die meisten meiner Arbeiten sind persönlich und/oder allegorisch. Manchmal illustriere ich auch,
aber ich konzentriere mich auf die Kunstwelt und stelle in Galerien und Museen aus."

1 Join or Die, 2007, personal work
2 Helper: Power #1, 2004, personal work
3 Scatterbrain, 2006, personal work

4 Golden Plague, 2004, personal work
5 Black Helium, 2004, personal work

5

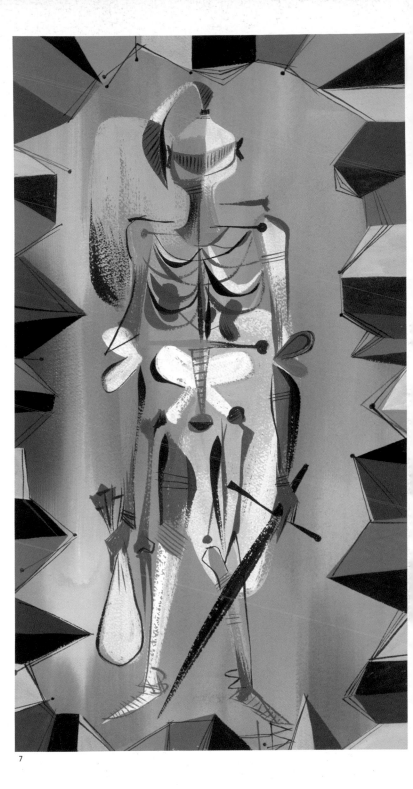

7

6 White Dragon, 2005, personal work
7 Pingala, 2006, personal work

ALEXANDER BLUE

NAME Alexander Blue
WEBSITE www.alexanderblue.com
LOCATION Seattle, WA, USA

AGENT Magnet Reps <www.magnetreps.com>
TOOLS Wacom Pad, Adobe Freehand, Adobe Photoshop, mixed media

CLIENTS Seventeen Magazine, The Stranger, San Francisco Chronicle, Target, Chickadee, Egreetings, Microsoft, MSN
AWARDS American Illustration

2

1 Michael, 2007, personal work
2 The Fox, 2006, personal work
3 Devil Cloud, 2006, personal work

"Based in colorful Seattle, Alexander Blue's irreverent illustrations poke fun at reality and make everyone from three to ninety-three, smile and snicker. Vibrant colors and pop imagery combine with creatures of his own creation and silly doodles to round out a wacky and whimsical style filled with energy and good cheer. Alexander Blue is eye-popping good fun."

« Inspirées par la ville riche en couleurs de Seattle, les illustrations irrévérencieuses d'Alexander Blue se moquent de la réalité et font rire et sourire tout le monde, de sept à soixante-dix-sept ans. Des couleurs vives et des images pop se mêlent à des créatures de son invention et à des ~~ri~~bouillages pour donner un style farfelu et étrange gonflé d'énergie et de joie. Avec Alexander Blue, c'est un festival d'amusement décalé. »

~~D~~er im bunten Seattle lebende Alexander Blue macht sich mit seinen ehrfurchtlosen Illustrationen über die Realität lustig und bringt ~~Me~~nschen zwischen drei und 93 zum Schmunzeln und Kichern. Er verbindet leuchtende Farben und Popsymbolik mit erfundenen Kreaturen ~~un~~d albernem Gekritzel zu einem verrückt-schrulligen Stil voller Energie und guter Laune. Alexander Blue steht für atemberaubenden Spaß."

4 Happy Bomb, 2007, J People Magazine
5 Mr. Wood, 2006, personal work
6 Sea Monster, 2006, personal work

MARC BOUTAVANT

NAME Marc Boutavant
LOCATION Paris, France
AGENT Heart <www.heartagency.com>

TOOLS Adobe Photoshop, pen tablet, pictures
CLIENTS Marks & Spencer, The New York Times,
Sky +, Martha Stewart Kids, Sony, Vodafone,
The New Yorker, Toyobo

AWARDS American Illustration,
Society of Publication Designers

1 Lapland, book Mouk's World Tour, 2007, Albin Michel Jeunesse
2 Elephant, 2005, Editions Sarbacane

2

"My work springs from a wry observation of life. My friends' personalities and mannerisms are transposed onto animals. These are creatures with a full range of emotions appealing to both adults and children alike. There's a lot of activity in my illustrations. Each scenario is felt and imagined in detail. Light-hearted horror, comedy and pathos are combined in a rich narrative."

« Mon travail naît d'une observation ironique de la vie. La personnalité et les manies de mes amis se métamorphosent en animaux, des créatures avec toute une gamme d'émotions qui plaisent autant aux adultes qu'aux enfants. Mes illustrations débordent d'activité. Chaque scénario est ressenti et pensé en détail. Une dose d'horreur plaisante, de comédie et de pathétique pour une narration riche. »

„Meine Arbeiten entspringen einem ironischen Blick auf das Leben. Ich übertrage die Persönlichkeiten und Eigenheiten meiner Freunde auf Tiere. Das sind dann Wesen mit einem vollständigen Gefühlsspektrum, die sowohl Erwachsene als auch Kinder ansprechen. In meinen Illustrationen ist viel los. Ich fühle und stelle mir jedes Szenarium vor. Beschwingter Horror, Komödie und Pathos sind zu einer komplexen narrativen Struktur verwoben."

3

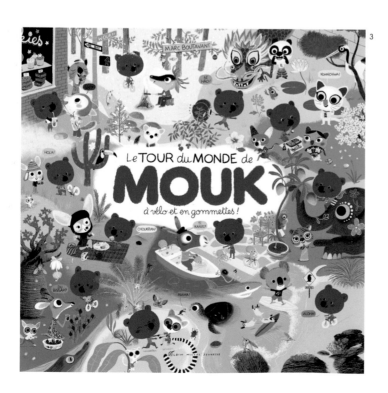

70

5

6

3 Book cover, Mouk's World Tour, 2007, Albin Michel Jeunesse
4 Abracadabra, 2004, DJECO
5 Momix, 2005, Momix Festival 2006
6 Sleepy, 2006, Éditions Nouvelles Images

JULIA
BRECKENREID

NAME Julia Breckenreid
WEBSITE www.breckenreid.com
LOCATION Toronto, Canada
AGENT Magnet Reps <www.magnetreps.com>

TOOLS Acrylic, watercolor, oil, glue, paper, mixed media
CLIENTS Chronicle Books, Mudpuppy, Intuit, Henry Holt, Parenting, Bride's, The New York Sun, The Week, Dance Magazine

AWARDS American Illustration, 3x3 ProShow, Society of Illustrators

2

1 Harbourfront Centre, 2007, Spacing Magazine
2 Untitled #2, 2007, Globe and Mail
3 Philip Seymour Hoffman, 2007, personal work

3

"Julia's vibrant painterly style has spanned the fields of magazines, book publishing, advertising, children's books, beauty, packaging, corporate identity, posters and newspapers. Julia was the curator of the travelling Boy's Club art exhibition, which showed in multiple cities in the USA and Canada. She has been teaching illustration since 2002 and is a chair of the ICON5 Illustration Conference."

« Le style vif et pictural de Julia a trouvé diffusion dans les magazines, l'édition, la publicité, les livres pour enfants, la cosmétique, les emballages, l'identité d'entreprise, les affiches et les journaux. Julia a été commissaire de l'exposition itinérante Boy's Club qui a parcouru plusieurs villes des États-Unis et du Canada. Elle enseigne l'illustration depuis 2002 et est à la présidence de la conférence ICON5 sur l'illustration. »

„Julias lebendiger, malerischer Stil wurde schon für Zeitschriften, Bücher, Werbung, Kinderbücher, Schönheitsprodukte, Verpackungsmaterial, Corporate Identity, Poster und Zeitungen eingesetzt. Julia war Kuratorin der Kunst-Wanderausstellung des ‚Boy's Club', die in vielen Städten in den USA und Kanada gezeigt wurde. Sie unterrichtet seit 2002 Illustration und ist Vorsitzende der ICON5 Illustration Conference."

4 Gentle Toxins, 2007, Howard Hughes Medical Institute
5 Feedbag, 2007, National Post
6 Untitled #1, 2007, Globe and Mail
7 Gillian Welch, 2005, personal work

GASTON CABA

NAME Gaston Caba
WEBSITE www.gastoncaba.com.ar
LOCATION Buenos Aires, Argentina

TOOLS Adobe Illustrator, Adobe Photoshop, pencil, paper

CLIENTS UNESCO, Orange, L.A. Gear, Benetton, Clarín, Milk Magazine, FRD Services

1 Brown Office, 2007, personal work
2 Petekooos!, 2007, personal work
3 At the Window, 2007, personal work
4 Gaston Custom, 2005, Gaston Custom,
FRD Services, What Productions (Hong Kong)

"I specialize in simple but strong concepts and colorful illustrations, not only for kids but also for adults who express themselves in a multi-colorful way and give a damn to be childish. I love to work on projects, managing multiple concepts to express either complex or simple ideas."

« Ma spécialité ? Les concepts simples mais forts et les illustrations riches en couleurs, non seulement pour les enfants, mais aussi pour les adultes qui s'expriment en multicolore et n'ont pas peur de paraître puériles. J'aime travailler sur des projets combinant plusieurs concepts pour exprimer des idées simples ou élaborées. »

Ich habe mich auf einfache, aber starke Konzepte und bunte Illustrationen spezialisiert – nicht nur für Kinder, sondern auch für Erwachsene, die sich vielfarbig ausdrücken und denen es nichts ausmacht, für kindisch gehalten zu werden. Ich arbeite gerne an Projekten, denen ich mit mehreren Konzepten jongliere, um sowohl komplexe als auch einfache Ideen auszudrücken."

BRIAN CAIRNS

NAME Brian Cairns
WEBSITE www.briancairns.com
LOCATION Glasgow, United Kingdom
AGENT Friend & Johnson
<www.friendandjohnson.com>

TOOLS Acrylic, ink, gouache, pen, pencil, brush, screenprint, letterpress, Adobe Photoshop, Adobe Illustrator, Adobe Flash, Adobe After Effects

CLIENTS Ridley Scott Associates, Warner Records, The New York Times, Channel 4, HP, BBC
AWARDS Society of Illustrators, Art Directors Club, D&AD, Society of Publication Designers, American Illustration, Communication Arts

3

1 Jake & Rhea invite, 2003, Ridey Scott Associates
2 Ridley Scott Associates logo, 2007, Ridey Scott Associates
3 SEE Magazine, 2006, Herman Miller / Cahan Associates

2

"I adopt an intuitive approach that explores a variety of ways to communicate an idea. The process employed in creating the work often informs the final solution. The work is visually concise with a sophisticated aesthetic that is open to multiple levels of interpretation."

« J'ai adopté une approche intuitive qui explore les diverses manières de faire passer une idée. Le processus créatif que j'emploie influe souvent sur le résultat final. Le travail est concis sur le plan visuel, avec une esthétique sophistiquée qui se prête à plusieurs niveaux d'interprétation. »

„Mein Ansatz ist intuitiv und erforscht eine Vielzahl von Wegen, eine Idee zu vermitteln. Der Arbeitsprozess regt oft die Lösung an. Das Werk ist visuell knapp und präzise und besitzt eine intellektuelle Ästhetik, die für mehrere Interpretationsebenen offen ist."

4

5

4 Howies, 2003, Howies. Silver Nomination for Design & Art Direction Annual
5 Warner Records Catalogue, 2006, Warner Records
6 24 Hour Skilift, 2005, Ski Magazine

ANDRÉ CARRILHO

NAME André Carrilho
WEBSITE www.andrecarrilho.com
LOCATION Lisbon, Portugal

TOOLS Pencil, pen, Adobe Photoshop
CLIENTS The New York Times, Vanity Fair, The Independent on Sunday, Diario de Noticias, Harper's, Word

AWARDS Society for News Design, World Press Cartoon

1 Billie Holiday, 2004, The Independent on Sunday, Carolyn Roberts (Art Director)
2 Katharine Hepburn, 2006, The Independent on Sunday, Colin Wilson (Art Director)
3 Queen Victoria, 2004, The Independent on Sunday, Carolyn Roberts (Art Director)
4 Frida Kahlo, 2004, Diario de Noticias, Henrique Cayette (Art Director)

2

3

4

"I try to combine different graphic languages into one, choosing between pencil hand drawing, computer-generated effects and texture sampling. My goal is to create a visual vocabulary that is at the same time flexible and varied, while maintaining its cohesiveness."

« Je tente de combiner différents langages graphiques en un seul : dessin au crayon, effets générés par ordinateur et échantillons de textures. L'objectif est de créer un vocabulaire visuel à la fois flexible et varié tout en conservant sa cohésion. »

„Ich versuche, mehrere grafische Sprachen zu einer zu vereinen. Ich wechsle zwischen manuellen Bleistiftzeichnungen, computergenerierten Effekten und Texture Sampling. Mein Ziel ist es, ein visuelles Vokabular zu erzeugen, das gleichzeitig flexibel, variantenreich und zusammenhängend ist."

5 Clint Eastwood, 2005, The Independent on Sunday, Carolyn Roberts (Art Director)
6 Bush does South America, 2006, Diario de Noticias, Paulo Freitas (Art Director)
7 Bono Vox, 2004, Word, Keith Drummond (Art Director)
8 Serge Gainsbourg, 2004, Word, Keith Drummond (Art Director)

NINA CHAKRABARTI

NAME Nina Chakrabarti
WEBSITE www.ninachakrabarti.com
LOCATION London, United Kingdom

TOOLS Rotring pen, felt-tip pen, watercolor, pencil, acrylic, ink, light box, Apple Mac

CLIENTS The Guardian, Parlaphone, Pentagram, Lawrence King, Babington House, Cass Arts, Collins, Topshop, Habitat

1 Seminal mugs 1999-2007, 2007, personal work
2 Ballpoint, 2004, Pentagram
3 I'm going to miss these walls, 2004, personal work

"I am incredulous that I can sit at a desk and scribble away with pens and pencils doodling for hours whilst listening to music, and then get paid for it. I consider myself a very fortunate person."

« Je n'arrive pas à croire que je peux passer des heures à ma table à griffonner au crayon et au stylo en écoutant de la musique et être payée pour le faire. Je me considère très chanceuse. »

„Ich kann kaum fassen, dass ich dafür bezahlt werde, stundenlang an einem Schreibtisch zu sitzen, mit Stiften herumzukritzeln und Musik zu hören. Ich schätze mich sehr glücklich."

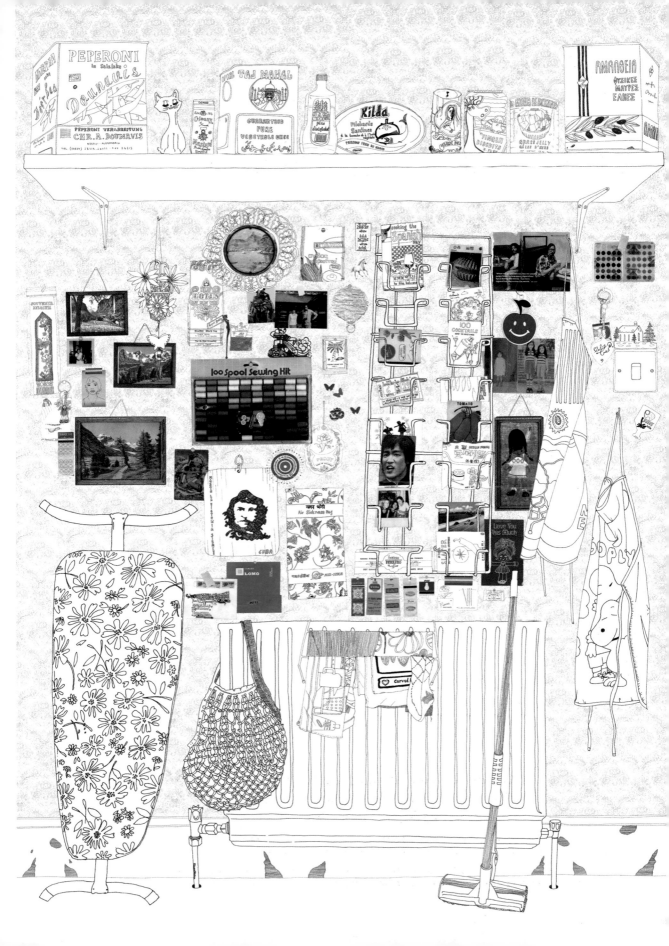

NISHANT CHOKSI

NAME Nishant Choksi
WEBSITE www.nishantchoksi.com

LOCATION London, United Kingdom
TOOLS Pencil, paper, Adobe Illustrator, Adobe Photoshop

CLIENTS Vodafone, Dyson, The Guardian, L.A. Times, New Scientist, Esquire, Vanity Fair, Time, Fast Company
AWARDS Association of Illustrators

Moon Explorer, 2007, personal work
Workforce, 2007, Print Week
Neuromarketing, 2006, Time Inc.

"When an image works, it works. The reason is sometimes indescribable, but I think it's something to do with the right combination of a good idea, drawing, colour and humour."

« Lorsqu'une image marche, elle marche. La raison est parfois indescriptible, mais je pense qu'elle a à voir avec la juste combinaison d'une bonne idée, du dessin, de la couleur et de l'humour. »

„Wenn ein Bild funktioniert, funktioniert es. Der Grund lässt sich nicht immer beschreiben, aber ich glaube, es hat etwas mit der richtigen Kombination von einer guten Idee, Zeichnung, Farbe und Humor zu tun."

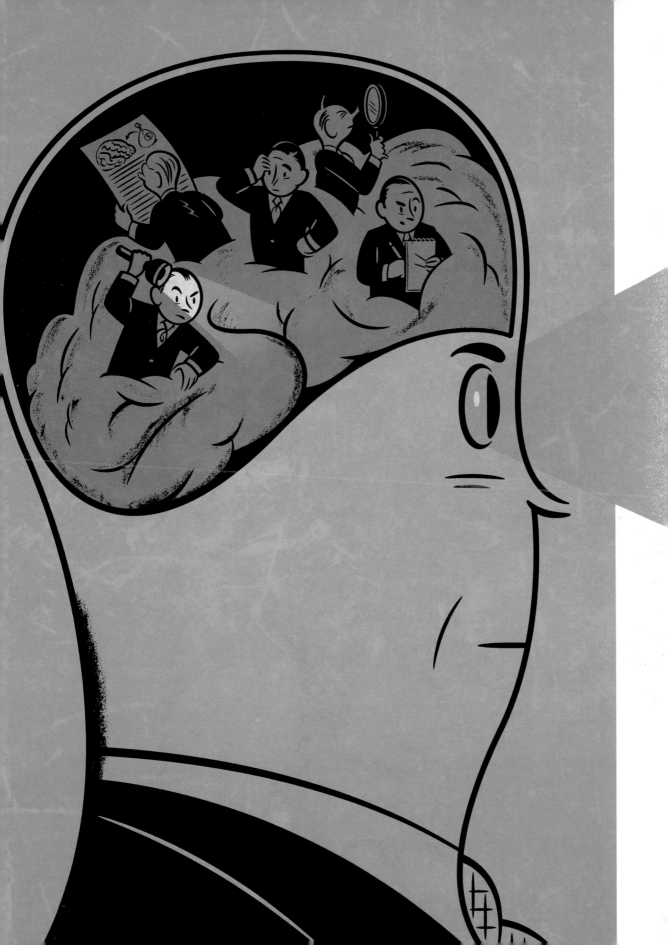

5

6

4 Eureka, 2005, personal work
5 Sales Promotion, 2006, 1576 Agency
6 Business Brains, 2007, Velocity Magazine

SEYMOUR CHWAST

NAME Seymour Chwast
WEBSITE www.pushpininc.com
LOCATION New York, NY, USA

AGENT Ronnie Herman
<www.hermanagencyinc.com>
TOOLS Pen, colored pencil, acrylic, woodcut

CLIENTS The New York Times, The New Yorker, BusinessWeek, The New York Observer, Chronicle, Harry N. Abrams,
AWARDS Art Directors Club, AIGA

3000 Years of Hair

1 The Nose 13: Hair Timeline, 2006, Push Pin Group Inc.
2 Seymour Chwast Poster Ehxibition, Warsaw Poster Museum

"I determine the style, attitude and technique from the material I am illustrating."

« Je choisis style, attitude et technique en fonction de ce que j'illustre. »

„Stil, Haltung und Technik einer Illustration lege ich aufgrund des Inhalts fest, der illustriert werden soll."

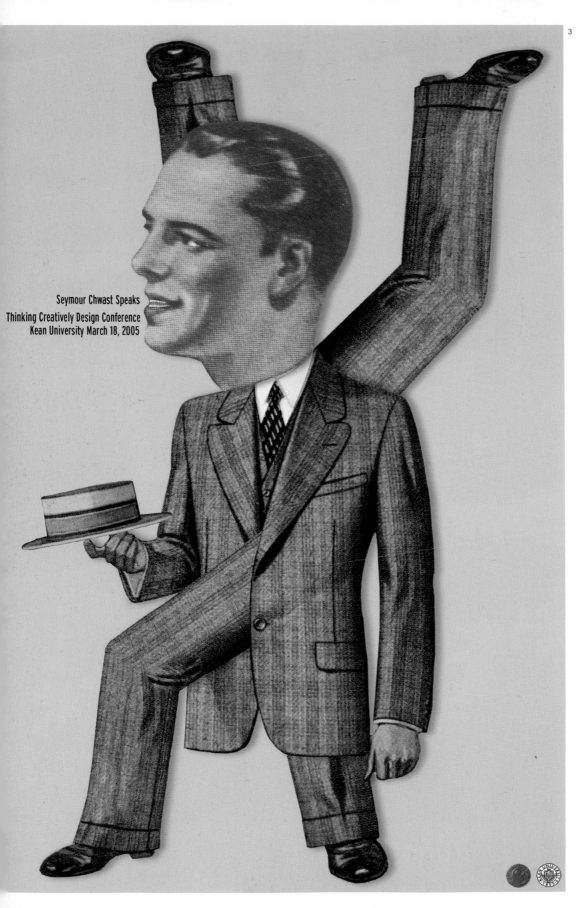

Seymour Chwast Speaks
Thinking Creatively Design Conference
Kean University March 18, 2005

LAURENT CILLUFFO

NAME Laurent Cilluffo
LOCATION Arras, France

AGENT 1 Illustrissimo, Paris,
<www.illustrissimo.com>
AGENT 2 Wanda Nowak, New York,
<www.wandanow.com>

TOOLS Mixed media, pencil
CLIENTS The New Yorker, The New York Times,
BusinessWeek, Newsweek Magazine, The Wall
Street Journal, The Financial Post, Denoël Graphic

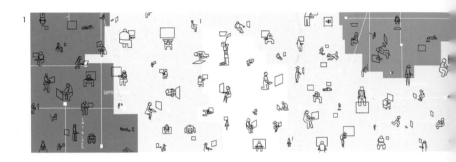

1 Everyone Blogging, 2002, Newsweek Magazine
2 Servicing the Community, 2006, Un Peu D'air Agency
3 Selling, 2006, The New York Times

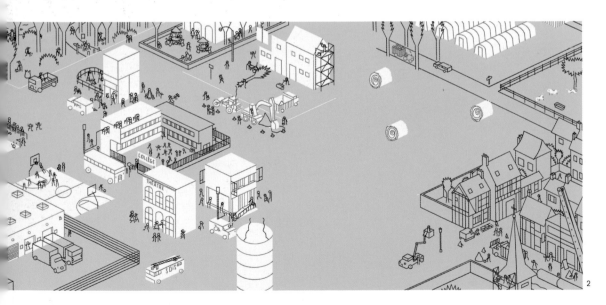

"To try and come up with a solution where
form is not mere decoration."

« Essayer de trouver une solution dans laquelle la forme est plus qu'une simple décoration. »

„Eine Lösung zu finden, bei der die Form nicht nur Dekoration ist."

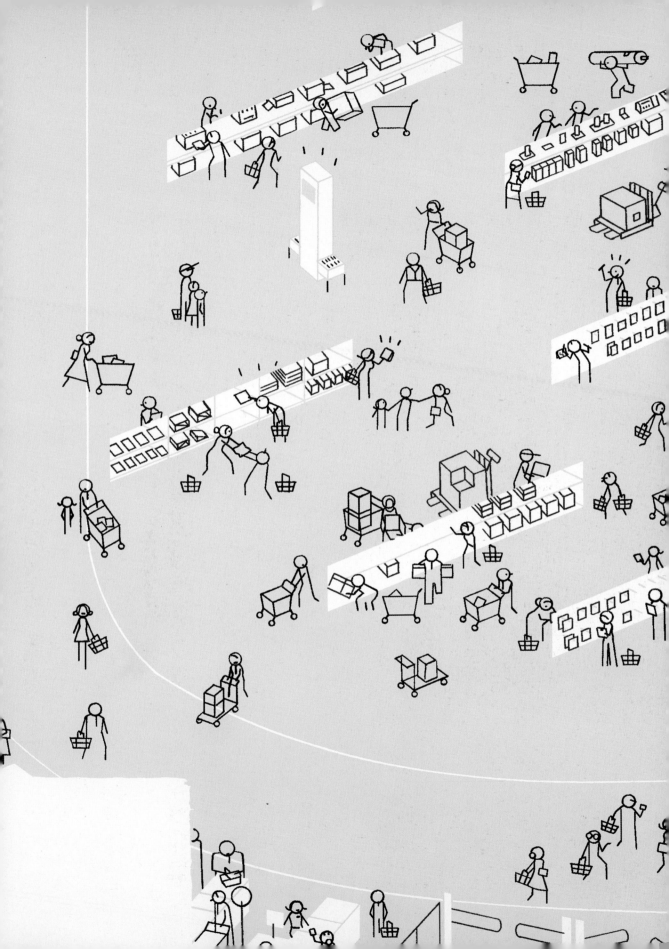

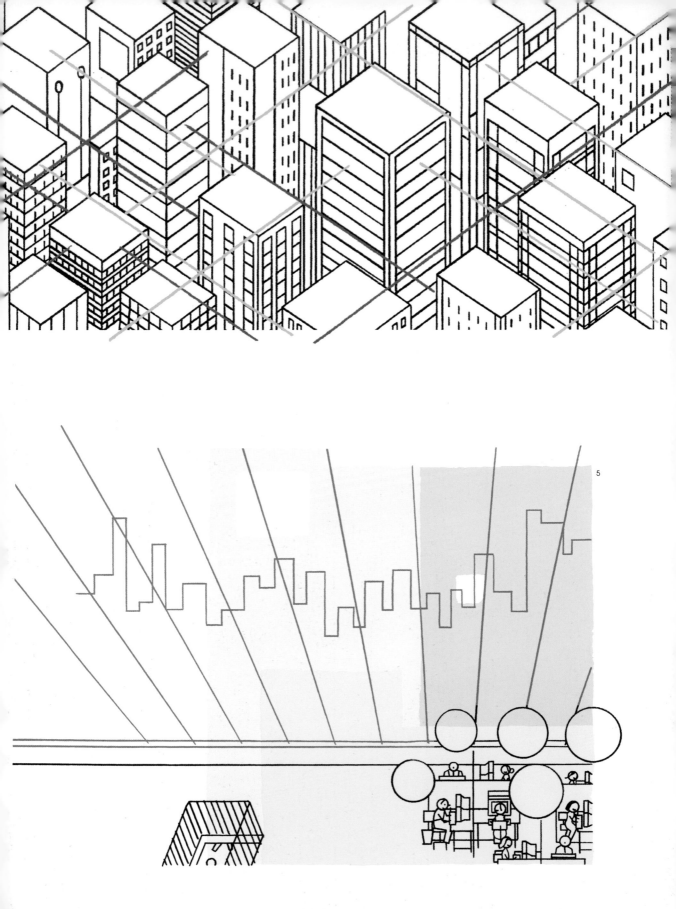

6

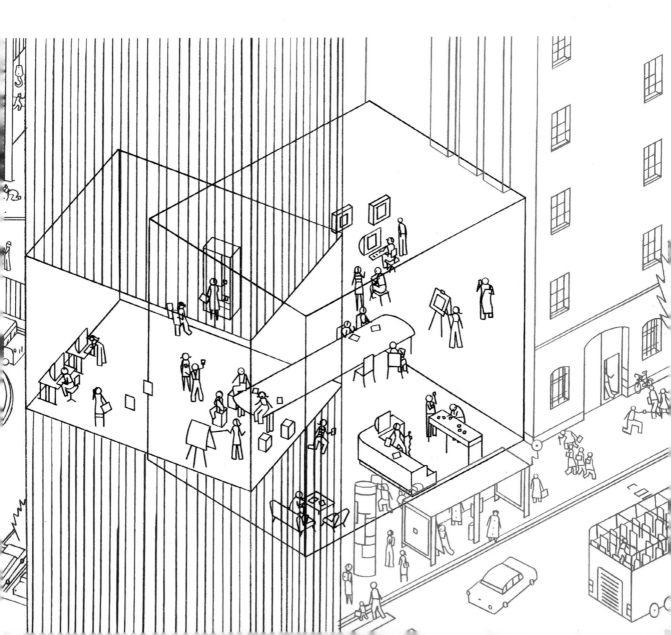

JOSH COCHRAN

NAME Josh Cochran
WEBSITE www.joshcochran.net
LOCATION Los Angeles, CA, USA
AGENT Louisa St. Pierre, New York, NY,
<www.boutique-art.com>

TOOLS Silkscreen, pencil, Adobe Photoshop
CLIENTS The New Yorker, Pepsi, Faber & Faber,
McSweeney's, Discovery Channel, MTV,
Sony Music, Entertainment Weekly

AWARDS Society of Illustrators, American
Illustration, Communication Arts, 3x3,
Society of Publication Designers, Luerzer's Archive

1 Tritons, 2006, Fantagraphics Books
2 Unbalanced, 2007, The Walrus
3 The Year That Was, 2007, Entertainment Weekly
4 100 Cars We Love, 2006, Esquire (Russia)

"My work creates unexpected juxtapositions with obsessive attention to detail. I get the most satisfaction from illustration when I improvise and find myself surprised with the outcome. My style is the complete culmination of everything that I have seen, heard or experienced. Hopefully it is something that is constantly shifting and evolving."

« Mon travail donne des juxtapositions inattendues avec des détails jusqu'à l'obsession. L'illustration me procure le plus de satisfaction lorsque j'improvise et me laisse surprendre par le résultat. Mon style est le résultat de tout ce que je vois, entends et expérimente. J'ai l'espoir qu'il ne cesse d'évoluer et de se renouveler. »

„In meinen Arbeiten entstehen durch eine obsessive Detailversessenheit oft überraschende Kontraste. Am meisten befleügt mich das Illustrieren, wenn ich improvisiere und vom Ergebnis überrascht werde. Mein Stil ist zusammengesetzt aus allem, was ich je gesehen, gehört oder erlebt habe. Ich hoffe, er verändert und entwickelt sich permanent."

5 Rooster, 2005, personal work
6 Friedrich Nietzsche, 2005, The New York Times Book Review
7 Make An Impact, Have An Impact, 2007, Cramer-Krasselt / Penfield Children Center
8 Map of Vancouver, 2007, Bugaboo / 72andSunny

6

7

8

NICK CRAINE

NAME Nick Craine
WEBSITE www.nickcraine.com
LOCATION Guelph, Ontario, Canada

TOOLS Brush, ink, Adobe Photoshop
CLIENTS The New York Times, The Globe and Mail, The Washington Post

AWARDS Dog Writers Association of America (Nominee)

"I try to give the subject a point of view and le
the approach to image construction reflect
that. I'm interested in creating images that are
specific in their character but broad in their
thematic make-up."

« Je m'efforce d'apporter un point de vue et de laisser l'élaboration de
l'image l'illustrer. J'aime créer des images à la fois spécifiques de par leur
caractère et de large portée de par leur composition thématique. »

„Ich nehme gerne eine bestimmte Perspektive ein und lass dies in den
Bildaufbau einfließen. Ich möchte Bilder erschaffen, die zwar in ihrem
Charakter spezifisch sind, in ihrer Thematik aber allgemein."

1

2

3

JORDAN CRANE

NAME Jordan Crane
WEBSITE www.reddingk.com
LOCATION Los Angeles, CA, USA

TOOLS India ink, bristol board, white paint,
Adobe Photoshop

CLIENTS Viking, Chronicle, Family Bookstore,
Fantagraphics, Blueprint, Nickelodeon, Critterbox,
Giant Robot
AWARDS AIGA Book Design

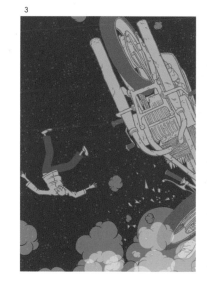

1 Light for Dark, 2005, personal work
2 Turned and Tousled, 2005, personal work
3 The Shade of Night Falls, 2007, personal work
4 Below the Dark Water, 2003, personal work

"Clean lines, all colour, representative rather than abstract. However, in representation there must, between the objects represented, emerge the indefinable feeling, that of mystery and abstraction. Therefore: abstraction through representation emerging in to the unknowable. Clean lines, all colour."

« Des lignes pures, tout en couleurs, avec un style plutôt représentatif qu'abstrait. Il doit toutefois se dégager de la représentation, entre les objets présentés, le sentiment indéfinissable du mystère et de l'abstraction. En d'autres termes, une abstraction obtenue par représentation débouchant sur l'inconnaissable. Des lignes pures, tout en couleurs. »

„Saubere Striche, bunt, eher gegenständlich als abstrakt. Es muss jedoch von den abgebildeten Objekten ein undefinierbares Gefühl von Rätselhaftigkeit und Abstraktion ausgehen. Also: Abstraktion durch Gegenständlichkeit, die das Unbekannte betritt. Saubere Striche, bunt."

5 All Wound Up, 2005, personal work
6 Don't Know if I'm Coming or Going, 2003, personal work
7 Toaster Oven and a Gas Leak, 2002, personal work
8 Hurts All Around, 2003, personal work

9

10

9 Oh! My Nellie, 2003, personal work
10 Germs Burn, 2005, personal work

PAUL DAVIS

NAME Paul Davis
WEBSITE www.okdavis.com
LOCATION New York, NY, USA
TOOLS Pen, pencil, acrylic, paper, canvas, watercolor, Adobe Photoshop, Adobe Illustrator

CLIENTS Vanity Fair, GQ, The New Yorker, The Public Theater, School of Visual Arts, The New York Times, Geffen Theater

AWARDS Society of Illustrators, Society of Publication Designers, Drama Desk Award, AIGA, Art Directors Club Hall of Fame

2

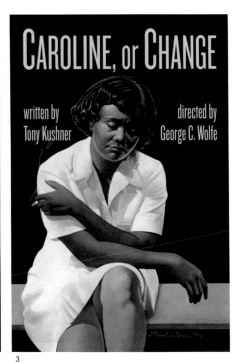

3

4

1 Geffen Playhouse 2002-2003, poster
2 Geffen Playhouse 2003-2004, poster
3 "Caroline, or Change", 2005, The Public Theater, book cover adapted from the poster advertising the Broadway musical created by Tony Kushner
4 Janus With a Yellow Hat, 2005, The Amerian Academy in Rome

"I am most satisfied in my work when I am able to convey some sense of the peculiar and particular emotional qualities that I perceive in daily life. Creating images often seems to me a self-conscious pursuit. At the same time, there is always the delicious possibility that in the process of making a picture something unexpected will occur."

« C'est lorsque je peux transmettre des qualités émotionnelles particulières que je perçois dans la vie quotidienne que mon travail me satisfait le plus. La création d'images m'apparaît souvent comme une poursuite de soi-même. En parallèle, il existe toujours la délicieuse possibilité que quelque chose d'imprévu survienne au cours du processus. »

„Ich bin dann mit meiner Arbeit zufrieden, wenn es mir gelingt, die seltsamen emotionalen Momente einzufangen, die mir im täglichen Leben begegnen. Oft erscheint mir das Erschaffen von Bildern als bewusster Vorgang. Gleichzeitig besteht die köstliche Möglichkeit, dass dabei etwas Unerwartetes passieren könnte."

Paul Dav
2005

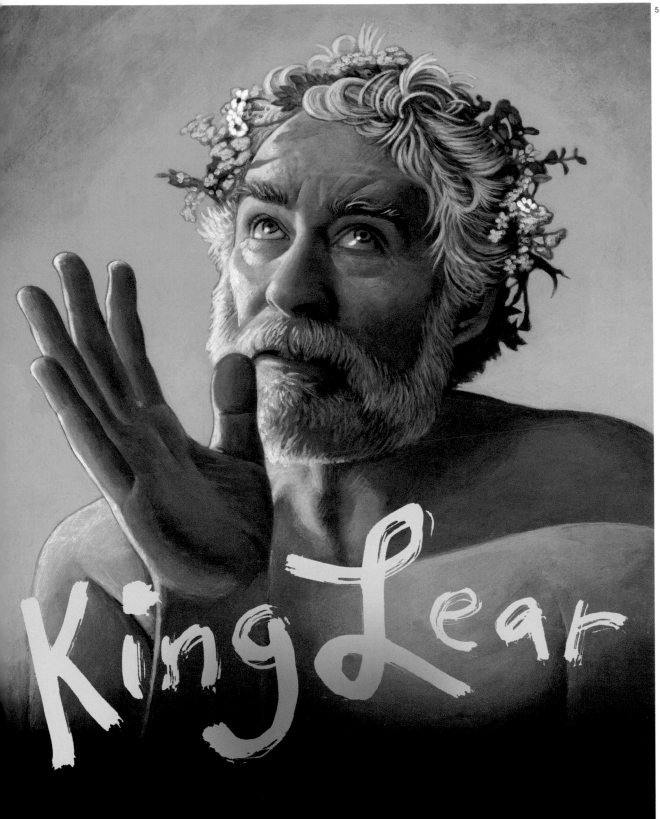

Paul Davis

6

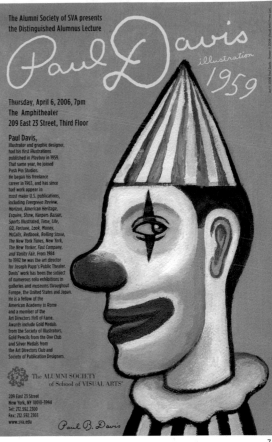

7

8

5 King Lear, 2007, The Public Theater
6 Paul Davis Posters, 2003, University of Arkansas
7 Paul Davis 1959, 2006, The Alumni Society of School of Visual Arts
8 Teatro Odeon 2006-2007, Teatro Communale di Lumezzane (Italy)

SELÇUK DEMIREL

NAME Selçuk Demirel
LOCATION Paris, France

AGENT Smart Magna <www.smartmagna.com>
TOOLS Ink, ecoline, watercolor, gouache, acrylic, pencil, collage

CLIENTS Le Monde, The Washington Post, The Wall Street Journal, The New York Times, Le Nouvel Observateur, How

1

1 Pour ou contre la Biographie, 1999, Le Nouvel Observateur
2 Gateau, 1991, Le Monde Diplomatique
3 How a 19th Century epidemic redefined life today, 2007, Yes Solutions / Bookspan

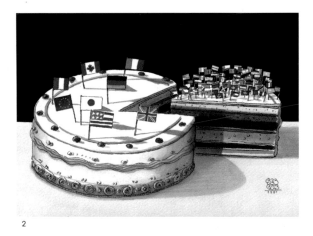

2

3

"It is an authentic miracle that the drawings I send to the four corners of the earth are understood and shared. Through this universal language I use, to be able to work with the same ease and in the same moment, whether it be for a magazine or for a newspaper in Paris, New York or Istanbul is, in a word, extraordinary. To me, drawing and painting is living."

« Que les dessins que j'envoie aux quatre coins du monde soient compris et diffusés est un vrai miracle. Par l'intermédiaire de cette langue universelle que j'utilise, pouvoir travailler avec la même aisance et au même moment, que ce soit pour une revue ou un journal de Paris, New York ou Istanbul est en un mot extraordinaire ! Dessiner et peindre, pour moi c'est vivre. »

„Dass die Illustrationen, die ich in alle vier Ecken des Erdballs schicke, überall verstanden und verbreitet werden, ist wirklich ein Wunder. Es ist einfach großartig, dass ich mit dieser universellen Sprache gleichzeitig für eine Zeitschrift oder eine Zeitung in Paris, New York oder Istanbul arbeiten kann. Zeichnen und malen sind für mich gleichbedeutend mit leben."

TIM DINTER

NAME Tim Dinter
WEBSITE www.timdinter.de
LOCATION Berlin, Germany

AGENT 2Agenten <www.2agenten.com>
TOOLS Pen, pencil, India ink, paper, Adobe Photoshop

CLIENTS Frankfurter Allgemeine Zeitung, Die Zeit, Stern, Max, Geo, Der Tagesspiegel, Die Welt, T-Online, Siemens, American Express
AWARDS ICOM (Independent Comic) Prize, Comic-Salon Erlangen

1 Superstars, 2003, Bolero
2 Sexy Pics, 2006, OCÉ
3 A A Alex, 2006, Illustrative

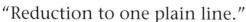

"Reduction to one plain line."

« Réduction à une simple ligne. »

„Reduktion auf einen einfachen Strich."

5

6

7

4 TV Family, 2006, Stern Magazine
5 Neighbour, 2006, Stern Magazine
6 Legs, 2006, Stern Magazine
7 E-generation, 2006, Stern Magazine

DOLCEQ

NAME DolceQ
WEBSITE www.dolceQ.com
LOCATION Rome, Italy

TOOLS Pencil, paper, Adobe Illustrator, Adobe Photoshop

CLIENTS Computer Arts, Arena Magazine, IdN, Coca-Cola, Shufflesome, Play Imaginative

1 Deconstruct, 2006, personal work
2 Passione, 2006, personal work
3 Geisha, 2006, personal work
4 Female2, 2007, personal work

2

3

"A sexy lovely world where butterflies, hearts,
stars and women live together in a minimal, erotic futuristic style."

« Un monde sexy et ravissant dans lequel papillons, cœurs, étoiles et femmes cohabitent
dans un style futuriste minimal et érotique. »

„Eine wunderschöne sexy Welt, in der Schmetterlinge, Herzen, Sterne und Frauen
in einem minimalen, erotischen, futuristischen Stil zusammenleben."

DRAGON

NAME Dragon
LOCATION Yokohama, Japan

AGENT Dutch Uncle Agency
<www.DutchUncle.co.uk>
TOOLS Acrylic, Adobe Photoshop

CLIENTS Vodafone, Blue Q, Trojan, 55DSL, Riddim Driven, Southern Comfort, Time Out, Vespa, Time Warner, VP Records

"My work is between illustration and live painting. I have a strong influence of music and culture in my work."

« Mon travail se situe entre l'illustration et le live painting. Il est fortement influencé par la musique et la culture. »

„Meine Arbeit ist zwischen Illustration und Livepainting angesiedelt. Sie ist stark durch Musik und Kultur beeinflusst."

1 Walk Bare Foot on the Earth, 2003, personal work
2 Mika Arisaka, 2006, Victor Entertainment
3 Cirlce of Life, 2004, personal work
4 Touch Your Soul, 2004, personal work

HENRIK DRESCHER

NAME Henrik Drescher
LOCATION 1 Toronto, Canada
LOCATION 2 Yunnan, China

AGENT Reactor Art <www.reactor.ca>
TOOLS Mixed media, mostly ink and color

CLIENTS The New York Times, Time Magazine, Harper's, LA Times

1 Visionary, 2000, Mark Murphy Design
2 Drug Haze, 2007, Neon Magazine
3 China, 2003, personal work

1

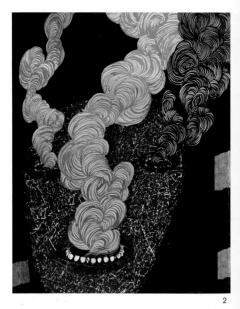

2

"I believe that it's important to create a constant flow of personal work as the central source of ideas and images for commercial work."

« Je crois qu'il est important de produire un flux continu de projets personnels comme source principale d'idées et d'images pour des projets commerciaux. »

„Ich bin der Ansicht, das es wichtig ist, einen steten Fluss an persönlichen Arbeiten zu schaffen, die dann die Hauptquelle für Ideen und Bilder für kommerzielle Aufträge sind."

CATALINA ESTRADA

NAME Catalina Estrada
WEBSITE www.catalinaestrada.com
LOCATION Barcelona, Spain

AGENT Folio <www.folioart.co.uk>
TOOLS Adobe Illustrator, Adobe Photoshop

CLIENTS Paul Smith, Coca-Cola, Nike, Honda, Custo Barcelona, Marks & Spencer, Salomon, Chronicle

1 Puscha Illustration, 2006, Puscha
2 Nike Air Magazine, 2007
3 Birds Gift Paper, 2007, Nineteenseventythree (UK)

"Born and raised in Colombia, and living in Barcelona since 1999, Catalina brings all the colors and power of Latin-American folklore and refines it with a subtle touch of European sophistication. Her ability for creating fascinating illusive worlds, full of colors, nature and enchanting characters bursts through in all of her works."

« Née et élevée en Colombie, Catalina vit à Barcelone depuis 1999. Elle transmet toutes les couleurs et la force du folklore d'Amérique latine en lui conférant une touche subtile de sophistication européenne. Toutes ses œuvres témoignent de sa capacité à créer des mondes irréels et fascinants, pleins de couleurs, de nature et de personnages enchanteurs. »

„Catalina ist in Kolumbien aufgewachsen und lebt seit 1999 in Barcelona. Ihre Arbeiten enthalten die ganze Farbenpracht und Kraft der lateinamerikanischen Folklore und verfeinern diese mit einem subtilen Hauch europäischer Raffinesse. In ihren Werken erschafft sie faszinierende Scheinwelten, prallvoll mit Farben, Natur und bezaubernden Figuren."

4 Noah and the Ark, 2006, Bizarre Tales
5 Anunciacao Brazilian Fashion Brand, 2007. Photo by Fernanda Calfat
6 Easter bottle, 2007, Coca Cola (Australia)
7 Easter poster, 2007, Coca Cola (Australia)

6

7

Easter on the **Coke** side of life

RYAN FEERER

NAME Ryan Feerer
WEBSITE 1 www.ryanfeerer.com
WEBSITE 2 www.murkville.com

LOCATION New York, NY, USA

TOOLS Pen, pencil, acrylic, old paper, coffee, Adobe Photoshop, Corel Painter

1 Yeah, 2007, personal work
2 Noch Fish, 2007, personal work
3 Band poster, 2007, Homer Hiccolm & the Rocketboys
3 Freestate Festival of the Arts, 2006

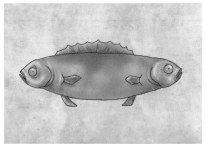

"Illustration is one of the most powerful forms of communication. It captivates us, and it makes us smile. Illustration makes a message or text of a story beautiful that may seem banal otherwise. It fills the communication gap that can't be explained with words and is something everyone in the world can relate to. Illustration also gives people the honor of experiencing my awesome imagination."

« L'illustration est l'une des formes de communication les plus puissantes. Elle fascine et fait sourire. Elle sait rendre attrayant un message ou le texte d'une histoire autrement banale. Elle comble le fossé de ce que l'on ne peut expliquer avec des mots et est accessible à tout le monde. Grâce à l'illustration, les gens ont aussi l'honneur de découvrir mon incroyable imagination. »

„Illustration ist eine der mächtigsten Kommunikationsmittel. Sie nimmt uns gefangen und bringt uns zum Schmunzeln. Illustration macht eine Nachricht oder einen Text oder eine Geschichte schön, die ansonsten vielleicht banal wirken würde. Sie füllt Kommunikationslücken, die Worte nicht füllen können, und spricht jeden an. Illustration gestaltet Menschen außerdem, an meiner beeindruckenden Fantasie teilzuhaben."

LIVE MUSIC, ARTIST'S DISPLAYS, LECTURERS,
MINISTRY-
BOOTHS.
GREAT FOOD!
BAND LIST.
FUN FAMILY ATMOSPHERE!
WALL CLIMBING!
& MORE.
FRIDAY, SATURDAY, SUNDAY!
DON'T MISS. OUT!!!!!!
May 19 THRU 21!
BE THERE!
HEADLINERS: FRIDAY, HOMER HICCOLM & the Rocketboys SATURDAY, RUSTIC SUNDAY, Rhythm
OTHER BANDS INCLUDE: Gatsby, Tableau Vivant, Doug Burr, Kelly wrecker, Canary, Transent Theory, Dylan Sneed, Modico, Clocktower showdown, Mid August Night, Not Called Common, The chemistry set, The Background, The Up Stairs Devine, Knockout Kings, Mahteo, Hundred Year Storm, Lanky, A Last Chance, Six Memphis Belle, Aaron and the Dusters Yellow Bird, Ramoth Gilead Clay and the People, Dwell Siddhartha, Ryan Ewing, Widows & Orphans (the Kirby) Whitman, Levi Smith The Pilots, NAOS Project, Paper Airline, South-East Crossing, Youth with a Mission, Treen Man
ALSO CAMPING & R.V. HOOK-UPS! (EXTRA)
HELP SUPPORT COMPASSION, HEART OF GRACE MINISTRIES
Brought to you by: THE MAD GOAT, The One P3: Fifteen
FREESTATE
FESTIVAL of the ARTS

LUKE FELDMAN

NAME Luke Feldman
WEBSITE www.skaffs.com
LOCATION 1 Melbourne, Australia

LOCATION 2 San Francisco, CA, USA
TOOLS Pen, marker, paper, Adobe Illustrator, Adobe Photoshop

CLIENTS Coca-Cola, Microsoft's Wallop, Desktop Magazine, Semi-Permanent, K-Swiss, STAF, Skinnie

1 Come Out and Play, 2006, Coca-Cola
2 Utopia, 2006, personal work
3 Miyu, 2007, personal work

"My pieces are minimalist, with defined lines, detailed characters, and vividly vibrant colours that give the images depth and movement. Sexy-girls: forms of stylized scantily dressed females reclining amongst surrealist backgrounds. The large, intense eyes and fluid bodies are strangely erotic; yet maintain a distant, unattainable feeling."

« Mes œuvres sont minimalistes, avec des lignes bien définies, des personnages détaillés et des couleurs très vives qui donnent profondeur et mouvement aux images. Filles sexy : des formes féminines stylisées et en tenue légère, allongées devant des arrière-plans surréalistes. Leurs grands yeux au regard intense et leurs corps fluides sont étrangement érotiques, tout en créant un sentiment de distance et d'inaccessible. »

„Meine Bilder sind minimalistisch, mit klaren Linien, detaillierten Figuren und lebendigen Farben, die Tiefe und Bewegung erzeugen. Sexy-Girls: stilisierte, leicht bekleidete weibliche Figuren vor surrealen Hintergründen. Die großen intensiven Augen und die fließenden Körper sind seltsam erotisch, doch gleichzeitig unnahbar."

DARREN FIRTH

NAME Darren Firth
WEBSITE www.keepsmesane.co.uk
LOCATION London, United Kingdom

TOOLS Adobe Photoshop, Adobe Illustrator, Adobe Freehand, Adobe Dreamweaver, Adobe Flash, pens, pencils, mixed media

CLIENTS Puma, Nike, Ben Sherman, HP, Next, Portsmouth FC, Boxfresh, Lee Cooper, IdN, Vodafone, Blanka, Design Week, L'Oréal, Dazed, Clerk & Teller, Stereohype, String Republic

1 Mc Faul, 2006
2 SFR, 2007
3 Yuck, 2006

"First and foremost I see myself as a designer; a designer that also illustrates. My profession is as a designer and thus my primary instinct is to solve a problem that is presented to me, whether it be a client brief or an independent creative project. I think the key as a creative is to know your strengths and limits, and ultimately what is the best solution for the job in hand. I see illustration as an extremely enjoyable hobby of mine, which often assists me with my daily duties as a designer."

« Tout d'abord, je me considère comme un designer qui fait aussi des illustrations. J'exerce en tant que designer et mon instinct premier est donc de résoudre les problèmes qui se présentent à moi, qu'il s'agisse de la commande d'un client ou d'un projet créatif indépendant. Pour moi, la clé en tant que créatif est de connaître ses forces et ses limites, ainsi que d'identifier la meilleure solution pour le travail à effectuer. Je vois l'illustration comme un passe-temps extrêmement agréable qui m'aide souvent dans mes tâches quotidiennes de designer. »

„Ich sehe mich in erster Linie als Designer – ein Designer, der auch illustriert. Mein Beruf ist der des Designers und deshalb geht es mir hauptsächlich darum, ein Problem zu lösen, egal ob es sich dabei um ein Kundenbriefing handelt oder ein unabhängiges Kreativprojekt. Als Kreativer sollte man seine Stärken und Grenzen kennen und immer daran denken, was für den gerade anliegenden Job die beste Lösung ist. Illustration betrachte ich als sehr angenehmes Hobby, das mir oft bei meinen täglichen Aufgaben als Designer hilft."

DREW FLAHERTY

NAME Drew Flaherty
WEBSITE www.drewflaherty.com
LOCATION Brisbane, Australia

TOOLS Ink, paper, pencil, Adobe Photoshop, Adobe Illustrator, Adobe Flash, Wacom tablet, 3D Studio Max, e frontier Poser, Corel Painter, Canon EOS 400d, scanner

CLIENTS Future Publishing, Future Entertainment, Sydney City Council, Yen magazine, Don't Panic, Fashionline, DirecTV

1 Club Famous Artwork, 2006, Club Famous / Future Entertainment
2 Dust Rush, 2006, personal work
3 Color Test, 2006, personal work

"Imagination is more important than knowledge."

« L'imagination est plus importante que le savoir. »

„Fantasie ist wichtiger als Wissen."

MARK FREDRICKSON

NAME Mark Fredrickson
LOCATION Hancock, USA
AGENT Gerald & Cullen Rapp <www.rappart.com>
TOOLS Adobe Photoshop

CLIENTS DC Comics, Mad Magazine, Village Voice, Time, Capital One, Entertainment Weekly, Sony, BusinessWeek, IndustryWeek, Atlantic Monthly, HarperCollins, Penguin Putnam

AWARDS Society of Illustrators, Communication Arts, Print

"After illustrating for over twenty years, I've finally realized that there are more important things to do in life; I just haven't found enough time to do them."

« Après avoir fait des illustrations pendant plus de vingt ans, j'ai finalement compris qu'il y a des choses plus importantes dans la vie, sauf que je n'ai pas trouvé le temps de les faire. »

„Nach über 20 Jahren als Illustrator habe ich nun endlich festgestellt, dass es im Leben wichtigere Dinge zu tun gibt. Ich habe nur noch nicht die Zeit gefunden, sie zu tun."

1

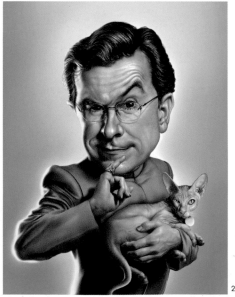

2

1 Barry Bonds (The Unnatural), 2007, Mad Magazine
2 Colbert, 2006, The Village Voice
3 Hillary Clinton as Harry Potter, 2003, The Village Voice

5

6

7

4 Phobias, 2001, Time Magazine
5 Little Shop of Horrors, 2003, Serino Coyne
6 Atrocity Archives, 2005, Penguin Putnam
7 Philip Seymore Hoffman, 2006, Time Magazine

4

GEZ FRY

NAME Gez Fry
WEBSITE www.gezfry.com
LOCATION Tebiro, Japan

AGENT Folio <www.folioart.co.uk>
TOOLS Pencil, Adobe Photoshop

CLIENTS New Riders, Plastic Animal Studios, A.P. Comics, Future Publishing, Carbon Industries, Namco Bandai Games, Firetrap

1

1 Ginza, 2006, Beacon Communications KK, Montblanc
2 Poplin, 2005, Firetrap

"Gez Fry's work is comprised of digitally painted illustrations, sequential and concept art. Born in Tokyo, he has since lived in several countries, is fluent in French, Italian, Japanese, and of course, English. This varied upbringing, and his Japanese/British nationality, is reflected in the multi-cultural nature of his work."

« Le travail de Gez Fry se compose d'illustrations peintes sur ordinateur, d'art séquentiel et d'art conceptuel. Né à Tokyo, il a vécu dans plusieurs pays et parle couramment le français, l'italien, le japonais et l'anglais, évidemment. Cette éducation plurielle et sa double nationalité japonaise/britannique se retrouvent dans la nature multiculturelle de son travail. »

„Gez Frys Arbeit umfasst digitale Illustrationen, sequenzielle Kunst und Konzeptkunst. Er wurde in Tokio geboren und lebte in verschiedenen Ländern. Er spricht Französisch, Italienisch, Japanisch und natürlich Englisch. Das Aufwachsen in unterschiedlichen Ländern und seine japanisch-britische Nationalität spiegeln sich in der Multikulturalität seiner Werke wieder."

3 Ukiyo-e, 2006, personal work

4

4 Hot Version, 2005
5 Causeway Bay, 2006, personal work
6 Sumera, 2005, Evisu

5

THOMAS FUCHS

NAME Thomas Fuchs
WEBSITE www.thomasfuchs.com
LOCATION New York, NY, USA
TOOLS Acrylic, Adobe Photoshop, Adobe Illustrator

CLIENTS The New York Times, Time Magazine, Newsweek, Rolling Stone, Esquire, ESPN, Entertainment Weekly

AWARDS Society of Publication Designers, Society of Illustrators, American Illustration, Communication Arts, Art Directors Club (Washington DC), Society for News Design

"Form follows function. Still true. Even in illustration...
I therefore try to keep my work as open as possible stylistically.
I think the idea should dictate what kind of visual translation it needs..."

« La forme obéit à la fonction. Un principe toujours vrai, même en illustration...
J'essaie donc que mon travail reste aussi ouvert que possible sur le plan stylistique.
Je crois que l'idée doit dicter le type de traduction visuelle requise... »

„Die Form folgt der Funktion. Das gilt immer noch. Auch für Illustrationen ...
Deshalb versuche ich, meine Arbeiten stilistisch so offen wie möglich zu halten.
Ich glaube, die Idee sollte bestimmen, welche Art von visueller Umsetzung sie braucht."

1

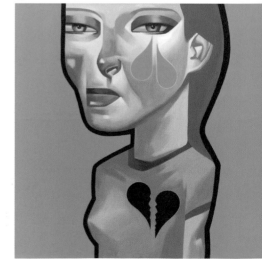

2

1 DJ, 2005, The New York Times Book Review
2 Heart Failure, 2006, Time Magazine
3 Sonic Youth, 2005, Rolling Stone Magazine

CHRIS GALL

NAME Chris Gall
WEBSITE www.chrisgall.com
LOCATION Tucson, AZ, USA
AGENT Richard Solomon, Artists Representative,
<www.richardsolomon.com>

TOOLS Engraving on heavy masonite board,
Adobe Illustrator
CLIENTS Time, Newsweek, Forbes, People, Pepsi,
GQ, The Washington Post, The New York Times,
Cider Jack Hard Cider

AWARDS Communication Arts, Print, Spectrum,
Society of Illustrators, Society of News Design,
Art Directors Club (New York)

1 Organic Food Growers, NRA 2007
2 Out of Control Media, NRA 2007
3 Government anti-smoking campaign, calendar, 2004,
Mark Murphy Design

1

2

"The role of the illustrator is unique within the arts, for an illustrator must be equal parts craftsman, engineer, and visionary. Above all he should be a problem solver, where the client's needs are carefully considered and then taken to a new level of creativity. The greatest goal is that of a solution that no one expects or foresees, but which arises from the collaboration of creative minds."

« Le rôle de l'illustrateur est unique dans le monde de l'art, car il doit être à la fois artisan, ingénieur et visionnaire. Avant tout, il doit savoir résoudre des problèmes, en analysant minutieusement les besoins du client et en les transposant à un nouveau niveau de créativité. L'objectif maximum est une solution que personne n'attend ni ne prévoit, mais qui voit le jour grâce à la collaboration d'esprits créatifs. »

„Die Rolle des Illustrators ist innerhalb der Künste einmalig, denn er muss zu gleichen Teilen Handwerker, Ingenieur und Visionär sein. Vor allem sollte er ein Problemlöser sein, der die Bedürfnisse des Kunden sorgfältig analysiert und dann auf eine neue Kreativitätsebene hebt. Das ultimative Ziel ist eine Lösung, die niemand erwartet oder vorhersieht, die aber aus der Zusammenarbeit kreativer Köpfe entsteht."

9

8 Hair Dresser, book "Dear Fish" – Little, Brown 2006
9 Lift Off, book "There's Nothing To Do On Mars"
– Little, Brown 2008
10 Pedaling for Wattage, 2005, Bicycling Magazine

AUDREY GESSAT

NAME Audrey Gessat
LOCATION Lyon, France

AGENT Illustrissimo <www.illustrissimo.com>
TOOLS Modeling material, watercolor, paper, and a good photograph

CLIENTS Peugeot, Perrier, Omo, Blédina, EDF, Le Point, Nathan, Milan Press, Editions Sarbacane

1

2

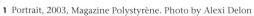

1 Portrait, 2003, Magazine Polystyrène. Photo by Alexi Delon
2 Coccinelle, 2006, personal work
3 Bleu, 2000, personal work. Photo by Jean-Louis Hess

"To me, illustrating means making images for other people. Their view is important. Although I have always drawn, I love to transform my drawings to give them volume. Afterwards they acquire all their essence under the light of the photographer. I love to live my passion."

« L'illustration, c'est pour moi réaliser des images pour les autres. Leur regard est important. J'ai toujours dessiné, mais ce que j'adore c'est transformer mes dessins en volumes. Ils prennent ensuite toute leur âme sous la lumière du photographe. Je suis heureuse de vivre ma passion. »

„Illustration bedeutet für mich, Bilder für andere zu erschaffen. Ihr Blick ist mir wichtig. Ich habe schon immer gezeichnet. Besonders gerne verändere ich die Größe meiner Illustrationen. Danach wird ihnen durch das Licht des Fotografen Seele eingehaucht. Ich bin glücklich, meine Leidenschaft ausleben zu können."

DYLAN GIBSON

NAME Dylan Gibson
WEBSITE www.dylangibsonillustration.co.uk
LOCATION Perthshire, United Kingdom

AGENT Eye Candy <www.eyecandy.co.uk>
TOOLS Pencil, pen, ink, paper, Adobe Photoshop, Adobe Illustrator

CLIENTS Atkins Global, Bank of Ireland, BBC, Clarks Shoes, The Guardian, Irish News, Kellogg's, Piaggio, Princes Trust, Tesco

1 Character Collage, 2006
2 Skateboarder, 2006, personal work
3 City, 2005, personal work
4 Light Festival, 2006, Glasgow City Council

3

2

"I draw on influences from every aspect of my life, from watching the countryside glide past through the windows of a train to flicking through comic books old and new. I am fascinated by the world around me and enjoy transforming all these thoughts and ideas into vibrant and varied illustrations."

« Je tire mes influences de tous les aspects de ma vie, qu'il s'agisse du paysage qui défile sous mes yeux à travers les vitres d'un train ou des bandes dessinées anciennes ou récentes que je feuillette. Je suis fasciné par le monde qui m'entoure et j'adore transformer toutes ces pensées et ces idées en illustrations dynamiques et variées. »

„Ich ziehe meine Ideen aus allen Lebenslagen, zum Beispiel, wenn ich aus dem Zugfenster heraus die Landschaft vorbeigleiten sehe oder alte und neue Comics durchblättere. Mich fasziniert die Welt um mich herum und ich verarbeite diese Eindrücke gerne zu lebendigen und vielseitigen Illustrationen."

VASSILIS GOGTZILAS

NAME Vassilis Gogtzilas
WEBSITE www.gogtzilas.com
LOCATION Thessaloniki, Greece

AGENT Studio Emotion
TOOLS Pen, pencil, ink, brushe, gouache, watercolor, paper, Adobe Photoshop

CLIENTS Image Comics, Athens Oice Books Greece

"I try to communicate the best way, while having fun with my work."

« J'essaie de m'exprimer de la meilleure façon possible tout en m'amusant dans mon travail. »

„Ich versuche, so gut wie möglich zu kommunizieren und gleichzeitig Spaß zu haben."

1 Between Her Legs, 2007, Athens Voice books
2 Vamvakaris, 2006, Epiloges Magazine
3 Bukowski, 2006, Epiloges Magazine

JASPER GOODALL

NAME Jasper Goodall
WEBSITE www.jaspergoodall.com
LOCATION Brighton, United Kingdom

AGENT Big Active <www.bigactive.com>
TOOLS Photography, Adobe Photoshop, Adobe Illustrator

CLIENTS Muse / Maverick Records, S Magazine, Nike, MTV

"I think illustration should be about producing artwork that is meaningful to many and not solely about self-expression. I think an image needs to resonate with the viewer, if not on an obvious communicating level, then it must appeal to an individual's sense of beauty, power or desire. Illustration is at it's richest when it has strong ideas behind the attractive imagery."

« Je pense que l'illustration devrait être une production d'images ayant un sens pour un large public, au lieu de se cantonner à l'expression de soi. Je crois qu'une image doit évoquer quelque chose chez la personne qui l'observe ; si ce n'est à un niveau évident de communication, elle doit parler à l'approche personnelle de la beauté, du pouvoir ou du désir de chacun. L'illustration est à son apogée lorsqu'elle renferme des idées fortes derrière des images attirantes. »

„Meiner Meinung nach sollte Illustration Kunstwerke hervorbringen, bei denen es nicht nur um Selbstausdruck geht, sondern die viele Menschen ansprechen. Das Bild muss etwas im Betrachter auslösen, entweder auf einer direkten Kommunikationsebene oder indem es seinen Sinn für Schönheit, Macht oder Sehnsucht berührt. Illustration ist dann am wirkunsvollsten, wenn hinter den attraktiven Bildern starke Ideen stehen."

1 Invincible DVD, 2007, Muse / Maverick Records
2 Knights of Cydonia DVD, 2006, Muse / Maverick Records
3 Knights of Cydonia CD, 2006, Muse / Maverick Records
4 Knights of Cydionia Picture Disk, 2006, Muse / Maverick Records
5 Nebula Kiss, Invincible CD, 2006, Muse / Maverick Records

6

7

6 Temptation Costume, 2006, JG4B Swimwear
7 Flamingo Park Costume, 2006, JG4B Swimwear
8 Wind Horse Bikini, 2006, JG4B Swimwear

RE-ANIMATRIX

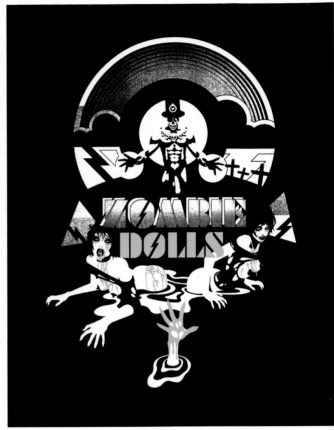

9 Sisters of Satan, 2007, 'S' Magazine
10 Re-Animatrix, 2007, 'S' Magazine
11 Zombie Dolls, 2007, 'S' Magazine
12 Virgin Blood, 2007, 'S' Magazine

12

SILJA GÖTZ

NAME Silja Götz
WEBSITE www.siljagoetz.com
LOCATION Madrid, Spain

AGENT Art Department <www.art-dept.com>
TOOLS Cut paper, ink, pencil, Adobe Photoshop

CLIENTS The New Yorker, Nylon, El País, Neon, The New York Times Magazine, Estrella Damm, Nordic Mist, Custo Barcelona, Marie Claire

1 Untitled, 2006, Nylon (USA)
2 Untitled, 2007, personal work

1

"With my illustrations I want to give a beautiful, tangible form to abstract ideas by using my imagination and any kind of material I have at hand. Rather than an artist, I see myself as an artisan."

« Avec mes illustrations, je veux donner une forme belle et tangible à des idées abstraites, grâce à mon imagination et à tout type de matériau disponible. Plutôt qu'un artiste, je me vois comme un artisan. »

„Ich möchte mit meinen Illustrationen abstrakten Ideen eine schöne und greifbare Form geben. Dabei setze ich meine Fantasie und jedes erdenkliche Material ein, das gerade zur Hand ist. Ich sehe mich eher als Kunsthandwerker als als Künstler."

3 Untitled, 2006, Nordic Mist Tonic Water
4 Untitled, 2007, Champagne Henriot
5 Untitled, 2007, El País (Spain)

ALEX GROSS

NAME Alex Gross
WEBSITE www.alexgross.com
LOCATION South Pasadena, CA, USA

TOOLS Oil, panel, canvas
CLIENTS Entertainment Weekly, Esquire, Nike, LA Times, Los Angeles Magazine, New Republic, Premiere, Runner's World

AWARDS Society of Illustrators, Communication Arts, American Illustration

1

1 Siren, 2004, BLAB
2 Despair, 2007, Akkochan Kaish.

"'Alex Gross' work conjoins irreconcilable contradictions; it unnaturally bridges gulfs of space and time – because that's what the world's peoples must do, nowadays. That dichotomy, that disjuncture between that which is packaged for us to consume and our own unspoken distress as human beings tumbled in dark streams of history – that's the variety of 'surrealism' that compels the work of Alex Gross. It's deeply repressed and hidden from conscious awareness, something like a covert bombing campaign that fails to appear on TV.' – Bruce Sterling"

«‹ Le travail d'Alex Gross associe des contradictions inconciliables : il comble des gouffres d'espace et de temps, car c'est ce que les peuples du monde doivent faire, à l'heure actuelle. Cette dichotomie, cette disjonction entre ce qui est emballé pour notre consommation et notre propre détresse inavouée en tant qu'êtres humains jetés dans les courants obscurs de l'histoire, tel est le type de ‹ surréalisme › qui marque le travail d'Alex Gross. Tout ceci est profondément réprimé et enfoui dans la conscience, un peu comme une opération de bombardements furtifs dont personne ne parle à la télévision. › – Bruce Sterling »

„‚Das Werk von Alex Gross verbindet unvereinbare Gegensätze; es überbrückt unnatürlicherweise Kluften von Raum und Zeit – weil das die Menschen auf der Welt heutzutage tun müssen. Der Zwiespalt zwischen dem, was wir verpackt zum Konsumieren vorgesetzt bekommen, und unseren unausgesprochenen Nöten als Menschen, die hilflos in den dunklen Strömen der Geschichte umhergeschleudert werden – dies ist die Art von ‚Surrealismus', die das Werk von Alex Gross ausmacht. Es wird stark unterdrückt und vom Bewusstsein versteckt, so wie ein geheimer Bombenangriff, den man nicht im Fernsehen zeigt.' – Bruce Sterling"

4

5

6

3 Birds Without Wings, 2005, Los Angeles Times Book Review
4 Monferrato Rosso, 2006, Bonny Doon Vineyard
5 Il Moscato Giallo, 2006, Bonny Doon Vineyard
6 Il Ciliegiolo, 2006, Bonny Doon Vineyard
7 Ca Del Solo, 2006, Bonny Doon Vineyard

7

JENS HARDER

NAME Jens Harder
WEBSITE www.hardercomics.de
LOCATION Berlin, Germany

TOOLS Pen, pencil, paper, Adobe Photoshop
CLIENTS Die Gestalten Verlag, Goethe-Institute, Greenpeace Magazine

AWARDS Fumetto, Comic-Salon

1-2 La Cité de Dieu, panel, 2007, Éditions de l'An 2 (France)
3 Fond of Travelling, 2006, personal work

"Nature is the best designer, life the best storyteller. So there is nothing left to do other than record everything and keep it alive on paper."

« La nature est le meilleur designer, la vie le meilleur conteur d'histoires. Il ne reste donc rien à faire, sauf tout enregistrer et le maintenir en vie sur papier. »

„Die Natur ist der beste Designer und das Leben der beste Geschichtenerzähler. Es bleibt also nichts weiter zu tun, als alles aufzuzeichnen und auf Papier am Leben zu erhalten."

GEORGE HARDIE

NAME George Hardie
LOCATION Chichester, United Kingdom
TOOLS Pen, white paint, paper, Adobe Photoshop, Adobe Illustrator

CLIENTS Pentagram, Advico Young & Rubicam, The Ganzfeld, Italo Lupi, Trickett & Webb, Royal Mail

AWARDS Design and Art Direction of Great Britain

1 Order by Number, 2003, Trickett and Webb
2 The Museum of Holes, 2002, Trickett and Web
3 Manual, 2006, Nagoya University of Arts

"Trained as a graphic designer, I am mainly commissioned to solve problems and make illustrations for a variety of clients in many countries (fourteen to date). I like playing visual games, sticking to strange rules and limitations, ideas, and geometry. My ambition is to notice things and get things noticed."

« Étant designer graphique de formation, je suis surtout chargé de résoudre des problèmes et de faire des illustrations pour des clients divers dans de nombreux pays (quatorze à ce jour). J'aime jouer à des jeux visuels, respecter des règles et des limites curieuses, les idées et la géométrie. J'aspire à remarquer des choses et à les faire remarquer. »

„Ich bin ausgebildeter Grafikdesigner und werde von unterschiedlichen Kunden in vielen Ländern (zur Zeit 14) hauptsächlich dafür engagiert, Probleme zu lösen und Illustrationen anzufertigen. Ich mag visuelle Spiele und Geometrie und halte mich gerne an seltsame Regeln und Beschränkungen. Mein Ziel ist es, Dinge zu bemerken und dazu beizutragen, dass sie bemerkt werden."

TARA HARDY

NAME Tara Hardy
WEBSITE www.tarahardyillustration.com
LOCATION Montreal, Canada

AGENT Colagene <www.colagene.com>
TOOLS Collage, drawing, paint, paper, canvas, Adobe Photoshop, oil, ink, experimental mixing

CLIENTS Coca-Cola, Elle (Quebec), Reader's Digest, EnRoute, The Globe and Mail, Quebec Science, The New Yorker
AWARDS National Magazine Awards, Grafika Lux, Applied Arts

1 Music is Within, 2007, Honens International Piano Competition, Wax
2 Protection, 2006, Quebec Science Magazine
3 Persona et Moi, 2006, Les Éditions Marchand de Feuilles

2

"Illustration can help make this world a little better."

« L'illustration peut contribuer à rendre ce monde un peu meilleur. »

„Illustration kann dazu beitragen, diese Welt ein kleines bisschen besser zu machen."

Persona et Moi

EVOLUTION MENTALE

DATE: 23-9-70

Dr Jacques Ferron, M.D.

te-Marie

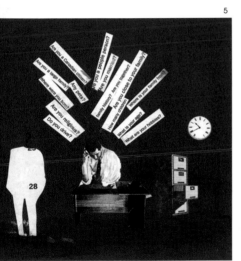

spring into the **Coke** side of life™

4 In Your Head, 2007, Editions Boréal
5 Too Many Questions, 2006, Report on Small Business, Globe and Mail
6 Urban Bloom, 2007, Coca-Cola, MacLaren McCann
7 Slow Moving, 2007, Report on Small Business, Globe and Mail

LYNDON HAYES

NAME Lyndon Hayes
WEBSITE www.lyndonscircus.co.uk
LOCATION London, United Kingdom

AGENT Dutch Uncle Agency
<www.DutchUncle.co.uk>

TOOLS Mixed media, Adobe Photoshop, Adobe Illustrator
CLIENTS Wallpaper, Faber, Volvo, The Guardian, Harper Collins, ALEF, Folio Society, Time Warner

1 James Dean, 2007
2 Tom Yorke, 2007
3 Girl With a Playboy Earing, 2007

"Nostalgic elements have always been at the heart of my work, incorporating innocent and sometimes real and gritty snapshots of life. Recently my style has been divided into two equal parts, painted pieces and also modern graphic pen and ink drawings, both incorporating flourishes of collage. My influences range from Sir Peter Blake, Euan Uglow, Robert Rauschenberg, American photographers such as Lee Friedlander, Saul Leiter and also graphic artists such as Saul Bass and the Blue Note sleeves."

« La nostalgie a toujours été au cœur de mon travail, auquel j'intègre des instantanés innocents et parfois réels et crus de la vie. Dernièrement, mon style s'est divisé à parts égales entre les peintures et les dessins modernes au stylo et à l'encre, les deux ornés de collages. Parmi mes influences, Sir Peter Blake, Euan Uglow, Robert Rauschenberg, des photographes américains comme Lee Friedlander, Saul Leiter, des artistes graphiques comme Saul Bass et les pochettes des disques Blue Note. »

„Nostalgische Elemente bildeten schon immer den Kern meiner Arbeit, die unschuldige und manchmal realistisch-düstere Schnappschüsse des Lebens enthält. Seit Kurzem ist mein Stil in zwei gleiche Teile gespalten: in gemalte und mit dem Grafikstift oder Tusche gezeichnete Werke – beide mit Collageelementen. Ich bin beeinflusst von Künstlern wie Sir Peter Blake, Euan Uglow und Robert Rauschenberg, amerikanischen Fotografen wie Lee Friedländer und Saul Leiter und auch Grafikern wie Saul Bass und den Designern der Blue-Note-Cover."

JOSEPH HEIDECKER

NAME Joseph Heidecker
WEBSITE www.josephheidecker.com

LOCATION Bellport, NY, USA
TOOLS X-acto blades, photocopy, hands

CLIENTS The New York Times Style Magazine, The New York Times, The New Yorker, Details Magazine, Men's Health, Seattle Weekly

1 Mind/Body Connection, 2006, Radcliffe Quaterly
2 Flawless, 2006, The New York Times "T" Style Magazine
3 Alice Waters, 2006, The New York Times "T" Style Magazine

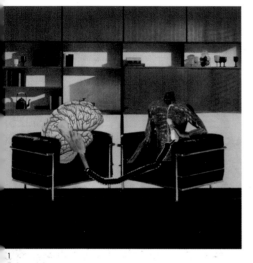

"I like to hand-manipulate/collage found images and reinterpret them in new ways."

« J'aime manipuler et faire des collages avec des images trouvées pour les réinterpréter. »

„Ich mag es, gefundene Bilder per Hand zu manipulieren oder zu Collagen zu verarbeiten und sie dadurch neu zu interpretieren."

ANTOINE HELBERT

NAME Antoine Helbert
WEBSITE www.antoine-helbert.com
LOCATION France

AGENT Agent 002 <www.agent002.com>
TOOLS Pen, pencil, oil, canvas, wood, Adobe Photoshop

CLIENTS Grimbergen, Canal+, Française des Jeux, Orchestre Philharmonique de Strasbourg, Festival de Musique Ancienne de Ribeauvillé, Vidéoselect

1

2

3

1 Hommpaon, 2006
2 Blackleo, 2006
3 Blackbird, 2006
4 Femmecoq, 2006

"Looking around you provides an unlimited source of inspiration. Past centuries and the present offer me a cultural gold-mine, extreme, varied, diverse, rich... The tone is given, the colour is found, eclecticism... My creation is made up of contemporary and past references combined on the canvas and the screen, mixing elements and figures which are never destroyed."

« Regarder devant soi et à la fois derrière soi est source d'inspiration illimitée, les siècles passés et le présent m'offrent un gisement culturel, extrême, varié, divers, riche... Le ton est donné, la couleur trouvée, « l'éclectisme ». Ma création composée de références contemporaines et passées se conjugue sur la toile et l'écran, mêlant éléments et figures qui jamais ne s'annihilent. »

„Nach vorne und zurück zu schauen, ist eine unendliche Quelle der Inspiration. Sowohl vergangene Jahrhunderte als auch die Gegenwart bieten mir eine kulturelle Fundgrube – extrem, vielseitig, voll ... Der Ton ist gegeben, die Farbe gefunden, „Eklektizismus". Meine Komposition enthält zeitgenössische und historische Referenzen, die sich auf der Leinwand vermischen, eine Mixtur an Elementen und Figuren, die nie zerstört werden."

HELLOVON

NAME Hellovon
WEBSITE www.hellovon.com

LOCATION London, United Kingdom
TOOLS Pencil, ink, computer

CLIENTS 4AD, Dazed & Confused, The Guardian, The New York Times, Non-Format, Ogilvy & Mather

1

2

1 Heartbreaker, 2006, Valentines Day Promotional Image
2 SVSV 01, 2006, Serum versus Venum. Photo by Kareem Black
3 Emily, 2007, If You Could Ehxibition

"To be better."

« S'améliorer. »

„Besser sein."

LARS HENKEL

NAME Lars Henkel
WEBSITE www.reflektorium.de
LOCATION Bonn, Germany

TOOLS Puppets, objects, camera, Adobe Photoshop
CLIENTS Universal Records, Ride Snowboards, Pittsburgh Dance Company, WDR, HAZ, StadtRevue

AWARDS Society of Illustrators, 3x3, American Illustration, Art Directors Club, Communication Arts, Freistil

1-3 Waldminiatur, 2006, personal work

"As with other work, intuitive access to the story and its subjects was important to me whilst working on the *Blinde Waldminiatur* comic series. It is much more interesting to awaken in the observer as many associations as possible using atmospheric images and a fantastic logic, than to tell a straightforward story."

« Tout comme pour d'autres projets, pour la série de bande dessinée *Blinde Waldminiatur* il était important pour moi d'avoir accès à l'histoire et à ses thèmes de manière intuitive. Il est bien plus intéressant d'éveiller chez le spectateur autant d'associations que possible grâce à des images atmosphériques et à une logique onirique que de raconter une histoire linéaire. »

„Wie auch bei anderen Arbeiten war mir bei der Serie ,Blinde Waldminiatur' ein intuitiver Zugang zu Geschichte und Motiven wichtig. Es ist viel reizvoller, mit atmosphärischen Bildern und einer traumhaften Logik möglichst viele Assoziationen beim Betrachter zu wecken, als eine konkrete Geschichte zu erzählen."

JOHN HERSEY

NAME John Hersey
WEBSITE www.hersey.com
LOCATION San Anselmo, CA, USA

TOOLS Brush, ink, Adobe Illustrator, Adobe Photoshop, Adobe Flash, Autodesk Maya
CLIENTS The New York Times, Absolut Vodka, Swatch, Esquire, Le Monde, Bandai, Apple, Microsoft, Corbis, United Airlines

AWARDS Print, Communication Arts, Etapes, SPD, How, Form, American Illustration

"Make a great picture... always."

« Créer une belle image... à chaque fois. »

„Ein gutes Bild zu machen ... immer."

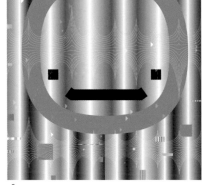

1 Yeti, 2006, Studio Camuffo
2 Newface, 2006, Pentagram
3 Nice, 2006, personal work
4 Forestrabbit, 2006, Studio Camuffo

HADLEY HOOPER

NAME Hadley Hooper
WEBSITE www.hadleyhooper.com
LOCATION Denver, CO, USA

AGENT Marlena Agency
<www.marlenaagency.com>
TOOLS Ink, house paint, acrylic, Venetian plaster,
Adobe Photoshop

CLIENTS The New York Times, Time, Harper's,
Herman Miller, Warner Bros, Rounder Records
AWARDS Society of Illustrators, American
Illustration, Communication Arts, Print Magazine,
Society of Puplication Designers

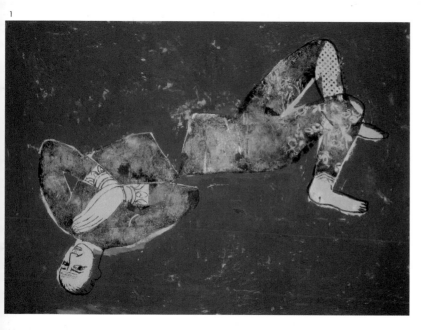

1 Man, 2006, personal work
2 The Coronation of Poppea, 2005, Central City Opera
3 Saturn Killing Time, 2005

"A creative life is one that is defined by problem solving. Whether you're working on a painting or an assignment from a client, the essence of the work is to answer the question. When asked about his approach to work, journalist David Halberstam quoted the basketball player Julius Irving: 'Being a professional is doing the things you love to do, on the days you don't feel like doing them'."

« Une vie créative est une vie passée à résoudre des problèmes. Qu'il s'agisse d'un tableau ou de la commande d'un client, l'essence du travail créatif consiste à répondre à une question. Interrogé sur son approche du travail, le journaliste David Halberstam a cité le joueur de basket-ball Julius Irving : ‹ Être un professionnel consiste à faire les choses qui vous plaisent, les jours où vous ne vous sentez pas de les faire ›. »

„Ein kreatives Leben wird durch das Lösen von Problemen definiert. Ob du nun an einem Gemälde arbeitest oder an einem Kundenauftrag, der Kern der Arbeit besteht darin, die Frage zu beantworten. Der Journalist David Halberstam, nach seiner Einstellung zur Arbeit gefragt, antwortete mit einem Zitat des Basketballspielers Julius Irving: ‚Ein Profi zu sein bedeutet, die Dinge, die du gern tust, an Tagen zu tun, an denen du keine Lust dazu hast'."

I LOVE DUST

NAME I Love Dust
WEBSITE www.ilovedust.com
LOCATION London, United Kingdom

AGENT Talkie Walkie <www.talkiewalkie.tw>
TOOLS Adobe Photoshop, Adobe Illustrator, pen, pencil

CLIENTS Microsoft, Coca-Cola, Nike, Pepsi

1 Sneaker Pimps, 2007
2 Zune, 2006

1

"Create and design in good conditions of work.
The atmosphere and the environment are very important
for good creations."

« Créer et concevoir dans de bonnes conditions de travail.
L'ambiance et l'environnement sont très importants pour obtenir de bonnes créations. »

„Kreiere und entwerfe unter guten Arbeitsbedingungen.
Atmosphäre und Umgebung sind sehr wichtig für gute schöpferische Leistungen."

4

3 Fish, 2006
4 Bliss, 2006
5 Q Bear, 2007

5

KAREEM ILIYA

NAME Kareem Iliya
LOCATION Shoreham, VT, USA
AGENT 1 Art Department, New York,
<www.art-dept.com>

AGENT 2 CWC, Tokyo, <www.cwctokyo.com>
TOOLS Watercolor, ink, charcoal, pastel, paper,
Adobe Photoshop

CLIENTS Vogue, W, The New Yorker, Nike,
Adidas, Visionaire, Harpers Bazaar, Interview,
Saks, Barneys, Bergdorf Goodman, Neiman
Marcus, Bloomingdales, Macy's, Tiffany & Co.,
Fendi, Shiseido

1 Untitled, 2005, Saks Fifth Avenue
2 Untitled, 2006, Neiman Marcus
3 Untitled, 2006, Frau Magazine
4 Untitled, 2005, personal work

"I'm driven by colour, texture and form, and avoid literal interpretations.
Rather than telling a story, I focus on the fundamentals of a subject."

« Je suis inspiré par les couleurs, les textures et les formes, et je fuis les interprétations littérales.
Au lieu de raconter une histoire, je me concentre sur l'essentiel d'un sujet. »

„Ich werde von Farbe, Material und Form motiviert und vermeide wortgetreue Interpretationen.
Anstatt eine Geschichte zu erzählen, konzentriere ich mich auf die fundamentalen Grundlagen eines Gegenstands."

MÄRT INFANGER

NAME Märt Infanger
LOCATION Lucerne, Switzerland

TOOLS Pen, Adobe Illustrator, Adobe Photoshop
CLIENTS Noman Records, Voodoo Rhythm Records, Memphisto Prod., Warner Music, Virgin

AWARDS 100 Best Posters (Germany), Jan Tschichold Prize (Switzerland)

"BLUES-TRASH-R'N'R-SWAMP-GARAGE-60'S-PUNK-CAJUN-TEX MEX-FUNERAL-JAVA-JAZZ PSYCHEDELIC-HARD-ROCK-MOD-FUNK-DEATH-COUNTRY-METAL-SPLATER-BEAT TWIST-BOOGII FOLK RHYTHM'N'BLUES-DOOWOP-BOOGALOO-MASALA."

1 The Fox, 2004, Memphisto Produktion
2 The Watzloves, 2002, Memphisto Produktion
3 Electric Polka, 2004, Jolly and the Flytrap

NATURAL
STEREO
BALANCE

JOLLY
AND THE
Flytrap

Live
ELECTRIC
POLKA

NEUE CD/LP

GRAFISTA
UltraBazar
MÄRZ 04

JAMES JARVIS

NAME James Jarvis
WEBSITE www.studiojarvis.com
LOCATION London, United Kingdom

TOOLS Pen, pencil, paper, digital processing
CLIENTS The Face, i-D, Nokia, Nova, Sony

1 King Ken III, Vinyl figurine, Amos, 2006
2 All Hail Silas, poster for Silas, Silas and Maria, 2003

1

"Modernist cartoon characters and drawing..."

« Dessins et personnages de bandes dessinées modernistes... »

„Klassische Cartoonfiguren und Zeichnen ..."

BILLIE JEAN

NAME Billie Jean
WEBSITE www.billiejean.co.uk
LOCATION London, United Kingdom

AGENT ZeegenRush <www.zeegenrush.com>
TOOLS Pencil, acrylic, biro, felt-tip, camera, Adobe Photoshop

CLIENTS Sony, Nike, Orange, Howies, GM Motors, The Samaritans, Hanes, Blueprint, Creative Review, Bloomsbury, Penguin, The Guardian, Wallpaper

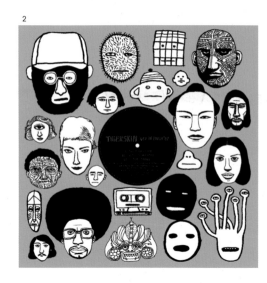

1 Chic, 2004, Native Weapom Magazine
2 Tiny Sticks, 2007, Tiny Sticks Records
3 Village People, 2005, Graphic Magazine #5

"I take a petticoat tail shortbread from my biscuit barrel and dunk it in my coffee. After the wet shortbread flops into my mouth, I can then put pencil to paper."

« Je prends un sablé en éventail dans ma boîte à biscuits et je le trempe dans mon café. Lorsque le sablé imbibé a fondu dans ma bouche, je peux poser une mine sur le papier. »

„Ich nehme einen Petticoat-Tail-Shortbread-Keks aus meiner Keksdose und tunke ihn in meinen Kaffee. Nachdem der feuchte Keks in meinen Mund geploppt ist, kann ich anfangen zu zeichnen."

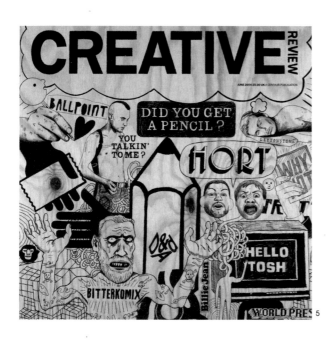

4 Vandal 1985, 2005, Nike
5 Creative Review, 2004
6 Back to the Old School, 2004, Parker Pens / Pentagram
7 Hello, 2006, Hanes

STUDIO
JEANCLODE

NAME Studio Jeanclode
WEBSITE www.jeanspezial.com
LOCATION Troyes, France

TOOLS Adobe Photoshop, Adobe Illustrator,
paper, canvas, pen, pencil, acrylic, spray, collage

CLIENTS Gaz de France, Hachette Filipacchi,
Contrex, Ricard, Rip Curl, String Republic,
E.Leclerc Supermarkets

1 Untitled, 2006
2 Untitled, 2007
3 Untitled, 2006
4 Untitled, 2006

"Three people work in the studio. It is not a question of highlighting individualism, but of complementing and enriching each other mutually. Consequently, the majority of our images are made by more than one of us. Three pairs of hands working together on the same support. Experimentation represents an important part of our work."

« Nous travaillons à trois personnes au sein du studio. Il ne s'agit pas de mettre en avant des individualités, mais bien de se compléter et de s'enrichir les uns les autres. Ainsi, la majorité de nos images sont réalisées à plusieurs, à trois paires de mains sur un même support. L'expérimentation représente une partie importante de notre travail. »

„Wir arbeiten zu dritt im Studio. Es geht nicht um Individualität, sondern darum, sich gegenseitig zu ergänzen und bereichern. Die meisten Illustrationen haben wir daher zusammen gemacht, 3 Paar Hände am selben Tisch. Experimentieren ist ein wichtiger Bestandteil unserer Arbeit."

JEREMYVILLE

NAME Jeremyville
WEBSITE www.jeremyville.com
LOCATION 1 Sydney, Australia
LOCATION 2 New York, NY, USA

AGENT Pocko People <www.pocko.com>
TOOLS Pen, sketchbook, ink and brush, acrylic, Adobe Photoshop, Adobe Freehand, Adobe Dreamweaver

CLIENTS MTV (Italy), Converse, Rossignol, IdN, Kidrobot, STRANGEco, Swindle, Colette, Corbis, Tiger Beer, Coca-Cola

1

1 "Gelati", "Monsieur Fromage",
"I Heart Cupcakes", Ceramic plate designs,
2007, Domestic, Paris
2 "Don't Panic! Let Love In...", poster, 2006,
Don't Panic UK and Australia (inaugural issue)

"To rescue drowning characters from my stream of consciousness."

« Sauver des personnages qui se noient dans le flot de ma conscience. »

„Figuren zu retten, die in meinem Bewusstseinsstrom ertrinken."

3

3 Ice Dreams, Snowboard designs, Rossignol
Snowboards, 2007 (released in 2008)
4 25 Hours in Jeremyville, Toy 2R, and Territory
Gallery, Cologne, 2006
5 'Shrooms, 55 DSL, Switzerland, 2 Steps Back
traveling art show, 2006

6

222

6 Stay Up!, Chuck Taylor shoe graphic, Converse (Red Project), 2007 (released in 2008)
7 Voices in My Head, George Lucas's 30th Anniversary of Star Wars, Los Angeles, 2007
8 Sketchel Kid, Sketchel custom art satchel project, 2007

VARSHESH JOSHI

NAME Varshesh Joshi
WEBSITE www.shoonyadesign.net
LOCATION Bangalore, India

TOOLS Pencil, pen, paper, photo ink, Adobe Flash, Adobe Illustrator, Adobe Photoshop

1-3 Untitled, 2003, personal work

"All my inspiration and learning behind my art has been through comics. I love to create characters; mostly inspired by people I come across in life. Personally, I like the possibility of comical exaggeration of expressions and emotions with realistic treatment."

« Toute l'inspiration et tout l'apprentissage derrière mon art proviennent des bandes dessinées. J'adore créer des personnages, le plus souvent inspirés par les personnes que je suis amené à rencontrer. Personnellement, j'aime la possibilité de l'exagération comique des expressions et des émotions avec un traitement réaliste. »

„Die Inspiration und das Wissen hinter meiner Kunst stammt von Comics. Ich liebe es, Figuren zu erfinden; sie sind meist von Leuten inspiriert, die mir wirklich begegnet sind. Mir gefällt, dass man realistische Sachverhalte mit übertriebenen Gesichtsausdrücken und Gefühlen darstellen kann."

KACCHI

NAME Kacchi
WEBSITE www.kacchiworld.com
LOCATION Tokyo, Japan

AGENT CWC International <www.cwc-i.com>
TOOLS Clay, acrylic

CLIENTS Sony, NHK, Paul Smith, NTT DoCoMo, Lumine, Nickelodeon, Seventeen

1

1 Superstar, 2006, Riot Magazine
2 Flower Tree, 2006, personal work

"I hope my work gives pleasure and happiness to all viewers, regardless of their age, gender, or ethnicity. I'd always like to create works where one can imagine the story."

« J'espère que mon travail procure plaisir et bonheur à tous ceux qui l'observent, quels que soient leur âge, leur genre ou leur ethnicité. J'ai toujours aimé créer des œuvres qui peuvent inspirer une histoire. »

„Ich hoffe, meine Arbeiten bereiten allen Betrachtern Vergnügen und Freude, egal welches Alter, Geschlecht oder welche Ethnizität sie haben. Ich erschaffe gerne Bilder, zu denen man sich eine Geschichte vorstellen kann."

MAIRA KALMAN

NAME Maira Kalman
WEBSITE www.mairakalman.com
LOCATION New York, NY, USA

TOOLS Gouache, paper
CLIENTS The New York Times, The New Yorker,
Interview, Newsweek, Travel & Leisure

AWARDS Society of Illustrators, Art Directors Club,
American Illustration, The New York Times, AIGA,
Society of Publication Designers

1

"I did not study illustration or design.
I studied literature. My paintings are
narrative, absurd, humorous,
and rely on personal storytelling."

« Je n'ai pas étudié l'illustration ou le design, mais la littérature.
Mes peintures sont narratives, absurdes, humoristiques
et reposent sur la narration personnelle. »

„Ich habe weder Illustration noch Design studiert,
sondern Literatur. Meine Bilder sind narrativ, absurd
und humorvoll und basieren auf persönlichen Geschichten."

1-3 Elements of Style, 2005, Penguin Press
4 Breakfast, 2006, Gourmet Magazine

2

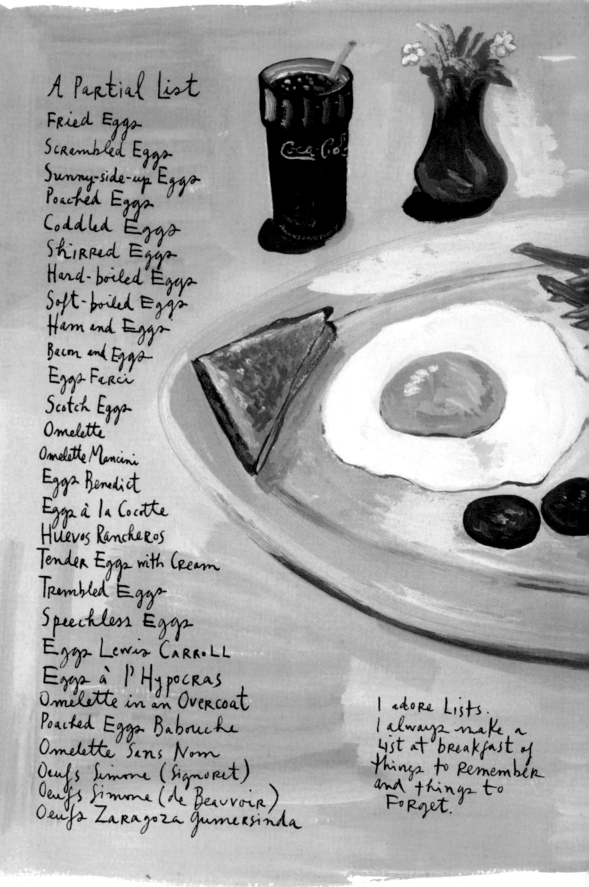

A Partial List
Fried Eggs
Scrambled Eggs
Sunny-side-up Eggs
Poached Eggs
Coddled Eggs
Shirred Eggs
Hard-boiled Eggs
Soft-boiled Eggs
Ham and Eggs
Bacon and Eggs
Eggs Farci
Scotch Eggs
Omelette
Omelette Mancini
Eggs Benedict
Eggs à la Cocotte
Huevos Rancheros
Tender Eggs with Cream
Trembled Eggs
Speechless Eggs
Eggs Lewis Carroll
Eggs à l'Hypocras
Omelette in an Overcoat
Poached Eggs Babouche
Omelette Sans Nom
Oeufs Simone (Signoret)
Oeufs Simone (de Beauvoir)
Oeufs Zaragoza Gumersinda

I adore Lists.
I always make a
list at breakfast of
things to Remember
and things to
Forget.

we came to America in 1954.
If you come to America, I advise you to
come in 1954.

It was the time of
unlimited TV watching.
We drank Coca-Cola for breakfast
in the coffee shop. That was
short-lived but memorable.
The coffee shop is the ultimate sensational way
to start the day. Everyone is in this mad Rush,
yelling "Whiskey Down" and "Adam and Eve on a Raft,
WRECK 'EM!" Where will you hear Language like that?
Everyone is polishing off This and washing it down with THAT.
It gives one HOPE.

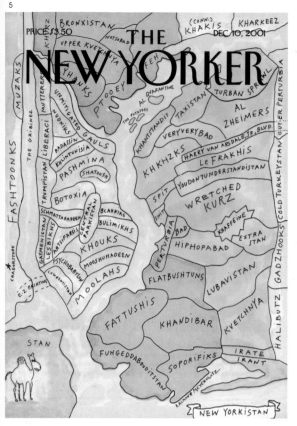

5 New Yorkistan, by Maira Kalman & Rick Meyerowitz, 2001, The New Yorker
6 Misery Day Parade, 2001, The New Yorker
7-8 Principles of Uncertainty, 2006-2007, The New York Times Select

NABOKOV'S FAMILY FLED RUSSIA.
How COULD the YOUNG NABOKOV, SITTING
INNOCENTLY and ELEGANTLY in a
Red chair. Leafing through a Book
on BUTTERFLIES imagine Such
displacement.   Such Loss.

DONALD KILPATRICK III

NAME Donald Kilpatrick III
WEBSITE www.illoz.com/donkilpatrick
LOCATION 1 Birmingham, MI, USA
LOCATION 2 New York, NY, USA

AGENT Morgan Gaynin Inc.
<www.morgangaynin.com>
TOOLS Acrylic, oil, found surfaces, ink, old paper,
Adobe Photoshop, Adobe Illustrator

CLIENTS DreamWorks, Fortune, Penguin,
Salt Lake Olympic Committee, Chrysler,
VH1, Bicycling Magazine
AWARDS Communication Arts, 3x3 Annual,
XIX Winter Olympic Games, SINY

1 Tied-up, 2006, personal work
2 Peace, 2006, personal work
3 Furniture Store, 2004, personal work

"I strive to make my work personal, and in doing so relate it to the individual as well as society in general. Most people haven't had an art education, so my work has to speak for itself. I make every effort not to overly control my process, and keep myself open to new experiences in the creation of my art."

« Je m'efforce de faire des créations à la fois personnelles et en rapport avec les personnes et la société en général. Les gens ne recevant généralement pas d'éducation artistique, mon travail doit parler de lui-même. Je me concentre pour ne pas trop contrôler le processus et rester ouvert à de nouvelles expériences. »

„Ich versuche, meine Arbeiten persönlich zu gestalten und schaffe dabei sowohl zum Individuum als auch zur Gesellschaft generell einen Bezug. Die meisten Menschen haben keine spezielle Kunstausbildung, meine Arbeit muss also für sich sprechen. Ich bemühe mich sehr, den Schaffensprozess nicht zu stark zu kontrollieren, und bin für neue Erfahrungen offen."

4 Through a Gate of Trees, 2006, CavanKerry Press
5 Icarus, 2006, personal work
6 Roma, 2006, personal work
7 S- Red Scoot, 2006, personal work

KIMI KIMOKI

NAME Kimi kimoki
WEBSITE www.kimikimoki.blogspot.com
LOCATION Marseille, France

AGENT 1 Lezilus, Paris, <www.lezilus.com>
AGENT 2 Colagene, Montreal, <www.colagene.com>
TOOLS Lead pencil, gouache, watercolor, felt-tip pen, Adobe Photoshop, Corel Painter

CLIENTS Le Coq Sportif, PMU, Bijouterie Frojo, Condat, Éditions Libre Expression, Sidlee, WAD, Hydro-Québec, TÊTU, Technikart, Air Canada

1 Untitled, 2005, Bijouterie Frojo
Ginette NY
2 Untitled, 2005, Coming Up Magazine
3 Untitled, 2007, Papier Condat
Stateus Agency

"Light, the work of the naked parts, finished elements juxtapositioned with spaces, are the points on which I centre all my attention. Get close to reality in order to go out into it and extrapolate it. Create a fiction in which the characters and objects are suspended between illusion and truth. My intention is to highlight the beauty of that which our view tends to trivialise."

« La lumière, le travail des chairs, les éléments aboutis juxtaposés aux espaces, sont les points sur lesquels je porte toute mon attention. M'approcher du réel pour en sortir, l'extrapoler. Créer une fiction où personnages et objets sont suspendus entre illusion et vérité. Mon intention est de souligner la beauté de ce que notre regard a tendance à banaliser. »

„Licht, Haut, abgeschlossene Elemente, die Räumen gegenübergestellt sind – das sind die Aspekte, auf die ich mich konzentriere. Ich nähere mich der Realität, um sie zu erkunden und zu erfassen. Eine Fiktion zu erschaffen, in der Figuren und Objekte sich zwischen Illusion und Wahrheit befinden. Ich möchte die Schönheit dessen betonen, was wir mit unserem Blick banalisieren."

TATSURO KIUCHI

NAME Tatsuro Kiuchi
WEBSITE www.tatsurokiuchi.com
LOCATION Tokyo, Japan

AGENT Heflinreps <www.heflinreps.com>
TOOLS Adobe Photoshop, paper, acrylic
CLIENTS The New Yorker, The Guardian, The New York Times, United Airlines, The Royal Mail, NHK, Kodansha, Bunshun, JAL, NEC, Sony, Asahi News

AWARDS Society of Illustrators, Bologna International Children's Book Fair, Communication Arts, Art Directors Club, American Illustration, 3x3, Kodansha Award

1 A traveler in Books, 2007, Kadokawa Shoten
2 Last Night, 2007, The Guardian,
3 Golf Orphans, 2007, Golf for Women Magazine

2

1

"The selection of colours is the most important thing to me when creating pieces, and secondly, compositions. Even though I like simplifying shapes and forms, I try to consult the reference materials as much as possible. This way I can avoid inventing things I don't know much of."

« Le choix des couleurs est ce qu'il y a de plus important à mes yeux au moment de créer des œuvres, puis viennent les compositions. Même si j'aime simplifier les formes, j'essaie autant que possible d'étudier les documents de référence. J'évite ainsi d'inventer des choses que je ne maîtrise pas. »

„Das wichtigste für mich ist die Auswahl der Farben. Dann kommt die Komposition. Obwohl ich Formen gerne vereinfache, schöpfe ich so viel wie möglich aus dem Referenzmaterial. So muss ich keine Dinge erfinden, über die ich nicht viel weiß."

6

7

5

4 Walking a shiba dog in the central park, 2007, Absolute Magazine
5 A pearl necklace, 2007, Good Housekeeping Magazine
6 The sharp decline in stock prices, 2007, Bunshun
7 Byakkotai, 2007, Kodansha

JEROME LAGARRIGUE

NAME Jerome Lagarrigue
WEBSITE www.jeromelagarrigue.com
LOCATION New York, NY, USA

AGENT Gerald & Cullen Rapp <www.rappart.com>
TOOLS Acrylic, board, paper

CLIENTS The New Yorker, The New York Times, Penguin, Simon & Schuster, Farrar, Time Warner, Straus & Giroux
AWARDS Coretta Scott King Award, Ezra Jack Keats Award, Society of Illustrators Award

1 Tony Soprano, 2004, Sterling Publishing
2 Suge Knight, 2003, personal work
3 Notorious BIG, 2006, Vibe Magazine
4 Tyson's True Colors, 2004, personal work

"My approach to illustration is painterly. I try to capture that specific blurred mood that permeates my entire body of work. I want my images to be as hazy as possible. My compositions are usually simple and straightforward, willing to achieve a high level of impact. I enjoy the notion that paint is loosely applied."

« Mon approche de l'illustration se fait par la peinture. J'essaie de capturer cette humeur floue qui imprègne toute mon œuvre. Je veux que mes images soient aussi troubles que possible. Mes compositions sont généralement simples pour que le niveau d'impact soit élevé. J'aime l'idée de la peinture appliquée de façon libre. »

„Ich habe einen malerischen Zugang zur Illustration. Ich versuche, eine ganz spezielle verschwommene Stimmung einzufangen, die sich durch alle meine Arbeiten zieht. Meine Bilder sollen so nebelhaft wie möglich sein. Meine Kompositionen sind in der Regel einfach und gradlinig, um eine starke Wirkung zu erzielen. Ich mag die Vorstellung von locker aufgetragener Farbe."

6

5 Poetry for young people: Maya Angelou, 2007, Sterling Publishing
6 Talib Kweli & DJ Hi-Tek, 2000, Rawkus
7 Airplane #1, 2004, personal work
8 Airplane #2, 2004, personal work

8

ZOHAR LAZAR

NAME Zohar Lazar
WEBSITE www.zoharlazar.com
LOCATION New York, NY, USA

TOOLS Watercolor, gouache, acrylic, Adobe Photoshop
CLIENTS The New Yorker, Time, Nickelodeon, The New York Times, GQ, Noggin, Nike, Microsoft

AWARDS Art Directors Club Young Guns, Spot Show, American Illustration

1

"Get the job in on time.
Don't forget to send the invoice."

« Faire le travail dans les délais. Ne pas oublier d'envoyer la facture. »

„Gib die Arbeit rechtzeitig ab. Vergiss nicht, die Rechnung zu stellen."

2   3

1 Katamine Girl, 2005, Katamine
2 Power Lines, 2005, They Might Be Giants (CD The Spine)
3 Pick Up, 2005, They Might Be Giants (CD The Spine)
4 Untitled, 2007, GQ Magazine

5 The Spine, 2005, They Might Be Giants (CD The Spine)
6 Wizard of Oz, 2006, Entertainment Weekly Magazine
7 Untitled, 2006, GQ Magazine
8 Rat Race, 2007, Plan Sponsor Magazine

CHOW LEE

NAME Chow Lee
WEBSITE www.chowlee.com

LOCATION Hong Kong, China
TOOLS Corel Painter, Adobe Photoshop

"Longman = Romance.
I try my best to create a mood of romance."

« Longman = Romance. Je m'efforce de créer une atmosphère romantique. »

„Longman = Romance. Ich versuche, eine romantische Stimmung zu erzeugen."

1 Longman #1, 2005, personal work
2 Longman #4, 2005, personal work
3 Longman #5, postcard, 2006, HK Society of Illustrators

4

4 Longman #2, 2005, personal work
5 Longman #3, 2006, Pacific Digital Picture Ltd.
6 Longman #6, 2005, personal work

WALDO LEE

NAME Waldo Lee
WEBSITE www.walee.com
LOCATION Paris, France

AGENT Talkie Walkie <www.talkiewalkie.tw>
TOOLS 3D Studio Max, Adobe Photoshop

CLIENTS Intermarché, Société Générale, Sony, Axa, Cartoon Network, Citroën, Lego, L'Oreal, P&G, Renault, SNCF, Garnier, Red Bull, Virtools, Soundlicious, Pepsi MAX

"Realising original illustrations, and enjoying it."

« Créer des illustrations originales et y prendre plaisir. »

„Originelle Illustrationen entstehen zu lassen und dabei Spaß zu haben."

1

2

1 Playstation 3, 2007, Sony / Dedicate Magazine. Photo by Marc da Cunha Lopes
2 Septembre, 2007, Talkie Walkie. Sahé Cibot (Model)
3 Game Over, 2006, Lady Caprice Magazine. Photo by Marc da Cunha Lopes

YOANN LEMOINE

NAME Yoann Lemoine
WEBSITE www.yoannlemoine.com
LOCATION 1 Paris, France
LOCATION 2 New York, NY, USA

AGENT Agent 002 <www.agent002.com>
TOOLS Ink, pencil, Adobe Photoshop

CLIENTS Wanda, Warner Music, TF1, Plon, Art Directors Club, Albin Michel, Rageot, Milan, TÊTU, Out Magazine

"Romanticism and nostalgia, sleeping boys and dancing girls, feathers, flowers, leaves, wool, milk, clouds."

« Romantisme et nostalgie, des garçons qui dorment et des filles qui dansent, des plumes, des fleurs, des feuilles, de la laine, du lait, des nuages. »

„Romantik und Nostalgie, schlafende Knaben und tanzende Mädchen, Federn, Blumen, Blätter, Wolle, Milch, Wolken."

1 Luka, album cover, 2007
2 Good Morning Brooklyn, 2007, personal work
3 K.N.I.T., 2007, personal work

3

KENNY LINDSTRÖM

NAME Kenny Lindström
WEBSITE www.organiclevel.com
LOCATION Umeå, Sweden

TOOLS Pen, marker, ink, acrylic, Adobe Flash, Adobe Photoshop, Adobe Illustrator

CLIENTS North Kingdom, Popcore Film, Save The Children, RFSU, Syrup NYC, DeVillain Guitar Company

1 Wet With Water, 2007, personal work
2 Untitled, 2005, Save the children
3 Untitled, 2005, Save the children

"I love drawing, always have, and always will. To be able to do this for a living is a dream come true. A really good illustration or work of art can give me so much energy and inspiration, and if my work can bring even half of that happiness and inspiration into other's lives, I would be more then happy."

« J'adore dessiner, j'ai toujours aimé et j'aimerai toujours. Pouvoir en vivre est un rêve devenu réalité. Une illustration ou une œuvre d'art vraiment bonne me procure une incroyable dose d'énergie et d'inspiration, et si mon travail peut transmettre ne serait-ce que la moitié de ce bonheur et de cette inspiration à autrui, je suis plus qu'heureux. »

„Ich habe schon immer gerne gezeichnet und werde es auch immer tun. Davon leben zu können, ist für mich ein wahrgewordener Traum. Eine richtig gute Illustration gibt mir unglaublich viel Energie und Inspiration. Wenn ich anderen mit meiner Arbeit auch nur halb soviel Freude und Inspiration geben kann, bin ich überglücklich."

NICE LOPES

NAME Nice Lopes
WEBSITE www.nicelopes.blogspot.com
LOCATION Sao Paulo, Brazil

TOOLS Corel Draw, Adobe Photoshop, Adobe Illustrator, pen, pencil

CLIENTS Posterlounge, Jacques Janine, Q-Vizu, Shopping ABC, Ciclo das Vinhas, Paula Barsotti

1 Red, 2007, personal work
2 Wine, 2007, Ciclo das Vinhas
3 Buzz, 2007, personal work

"I love to experiment with new forms and styles of expression, and my greatest passion is to embody the feminine soul in my illustrations."

« J'aime faire des essais avec de nouvelles formes et des styles d'expression inédits. Ma plus grande passion est de représenter l'âme féminine dans mes illustrations. »

„Ich experimentiere gerne mit neuen Formen und Ausdrucksstilen. Meine größte Leidenschaft ist es, in meinen Illustrationen die weibliche Seele einzufangen."

DON MAK

NAME Don Mak
WEBSITE www.don.hk
LOCATION Hong Kong, China

TOOLS Pencil, ink, acrylic, paper,
Adobe Photoshop, Corel Painter

CLIENTS Maxim (Hong Kong), Spiral (Hong Kong),
Jade Dynasty Group
AWARDS Society of Illustrators (Hong Kong)

1 Siddhartha and Jesus, 2005, personal work
2 I Love Money, 2005, personal work
3 Madman Diary, 2005, personal work

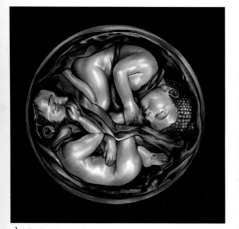
1

2

"In this moment, I am looking for a balance between drawing and doing illustration."

« En ce moment, je recherche l'équilibre entre dessiner et faire de l'illustration. »

„Zur Zeit suche ich nach einer Balance zwischen Zeichnen und Illustrieren."

TIM MARRS

NAME Tim Marrs
WEBSITE www.timmarrs.co.uk
LOCATION Hastings, United Kingdom

AGENT 1 Central Illustration Agency, London,
<www.centralillustration.com>
AGENT 2 Bernstein & Andriulli, New York,
<www.ba-reps.com>

TOOLS Adobe Photoshop, screen painting, paint, pencil, papermate pen, digital camera, photocopy
CLIENTS Jordan Brand, Ogilvy & Mather, LA Times, W+K, Nike, Entertainment Weekly, The Guardian, Saatchi & Saatchi, Time Out, Rolling Stone

1 Music Ressurection, 2007, The Guardian
2 Firecracker, 2002, personal work
3 Young Bob, 2005, Entertainment Weekly

"I hope that my works reflect the passion I have for textures, coloured mess and colour. Although made in Photoshop I try to keep the imagery as handmade looking as possible. No fancy filters, obsessive scrolling patterns, no vector shapes, just down and dirty rocking illustration with a cheeky nod and wink, that's me!"

« J'espère que mon travail reflète ma passion pour les textures, le désordre coloré et les couleurs. Même si j'utilise Photoshop, j'essaie que mes images semblent le plus possible faites à la main. Pas de filtres fantaisistes, pas de motifs qui se répètent, pas de formes vectorielles, mais rien que de l'illustration brute de décoffrage avec une touche d'impertinence, tout moi en somme ! »

„Ich hoffe, dass meine Arbeiten meine Leidenschaft für Materialien, buntes Chaos und Farben widerspiegeln. Obwohl die Bilder in Photoshop erstellt sind, versuche ich, sie so handgemacht wie möglich aussehen zu lassen. Keine ausgefallenen Filter, obzessiven Schnörkelmuster oder Vektorformen, nur bodenständige rockig-dreckige Illustration mit einem frechen Augenzwinkern – das bin ich!"

4

4 Young Cobain, 2003/2004, Uncut Magazine
5 Missy, 2003, Mojo Magazine
6 New York City Marathon, 2006, Asics
7 Out Side of the Box, 2007, Nike / Wieden+Kennedy

5

6

7

MONE MAURER

NAME Mone Maurer
WEBSITE www.monemaurer.com
LOCATION Offenbach am Main, Germany

TOOLS Mixed media, printing, acrylic, pencil, marker pen, India ink, stickers, Adobe Photoshop

CLIENTS Brand Eins, Die Zeit, Design Hotels, Guj, Gigolo Records, M Publication, Neon, Rojo, Rosebud, Spex, Style Magazine

1 Recover Beauty – Claudia Schiffer, 2007, Vorn Magazine
2 Perspective, 2005, Brand Eins
3 Bruce Lee, 2005, personal work
3 Recover Privacy, 2006, Rosebud Magazine

"Illustration is like visual Djing, and in this spirit I'm a DJ! There are plenty of existing images, a visual overflow. Why should I create anything new? Firstly, I'm looking for existing material that works with the idea and then I remix it. Secondly, if I can't find something specific, I draw or photograph what I need and start to sample myself."

« L'illustration c'est du mixage visuel, ce qui fait de moi un DJ dans l'âme ! Il existe déjà des tonnes d'images, une saturation visuelle : pourquoi alors créer quoi que ce soit de nouveau ? Je commence par rechercher du matériel existant adapté à l'idée, puis je le remixe. Et si je n'arrive à rien de concret, je dessine ou photographie ce dont j'ai besoin et je commence à me sampler moi-même. »

„Illustration ist eine Art visuelles Djing und in diesem Sinne bin ich ein DJ! Es gibt schon so viele Bilder, ein visuelles Overflow. Warum also etwas Neues schaffen? Zuerst suche ich nach bestehendem Material, das zur Idee passt, und remixe es. Wenn ich nichts Passendes finde, zeichne oder fotografiere ich, was ich brauche, und sample mich dann selbst."

TED MCGRATH

NAME Ted McGrath
WEBSITE www.tedmcgrath.com
LOCATION Brooklyn, NY, USA

TOOLS Brush, ink, gouache, pencil, crayon, watercolor, pen, paper, cardboard, digital media, various tapes and adhesives

CLIENTS MTV Networks, The New York Times, Bust Magazine, Esquire (Russia), Texas Monthly, Plan Sponsor, Cottage Life, MacLean's
AWARDS Art Directors Club Young Guns, American Illustration

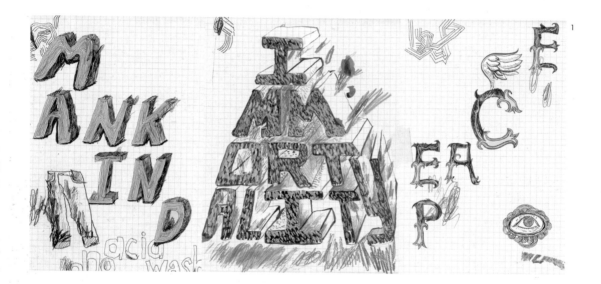

1 The Future of Jean Branding, 2006, Nylon Magazine
2 We Melted It AAALLLLLLLL..., 2007, personal work
3 Wave Tiger, 2007, Plan Sponsor Magazine

"What I enjoy most about being an illustrator is the broad and somewhat unimaginable audience that encounters and interacts with every piece you create. Every assignment becomes a chance to change someone's mind, force them to reconsider an opinion or maybe just alter their day for the better by surprising them with an unexpected image. It is this aspect of illustration that I hope most informs my work – the task of creating something that I want to look at compulsively and then, hopefully and by extension, the viewer will as well."

« Ce qui me plaît le plus dans le métier d'illustrateur, c'est le public infini et inimaginable qui est amené à voir et à interagir avec chacune de vos œuvres. Chaque commande offre la chance de faire changer quelqu'un d'avis, de forcer la remise à plat d'une opinion ou simplement d'améliorer la journée d'une personne en la surprenant avec une image inattendue. J'espère que mon travail montre surtout cet aspect de l'illustration, la tâche de créer quelque chose que je veux observer de façon compulsive puis, avec un peu de chance et par extension, que le public en fasse autant. »

„Am meisten gefällt mir am Illustratorendasein das breite und etwas undefinierte Publikum, das meinen Werken begegnet und mit ihnen interagiert. Jeder Auftrag birgt die Chance, jemandes Meinung zu ändern, ihn oder sie zu zwingen, eine vorgefasste Meinung zu überdenken. Oder man heitert jemanden auf, indem man ihn einfach mit einem unerwarteten Bild überrascht. Dieser Aspekt der Illustration bestimmt meine Arbeit am meisten, hoffe ich – etwas zu schaffen, das ich mir zwanghaft anschauen möchte, und das Publikum dann hoffentlich auch."

2

3

4 Toxic Waste in the Urals Mountains, 2005, Esquire (Russia)
5 EP / Cassette (Codex : Elvis), 2004, personal work
6 Mirror Match / Endless Winter, 2007, personal work
7 Sphinx Mountain / OK OK!, 2007, personal work
8 False Hopes And Natural Disasters, 2006, The New York Times. Brian Rea (Art Direction)

6

7

8

JASON MECIER

NAME Jason Mecier
WEBSITE www.jasonmecier.com
LOCATION San Francisco, CA, USA

AGENT Maslov & Weinberg <www.maslov.com>
TOOLS Mosaic illustration, found objects, food, make-up, celebrities' personal items, glue, board, anything...

CLIENTS Ford, Quaker, Wrigley's, Showtime, Entertainment Weekly, Harper's, Farrah Fawcett, Melissa Etheridge

1 Condoleezza Rice, 2007, Seven Stories Press, Amy Scholder
2 Phyllis Diller, 2006, personal work
3 Donald Trump, 2005, Radar Magazine

"These are one-of-a-kind handcrafted mosaics. I use a folksy, arts and crafts approach to my artwork, and then reapply it to the modern world. My subject matter primarily focuses on pop culture and celebrities. Any subject can be created using any materials."

« Il s'agit de mosaïques uniques en leur genre, faites à la main. J'ai adopté une approche artisanale et populaire de mon travail et je l'applique au monde moderne. Ma thématique concerne principalement la culture pop et les célébrités, mais n'importe quel sujet peut être représenté avec n'importe quel matériau. »

„Das sind einmalige handgearbeitete Mosaike. Ich habe einen folkloristischen kunsthandwerklichen Ansatz, den ich dann auf die moderne Welt anwende. Thematisch befasse ich mich vorwiegend mit Popkultur und Prominenten. Jedes Thema kann durch die Verwendung jeglichen Materials illustriert werden."

4 Pink, 2006, Bill Graham Presents
5 Rosie O'Donell, 2007, personal work
6 Missy Elliott, 2004, Suede Magazine
7 W Hotel, 2006, Assoline

MEGA

NAME Mega
WEBSITE www.ilovemega.com
LOCATION 1 Paris, France
LOCATION 2 Sao Paulo, Brazil

LOCATION 3 Sydney, Australia
AGENT Lezilus, Paris, <www.lezilus.com>
TOOLS Adobe Illustrator, paper, pen

CLIENTS Nike iD, Virgin Music, SFR, EMI, Cartel Skateboards, Complex Magazine, WAD Magazine, Clark Magazine
AWARDS Kink Magazine, WAD Magazine, Acclaim

1

1 DJ Diplo, 2006, Clark Magazine
2 Nori21 by Mega, 2007, Nori21
3 Lezilus Megastore, 2006, Lezilus

2

"I try to stay open to everything new, from music to fashion to art, so there is always something fresh I can incorporate in my work. I blend hand illustrations, graffiti, vector graphics and typography seamlessly in a very natural way, as expressions of my different experiences and influences."

« J'essaie de rester ouvert à toutes les nouveautés, de la musique à l'art en passant par la mode, ce qui me donne toujours quelque chose de frais à intégrer à mon travail. Je mélange illustrations à la main, graffiti, graphisme vectoriel et typographie de façon homogène et très naturelle, comme des expressions de mes diverses expériences et influences. »

„Ich versuche, für alles Neue offen zu bleiben – von Musik über Mode bis hin zur bildenden Kunst – damit ich immer etwas Frisches in meine Arbeit einbinden kann. Als Ausdruck meiner verschiedenen Erfahrungen und Einflüsse vermische ich Handzeichnungen, Graffiti, Vektorgrafiken und Typografie nahtlos und auf eine sehr natürliche Weise."

LEZILUS MEGASTORE
All you need and more.

SONIA MENDI

NAME Sonia Mendi
LOCATION Athens, Greece

AGENT Smart Magna <www.smartmagna.com>
TOOLS Pen, pencil, Adobe Photoshop

CLIENTS Lambrakis Press, Imako Press, Euro RSCG Calgon, Adel Saatchi & Saatchi, Diva, Getty Images, Harpers Bazaar

1 ASSM5, 2005, personal work
2 SM7, 2006, Smart Magna
3 SM3, 2006, Smart Magna
4 SM1, 2007, personal work

"I firmly believe that in every sketch a personal style is definitely more important than the technique itself. An essential aim for my drawings is for them not to be static, but to be filled with movement, to be elegant and interesting… like an abstract from a movie. I am very passionate about fashion, hence adapting it to the female body forms I design."

« Je suis fermement convaincue que dans chaque croquis, le style personnel l'emporte nettement sur la technique à proprement parler. L'un des principaux objectifs de mes dessins est qu'ils ne soient pas statiques, mais pleins d'élégance et de mouvement et intéressants… comme un extrait de film. J'ai une grande passion pour la mode, que j'adapte aux formes féminines que je crée. »

„Ich glaube fest daran, dass ein persönlicher Stil wichtiger ist als die Technik selber. Ich möchte, dass meine Zeichnungen nicht statisch, sondern voller Bewegung, dass sie elegant und interessant sind ... wie ein Filmabriss. Ich habe einen sehr leidenschaftlichen Zugang zu Mode und passe sie deshalb an die weiblichen Körperformen an, die ich entwerfe."

RODERICK MILLS

NAME Roderick Mills
LOCATION London, United Kingdom

AGENT Heart <www.heartagency.com>
TOOLS Pilot G-Tec-C4 and G-1 0.5 pens, scribble pad by Muji, mixed media

CLIENTS United Technologies, Volkswagen, The New York Times, Royal Mail, The BBC, Howies, Bloomsbury, The Guardian
AWARDS Society of Publication Designers

1 Suzanne Vega, 2007, Barnard Magazine
2 Welcome to the South West, 2006, Landscape Magazine

1

"Drawing for me is a direct way of communicating. I don't labour over reference material. I'm intuitive after studying source material. I quote elements rather than produce something that is representational. Rarely do I set out to illustrate, I draw around the subject. This allows the work to exist on many levels, as a piece of communication, but also as something which is inexplicable."

« Pour moi, le fait de dessiner est un mode de communication directe. Je ne m'étends pas sur le matériel de référence, j'agis intuitivement après avoir étudié le matériel source. Je rappelle des éléments plutôt que de construire quelque chose de figuratif. Il est rare que je cherche à illustrer. Je dessine autour du sujet. De cette façon, le travail peut exister à de nombreux niveaux, comme élément de communication, mais aussi comme quelque chose d'inexplicable. »

„Zeichnen ist für mich ein direkter Kommunikationsweg. Ich wälze kein Referenzmaterial. Ich arbeite intuitiv, nachdem ich das Quellenmaterial gesichtet habe. Ich zitiere Elemente, anstatt etwas Repräsentatives zu produzieren. Selten gehe ich eine Illustration gezielt an. Ich zeichne um das Thema herum. Dadurch existiert das Werk auf vielen Ebenen, als ein Stück Kommunikation, aber auch als etwas Unerklärliches."

JÉRÔME MIREAULT

NAME Jérôme Mireault
LOCATION Montreal, Canada

AGENT Colagene <www.colagene.com>
TOOLS Pencil, Col-Erase, Wacom tablet, Adobe Photoshop, Adobe Illustrator

CLIENTS Agency, Marketel, Cossette, Sidlee, Euro RSCG BETC, 52 Pick-Up, Elle, Pure, ATI, Clin d'Œil Magazine

1

1 Horoscope, 2007, Filles Clin d'Œil Magazine
2 Good Morning, 2005, personal work

"As a huge melting pot of everything that surrounds and inspires me, my style is often redefined to constantly reflect me. My many everyday influences are all recognizable in each piece I do, that's what makes the way I draw so unique to my eyes."

« Mon style est un énorme melting-pot de tout ce qui m'entoure et m'inspire, et il se redéfinit souvent pour être toujours à mon image. Les nombreuses influences que je subis chaque jour se reconnaissent bien dans chacune de mes œuvres, c'est ce qui à mes yeux rend unique ma façon de dessiner. »

„Mein Stil ist ein riesiger Schmelztiegel von allem, was mich umgibt und inspiriert, und wird häufig neu definiert, um mich ständig widerzuspiegeln. Meine vielen alltäglichen Einflüsse sind in jeder einzelnen Arbeit erkennbar. Das macht meine Art zu zeichnen in meinen Augen so einzigartig."

MKLANE

NAME Mklane
WEBSITE www.mklane.com
LOCATION Rome, Italy

TOOLS Pen, pencil, ink, watercolor, acrylic, collage, Adobe Photoshop, Adobe Illustrator

CLIENTS Clone, Cover, Head, Mekkanografici, NADA, Rosebud, Sportswear International
AWARDS Eulda, Quanto Project

1 Shibuya boy, 2007, Head Magazine
2 Salvador, 2007, Don't Panic Online Magazine
3 Bounds by Conditions, 2006, Destructed Magazine
4 People, 2006, personal work

1

2

3

"I observe everything around me, always setting out different visions, and all this influences me and vibrates my personality as well as my way of expressing myself through a sign. It is a game of unstable balances, between full and empty, between white and black. There is no particular philosophy in my work, but an irrepressible need to communicate to others who I am, what I see and how I see it."

« J'observe tout ce qui m'entoure, en proposant toujours plusieurs visions, et tout cela influence ma personnalité et la fait vibrer, ainsi que ma façon de m'exprimer à travers un signe. C'est un jeu d'équilibres instables, entre pleins et déliés, entre le blanc et le noir. Il n'y a aucune philosophie particulière derrière mon travail, juste un besoin impérieux de communiquer aux autres qui je suis, ce que je vois et comment je le vois. »

„Ich beobachte alles, was um mich herum passiert, aus verschiedenen Blickwinkeln. Dies beeinflusst meine Persönlichkeit sowie die Art, wie ich mich ausdrücke. Es ist ein Spiel voller instabiler Balancen, zwischen voll und leer, zwischen weiß und schwarz. Meiner Arbeit liegt keine bestimmte Philosophie zugrunde. Sie ist nur Ausdruck eines ununterdrückbaren Bedürfnisses, anderen mitzuteilen, wer ich bin, was ich sehe und wie ich es sehe."

CHRISTIAN MONTENEGRO

NAME Christian Montenegro
WEBSITE www.christianmontenegro.com.ar
LOCATION Buenos Aires, Argentina

AGENT Dutch Uncle Agency
<www.DutchUncle.co.uk>

CLIENTS Vodafone, Becks, The Economist, Levi's, The Guardian, Die Gestalten, Macmillan, GE, Vespa, Volkswagen, New Scientist, FOX

1 Kat, 2007, Templin Brink Design
2 Zutana, 2006, book "Peleadoras, Mentirosas y Haraganas"
3 Hawking's Flexiverse, 2006, News Cientist Magazine

"An attempt to fuse personal and commercial work into one."

« Une tentative de fusion du travail personnel et du travail commercial. »

„Der Versuch, persönliche und kommerzielle Arbeit zu verbinden."

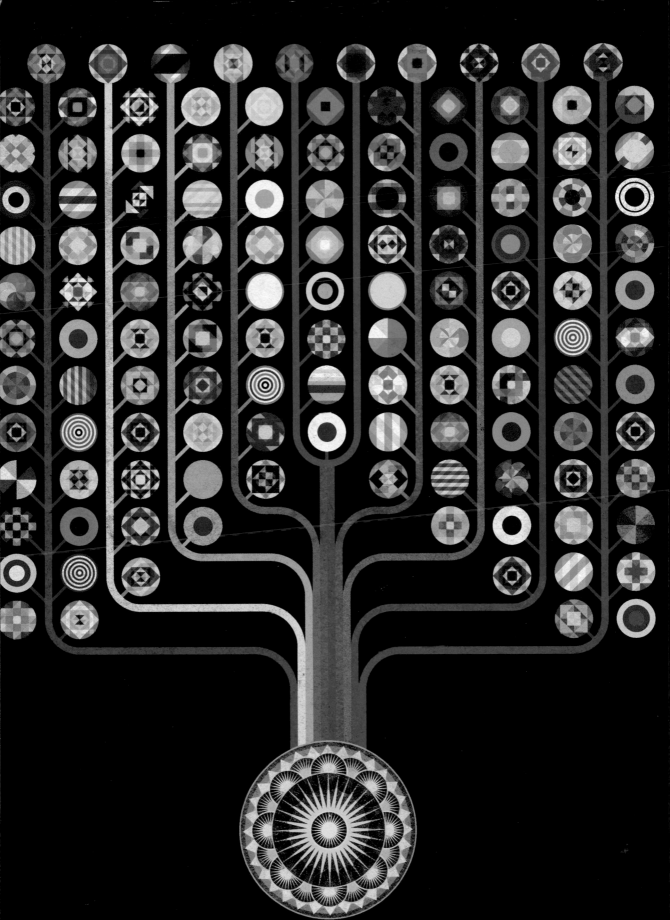

4 Basilisk, 2005, Zoda Magazine
5 Untitled, 2006, The Guardian
6 Envy, 2006, Grin and Shein Haus
7 This is My Generation, 2006, Levi's Argentina

HERR MUELLER

NAME Herr Mueller
WEBSITE www.ilikeyourbadbreathdaddy.de
LOCATION Berlin, Germany

AGENT UpperOrange <www.upperorange.com>
TOOLS Adhesive tape, paper, cutter, dirt, pen tablet, Adobe Photoshop, vintage books, pencil, paint

CLIENTS Neon Magazine, Feld Hommes, Zeit Wissen, Rund, Fleurop, Exberliner, DKdL
AWARDS Epica Award, Art Directors Club (Switzerland & Germany)

1 Ed Gein – Waistcoat, 2006, Feld Hommes
2 Tiger, 2006, Feld Hommes, photos by Philip Schneider for 747 Studios, Hamburg
3 Hand, 2006, Walker Werbeagentur / Fleurop, Mieke Haase (Art Direction)

"I developed a strange protestant work ethic, perhaps out of my teenage boredom. This, mashed up with my enthusiasm for bodies, shapes, textures, materials and structures, leads me to compose my illustrations. Maybe it's just a professional habit."

« J'ai développé une étrange éthique protestante du travail, qui résulte peut-être de l'ennui que j'ai ressenti pendant l'adolescence. Associée à ma passion pour les corps, les formes, les textures, les matériaux et les structures, elle me conduit à composer des illustrations. Mais peut-être s'agit-il juste d'une habitude professionnelle. »

„Ich entwickelte, vielleicht aus jugendlicher Langeweile heraus, eine seltsame protestantische Arbeitsmoral. Diese, vermengt mit meiner Begeisterung für Körper, Formen, Materialien und Strukturen, veranlasst mich zu illustrieren. Vielleicht ist es auch nur eine berufliche Angewohnheit."

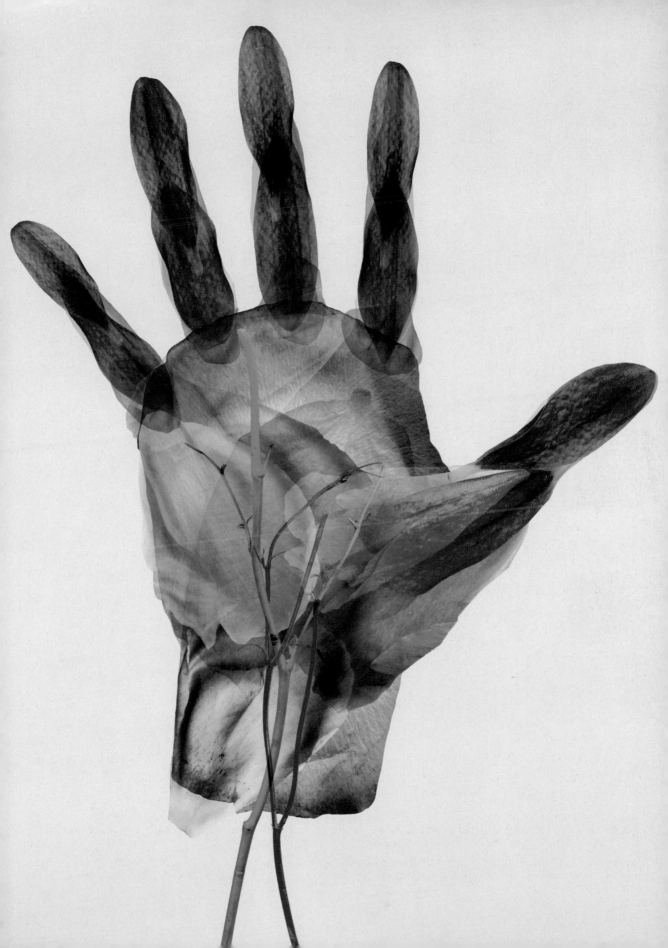

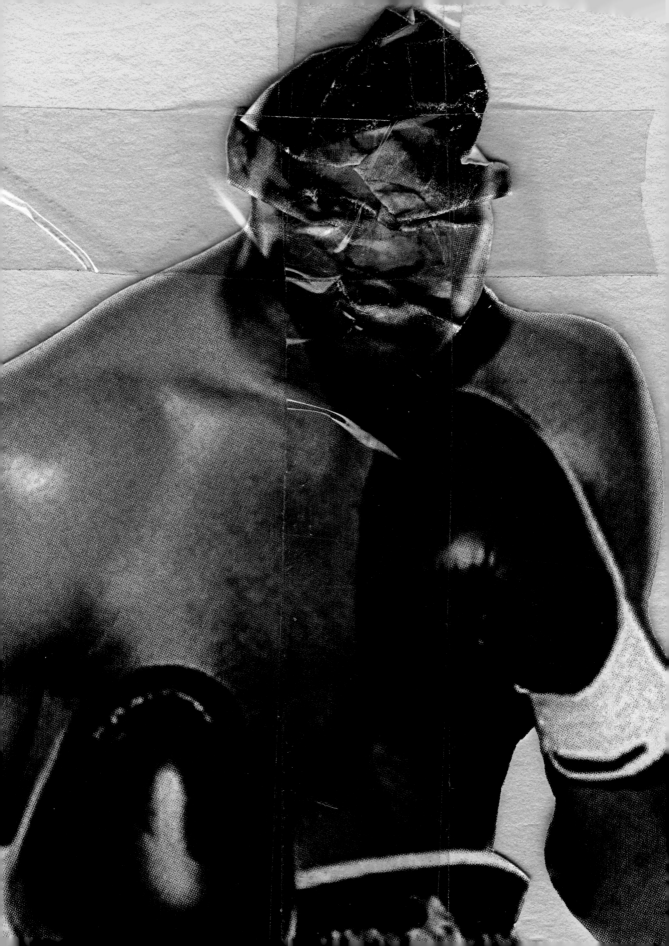

5

6

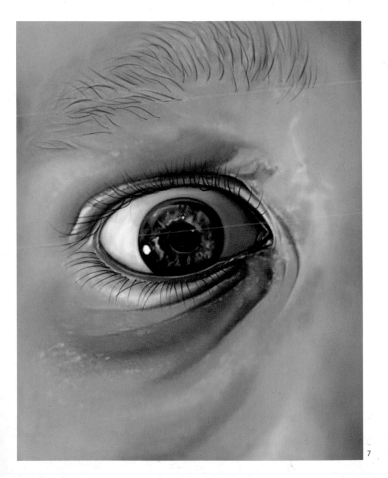

4 Boxer, 2006, Feld Hommes
5 Nobby Stiles, 2006, Feld Hommes
6 Implosion, 2007, perosnal work
7 Awake, 2007, Feld Hommes

7

ALEX NABAUM

NAME Alex Nabaum
WEBSITE www.alexnabaum.com
LOCATION Heber, UT, USA

TOOLS Gouache, brush, ink roller, embossing tools, paper board, pencil, Adobe Photoshop
CLIENTS Time, Newsweek, ESPN, Rolling Stone, The New York Times, National Geographic, FastCompany, Harvard, LA Times

AWARDS Communication Arts, 3x3 ProShow, Society of Illustrators, American Illustration

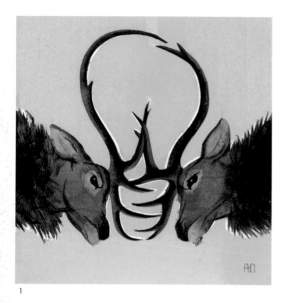

1

2

1 Creative Conflict, 2005, Inc. Magazine, Lou Vega (Art Director)
2 HGH in the NFL, 2006, ESPN The Magazine, Lou Vega (Art Director)
3 Super Pelvis, 2006, Minnesota Monthly, Brian Johnson (Art Director)

"Dig until I find a fresh and memorable idea that communicates. Tease and surprise the viewer's intellect and sometimes the heart. Add the right amount of beauty. And if I'm lucky the illustration will live on to create it's own story after the words have faded."

« Fouiner jusqu'à trouver une idée neuve et mémorable porteuse d'un message. Taquiner et surprendre l'intellect du public, parfois son cœur. Ajouter la juste dose de beauté. Avec de la chance, l'illustration perdurera pour créer sa propre histoire une fois les mots disparus. »

„So lange graben, bis ich eine frische und einprägsame Idee finde, die sich kommunizieren lässt. Den Intellekt und manchmal auch das Herz des Betrachters anregen und überraschen. Das richtige Maß an Schönheit hinzufügen. Und wenn ich Glück habe, lebt die Illustration weiter und entwickelt ihre eigene Geschichte, nachdem die Wörter verblasst sind."

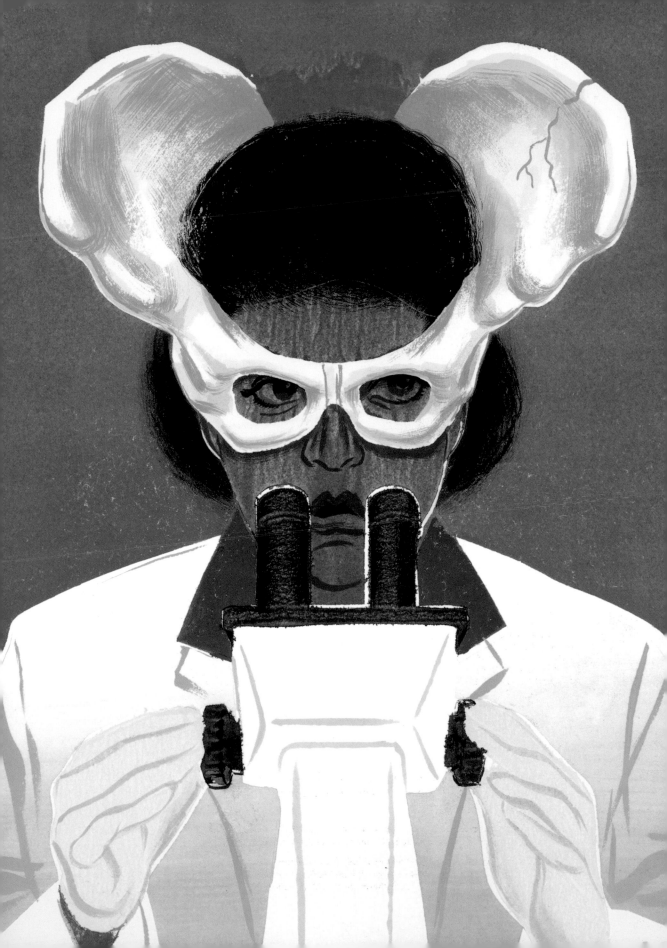

4 Hawk Mentality, 2005, Foreign Policy Magazine, Sarah Schumacher (Art Director)
5 Europe Central, 2005, The Los Angeles Times, Wesley Bausmith (Art Director)
6 Merry Christmas from Bethlehem, 2006, Minnesota Monthly, Brian Johnson (Art Director)
7 Dogs of War, 2006, The New York Times, Brian Rea (Art Director)

JULIAN DE NARVAEZ

NAME Julian de Narvaez
WEBSITE www.jdenarvaez.com
LOCATION Bogota, Colombia

AGENT Folio <www.folioart.co.uk>
TOOLS Fountain pen, Chinese ink, digital media

CLIENTS JWT, Alfaguara, Santillana, Panamericana, Norma, El Malpensante

1 Tratante de alas, 2007, personal work
2 The Magician, 2006, El Malpensante Magazine, cover of the magazine's 10th anniversary edition
3 The Juggler, 2006, El Malpensante Magazine, supplement of the magazine's 10th anniversary edition
4 The Writer, 2006, El Malpensante Magazine

"Julian has a unique eclectic style. His experience and knowledge of publishing and advertising have helped to create his diverse portfolio of work."

« Julian possède un style éclectique unique. Son expérience et ses connaissances dans les domaines de l'édition et de la publicité l'ont aidé à bâtir un portfolio très varié. »

„Julian hat einen einzigartigen eklektischen Stil. Seine Erfahrung und seine Kenntnisse des Verlagswesens und der Werbebranche haben dazu beigetragen, dass sein Arbeitsportfolio sehr vielseitig ist."

6

5 The Tiger and the Tamer, 2006, personal work
6 Sir with Hat, 2006, El Malpensante Magazine
7 Machine, 2006, personal work
8 Sasteria El Newyorkino, 2006, El Malpensante Magazine
9 El Cultur Generator, 2006, El Malpensante Magazine

8

9

IZUMI NOGAWA

NAME Izumi Nogawa
WEBSITE www.quietblue.org
LOCATION Tokyo, Japan

AGENT Dutch Uncle Agency
<www.DutchUncle.co.uk>
TOOLS Adobe Photoshop, Adobe Illustrator

CLIENTS Shu uemura, HMV, Condé Nast Traveler, Vespa, WDD, The Telegraph, Häagan Dazs

1 Nude Bike, 2003
2 Fruit, 2006, WWD
3 Hypnotic, 2006, MdN Magazine

2

1

"My focus is the female form. I take the dream girl silhouette on holiday to Japan, draping her in flowers and finery to produce gorgeous imagery. I want Izumi girls to be enchanting creations!"

« Je mise tout sur les formes féminines. Je prends la silhouette d'une fille de rêve en vacances au Japon et je la drape de fleurs et des plus beaux atours pour obtenir une image splendide. Je veux que les filles Izumi soient des créations enchanteresses ! »

„Der weibliche Körper bildet den Mittelpunkt meiner Arbeit. Ich entführe die Silhouette der Traumfrau nach Japan und schmücke sie mit Blumen und schönen Gewändern, um großartige Bilder zu erschaffen. Ich möchte, dass die Izumi-Mädchen bezaubernde Kreationen sind."

CHRIS O'LEARY

NAME Chris O'Leary
WEBSITE www.olearyillustration.com
LOCATION Columbus, OH, USA

AGENT Lindgren & Smith
<www.lindgrensmith.com>
TOOLS Acrylic, oil

CLIENTS Atlantic Monthly, Barnes & Noble, Chronicle Books, Boston Globe, LA Times, Henry Holt, Harcourt

1 Needled to Death, 2006, Penguin Putnam Publishing
2 The Fireballer, 2005, personal work
3 Untitled

1

2

"I try to create simple images that intimate the beginnings of a story."

« J'essaie de créer des images simples qui suggèrent le début d'une histoire. »

„Ich versuche, einfache Bilder zu erzeugen, die den Anfang einer Geschichte andeuten."

5

1 Untitled, 2006, Vegetarian Times Magazine
2 Untitled, Simon and Schuster
3 Mr. Vertigo, 2005, Playboy Magazine

ANDREA OFFERMANN

NAME Andrea Offermann
WEBSITE www.andreaoffermann.com
LOCATION Lübeck, Germany

TOOLS Pen, ink, oil, acrylic, etching, collage, Adobe Photoshop
CLIENTS The Times, Canongate, Random House, Flight Magazine, Amnesty International

AWARDS American Illustration, 3x3 ProShow, Communication Arts, CMYK, AltPick, Bologna Illustrators Exhibition

1 Life of Pi, Battle of the minds, 2006, London Times, Canongate Books
2 Life of Pi, Their Bodies, 2006, London Times, Canongate Books
3 Pink Elephants, 2006, personal work

"I love stories. They inspire me and challenge me to catch the intention of the author and solve it visually. My work is full of detail, because I like to imagine the viewer getting lost in it and entering the world of the story. To me that's what an illustration should do, invite the reader in and offer an interpretation, take this imagination a little further than the text would have, in a language that is universally understood."

« J'adore les histoires. Elles m'inspirent et me poussent à saisir l'intention de l'auteur pour la résoudre de façon graphique. Mon travail regorge de détails, car j'aime imaginer comment le spectateur s'y perd et pénètre dans l'univers de l'histoire. Telle est à mon sens la mission d'une illustration : inviter le lecteur à y entrer et proposer une interprétation, projeter son imagination un peu plus loin que le texte ne l'aurait fait, dans un langage universel. »

„Ich liebe Geschichten. Sie inspirieren mich und fordern dazu heraus, die Intention des Autors zu begreifen und visuell umzusetzen. Meine Arbeiten sind voller Details, weil ich mir gerne vorstelle, dass der Betrachter sich darin verliert und in die Welt der Geschichte eintritt. Das sollte eine Illustration meiner Meinung nach leisten: den Leser zum Eintreten einladen und eine Interpretation anbieten. Die Fantasie ein wenig weiter führen, als der Text es täte, und zwar in einer universell verständlichen Sprache."

TOKO OHMORI

NAME Toko Ohmori
LOCATION Tokyo, Japan

AGENT Kate Larkworthy Artist Representation, <www.larkworthy.com>
TOOLS Adobe Photoshop

CLIENTS Magazine House, Kodansha, Gakken, Lumine Omiya, Pace Communications, Sweet 16

1 Fruits, 2006, Gakken Co., Ltd.
2 Summer Vacation 02/2007, World Co., Ltd/grove
3 Summer Vacation 03/2007, World Co., Ltd/grove
4 Girlfriend Summer 2006, World Co., Ltd/index

"I try to bring the essence and ambience of eroticism and romanticism into my illustrations. I find it thrilling every time I draw a new illustration."

« J'essaie de transposer dans mes illustrations toute l'essence et l'atmosphère de l'érotisme et du romantisme. Chaque fois que je dessine une nouvelle illustration, je trouve cela palpitant. »

„Ich versuche, die Essenz und Atmosphäre von Erotik und Romantik in meinen Illustrationen einzufangen. Ich finde es jedes Mal erregend, eine neue Illustration zu zeichnen."

JULIEN PACAUD

NAME Julien Pacaud
WEBSITE www.institutdrahomira.com
LOCATION Paris, France

AGENT Talkie Walkie <www.talkiewalkie.tw>
TOOLS Adobe Photoshop

CLIENTS Remark Records, Sony BMG, The New York Times, Stick, Transworld, Le Nouveau Casino, Fast Company

1 The Illness, 2007, Goodbooks
2 Leni, 2006, Goodbooks
3 Memories of Tomorrow, 2006
4 Anonymous Calls from the Future, 2006

"Creating digital collages from old magazines, Julien Pacaud delights himself in building parallel worlds whose main ingredients are a touch of humour, a hint of retro futurism and a good pinch of 'happy apocalypse'."

« Auteur de collages numériques à partir de vieux magazines, Julien Pacaud s'amuse à construire des mondes parallèles dont les principaux ingrédients sont une touche d'humour, un soupçon de futurisme rétro et une bonne pincée de ‹ joyeuse apocalypse ›. »

„Julien Pacaud stellt aus alten Zeitschriften digitale Collagen her. Es amüsiert ihn, Parallelwelten zu erschaffen, deren Hauptbestandteile ein Schuss Humor, ein Hauch von Retro-Futurismus und eine Prise ‚glückliche Apokalypse' sind."

TASSOS PAPAIOANNOU

NAME Tassos Papaioannou
LOCATION Athens, Greece

AGENT Smart Magna <www.smartmagna.com>
TOOLS Pencil, marker, Pentel brush pen, paper, Adobe Photoshop

CLIENTS Giganto, Poor Designers, Klik Records, Athens Voice Newspaper, Eleftherotipia Newspaper, Sonik Magazine

1 Popular Art 2, 2006, Giganto Books
2 Self Portrait, 2007, personal work
3 Greek Island, 2006, personal work

"My illustrations are heavily influenced by pop culture and usually revolve around people. I use vivid colours as a response to the world around me. A world lit by the harsh Mediterranean sun."

« Mes illustrations sont largement influencées par la culture pop et portent généralement sur des personnes. Je me sers de couleurs vives pour répondre au monde qui m'entoure. Un monde illuminé par le rude soleil méditerranéen. »

„Meine Illustrationen sind stark von Popkultur beeinflusst und drehen sich meist um Menschen. Ich verwende grelle Farben, um die Welt um mich herum darzustellen. Eine Welt, die von der sengenden mediterranen Sonne beschienen wird."

ROBERTO PARADA

NAME Roberto Parada
WEBSITE www.robertoparada.com
LOCATION Arlington, VA, USA

TOOLS Oil, canvas
CLIENTS Time, Rolling Stone, Vanity, Esquire, Fortune, Der Spiegel

AWARDS Society of Illustrators, American Illustration, Communication Arts

1 The Last Scalpers, 2005, Playboy Magazine
2 Ted Haggard, 2007, Details Magazine
3 Crucified, 2007, Details Magazine

"I try to make thought provoking portraits of politicians, celebrities and the unknown."

« J'essaie de créer des portraits provocants d'hommes politiques, de vedettes et d'inconnus. »

„Ich versuche zum Nachdenken anregende Porträts von Politikern, Prominenten und Unbekannten zu machen."

4 Icons, 2003, Rolling Stone Magazine
5 Elvis Costello, 2005, Rolling Stone Magazine
6 Sex Pistols, 2005, Rolling Stone Magazine
7 Clint Eastwood, 2005, Time Magazine
8 Chinatown, 2003, Los Angeles Magazine

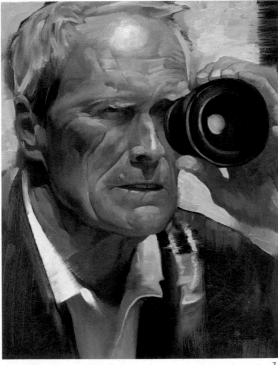

LEIF PARSONS

NAME Leif Parsons
WEBSITE www.leifparsons.com
LOCATION New York, NY, USA

TOOLS Pen, pencil, ink, watercolor, computer
CLIENTS Harper's, The New York Times, McSweeney's, The New York Times Magazine, Nike, Walrus, Atlantic Monthly

AWARDS Art Directors Club Young Guns, Society of Illustrators, Design Club of Canada, National Magazine Awards, American Illustration

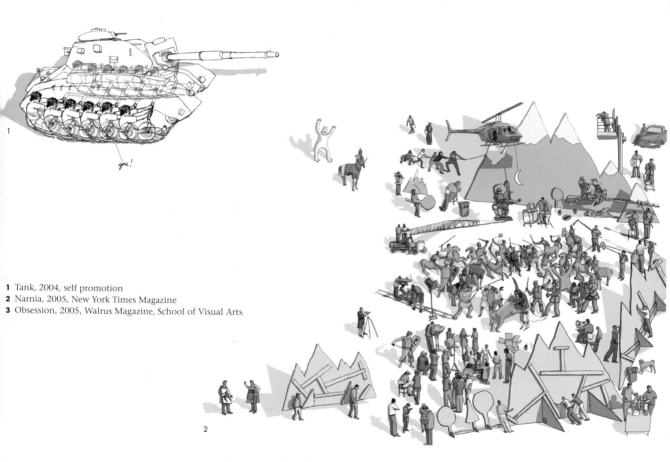

1 Tank, 2004, self promotion
2 Narnia, 2005, New York Times Magazine
3 Obsession, 2005, Walrus Magazine, School of Visual Arts

"I have recently been focused on trying to find the line between looseness and tightness, between deliberate idea and spontaneous expression, between observation and imagination."

« Dernièrement, je me concentre sur la recherche de la frontière entre l'imprécision et la rigueur, entre les idées mûrement réfléchies et l'expression spontanée, entre l'observation et l'imagination. »

„Seit Kurzem beschäftige ich mich damit, die Balance zu finden zwischen Lockerheit und Straffheit, einer bewussten Idee und einem spontanen Ausdruck, Beobachtung und Fantasie."

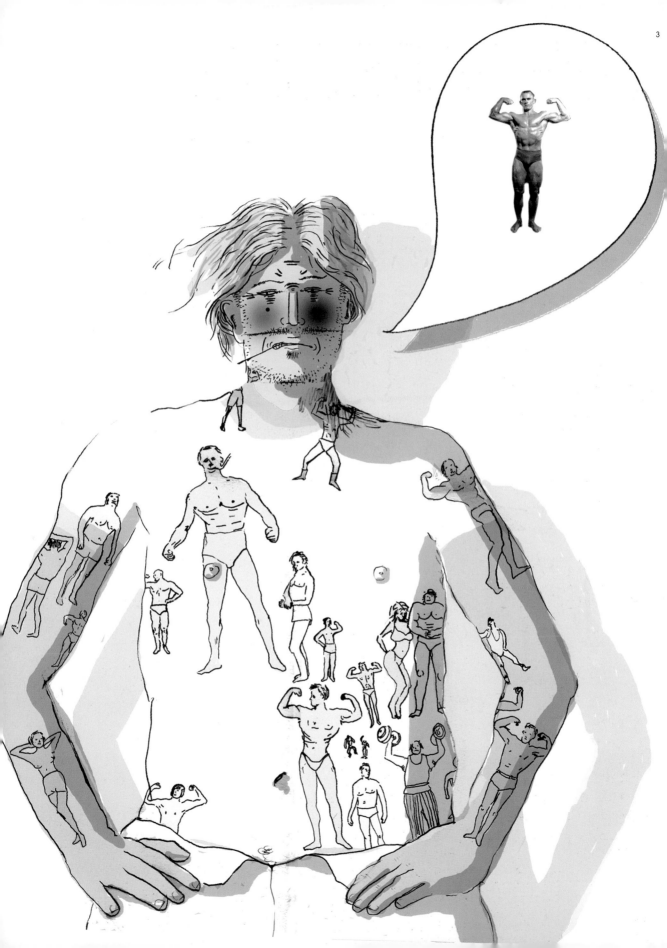

C. F. PAYNE

NAME C. F. Payne
LOCATION Cincinnati, OH, USA
AGENT Richard Solomon, Artists Representative
<www.richardsolomon.com>

TOOLS Graphite, colored pencil, acrylic, watercolor
CLIENTS Rolling Stone, Time, Reader's Digest, Mad, Atlantic Monthly, GQ, Esquire, Penthouse, Simon & Schuster, Penguin

AWARDS Society of Illustrators, Print, Communication Arts, Step-by-Step Graphics

1 "Jack Nicholson", self-promotion, 2004
2 "Andrew Wyeth", commissioned by Betsy Wyeth, 1998

"I like to draw. Good drawing is the foundation for my art. The history of illustration inspires me. Illustration is the art form that tells a story. I believe that to be a good illustrator you need to be a good artist, with good communication skills, good drawing and design skills, and a personal demand for excellence in craftsmanship and service to the job at hand."

« J'aime dessiner. Un bon dessin sert de point de départ à mon art. L'histoire de l'illustration m'inspire. L'illustration est une forme artistique qui raconte une histoire. Je crois que pour être un bon illustrateur, il faut être un bon artiste, doté de dons de communication, d'un talent de dessinateur et de designer, et être en quête personnelle d'excellence dans le travail et le service réalisés. »

„Ich zeichne gerne. Gute Zeichnungen sind das Fundament meiner Kunst. Die Geschichte der Illustration inspiriert mich. Illustration ist die Kunstform, die eine Geschichte erzählt. Als guter Illustrator musst du ein guter Künstler sein, kommunikative Fähigkeiten besitzen, gut zeichnen und entwerfen können und deine Kunst ganz in den Dienst des jeweiligen Auftrags stellen."

3

4

3 "Garage Band", back cover series, Reader's Digest Magazine, 2006
4 "Love Notes", back cover series, Reader's Digest Magazine, 2005
5 "Bagpipe Frog", promotional calendar, Dellas Graphics, 2005
6 "Jim Thorpe: All American", self-promotion, 2003

5

7 "W.C. Fields", 2004, The New York Times Book Review
8 "The Ageing Face of Germany", 2006, Der Spiegel Magazine
9 "Do Kids Have Too Much Power?", cover, 2001, Time Magazine
10 "Home $weet Home", cover, 2005, Time Magazine

8

9

10

JOSH PETHERICK

NAME Josh Petherick
WEBSITE www.joshpetherick.com
LOCATION Melbourne, Australia

TOOLS Pencil, pen, marker, paint, paper,
Adobe programs

CLIENTS Vitra Design Museum, Colette,
PAM, Nieves Books, Vans, Tokion, Stüssy,
2K by Gingham, Colab Eyewear

1 Crack in the Cosmic Egg, 2007, Perks and Mini
2 Sifting Sunlight, 2006, personal work
3 Listen, 2006, 2K by Gingham

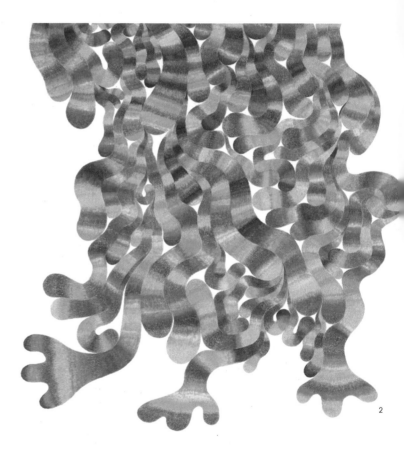

1

2

"Illustration to me inhabits the exact same space as graphic design, fine art, philosophy, film, object making and music. This is how I treat it within my practice. It's about creating an entire language without any clear division. Humor, abstraction, celebration and the imagination of the viewer/listener/participant are all integral parts."

« Pour moi, l'illustration occupe le même espace que le design graphique, les beaux arts, la philosophie, le cinéma, l'artisanat et la musique. Telle est ma façon de l'aborder dans la pratique. Il s'agit de créer tout un langage sans division claire. Humour, abstraction, célébration et imagination du spectateur/auditeur/participant en font partie intégrante. »

„Illustration ist für mich am selben Ort angesiedelt wie Grafikdesign, bildende Kunst, Philosophie, Film, Objektkunst und Musik. Es geht darum, eine komplette Sprache ohne klare Abgrenzungen zu erschaffen. Humor, Abstraktion, Zelebrierung und die Fantasie des Betrachters/Zuhörers/Teilnehmers sind integrale Bestandteile davon."

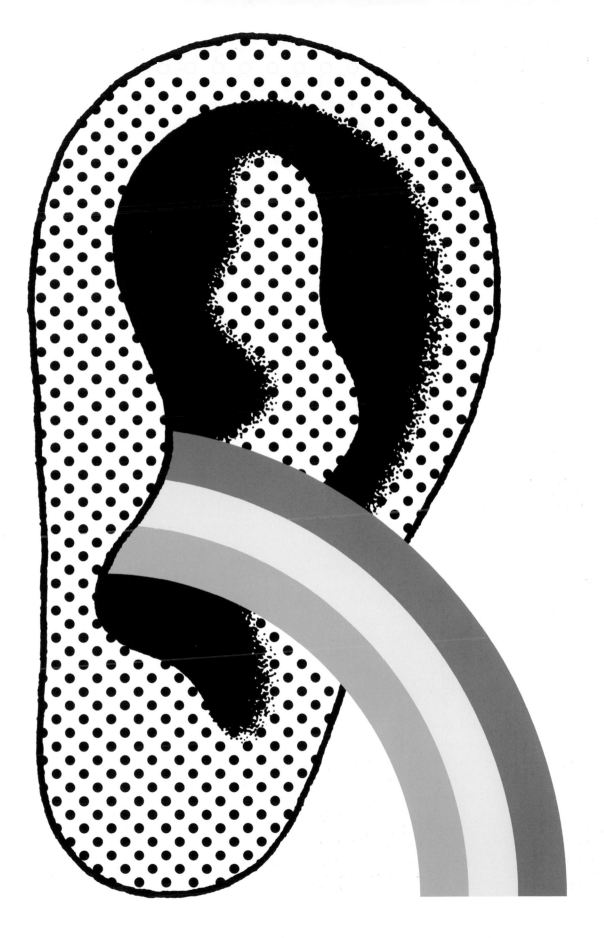

WENDY PLOVMAND

NAME Wendy Plovmand
WEBSITE www.wendyplovmand.com
LOCATION Copenhagen, Denmark

AGENT Central Illustration Agency
<www.centralillustration.com>
TOOLS Pen, pencil, watercolor, acrylic, collage,
Adobe Photoshop, photos

CLIENTS Nylon, Shape, Die Gestalten Verlag,
Victionary, Eurowoman, Costume, Gyldendal

1 To Conquer the One and Only, 2006, Costume Fashion Magazin
2 Scarf, 2007, Eurowoman Fashion Magazine
3 Female Fantasies #3, 2006, personal work

"My work is a hybrid between illustration, art and design. I like to experiment and I'm always focused on developing my style and work very curiously with different media. To me drawing and making visuals in all forms is an exploration into new undefined territories. My inspiration comes from a broad range of areas such as nature, music and fashion."

« Mon travail est un hybride entre illustration, art et design. J'aime faire des expériences et je cherche toujours à développer mon style en gardant une grande curiosité pour les différents supports. Je vois le dessin et les créations visuelles comme l'exploration de territoires inconnus et indéfinis. Je puise mon inspiration dans une large gamme de domaines, comme la nature, la musique et la mode. »

„Meine Arbeit ist eine Mischung aus Illustration, Kunst und Design. Ich experimentiere gerne, versuche immer, meinen Stil weiterzu-entwickeln, und interessiere mich für unterschiedliche Medien. Für mich bedeuten Zeichnen und das Erschaffen von Bildern aller Art die Erforschung von neuen, noch unentdeckten Gebieten. Meine Inspiration ziehe ich aus vielen Bereichen, wie zum Beispiel Natur, Musik und Mode."

ANDY RASH

NAME Andy Rash
WEBSITE www.rashworks.com
LOCATION Brooklyn, NY, USA
AGENT Pippin Properties, Inc.
<www.pippinproperties.com>

TOOLS Gouache, India ink, pencil,
Adobe Photoshop
CLIENTS The New York Times, The New Yorker,
Entertainment Weekly, Scholastic Press,
Newsweek, Time, Herald Tribune, Barrons

AWARDS Society of Publication Designers,
Society of Illustrators, Communication Arts,
American Illustration

2

1

1 The CEO Percentage, 2006, Time Magazine
2 Senator Joe McCarthy, 2004,
The New York Times Book Review
3 Agent K, 2004, Scholastic

"I really enjoy communicating a story in a single image. Hunting for the right metaphor to express an abstract idea is the big challenge. Creating an image that can express that idea, and also allow the viewer to empathize with a drawing of a person, animal, or object is the fun part."

« Je prends vraiment plaisir à raconter une histoire en une seule une image. Il est délicat de trouver la métaphore juste pour exprimer une idée abstraite. Je m'amuse à créer une image illustrant cette idée et permettant par la même occasion au public d'établir une relation avec le dessin d'une personne, d'un animal ou d'un objet. »

„Mir macht es Spaß, eine Geschichte in einem einzigen Bild zu übermitteln. Die größte Herausforderung besteht darin, die richtige Metapher für eine abstrakte Idee zu finden. Dann kommt der einfachere Teil: Ein Bild zu kreieren, das diese Idee ausdrücken kann und es dem Betrachter ermöglicht, sich in die Zeichnung einer Person, eines Tieres oder eines Gegenstandes einzufühlen."

REILLY

NAME Reilly
WEBSITE www.reilly69.com
LOCATION London, United Kingdom
AGENT 1 Art Department, NY, <www.art-dept.com>

AGENT 2 Vision Licensing, London, <www.visionlicensing.com>
TOOLS Felt pen, ink, pencil, acrylic, paper, canvas, camera, Adobe Photoshop, Adobe Illustrator, Corel Draw, Corel PhotoPaint, Corel Painter

CLIENTS Chloé, JD Sports, Tommy Hilfiger, Speedo, idN, Complex, Time Out, Cosmopolitan, Loaded Fashion, RADAR, Food & Wine, Surface, Vogue, Diageo, Macy's, Microsoft, Coca-Cola, Adobe, Old Navy, Leo Burnett

1 Butterfly, 2006, Vision Licensing
2 Untitled, 2007, Art Department promotional
3 Tokyo #1, 2004, Exposure Exhibition, Life of Reilly

"I have a desirous imagination and strive to be the most creative I can be in every job I do."

« J'ai une imagination avide et m'efforce d'être le plus créatif possible dans chacun de mes projets. »

„Ich habe eine begierige Einbildungskraft und versucht, bei jeder Arbeit, die ich mache, so kreativ wie möglich zu sein."

5

6

4 Lover, 2004, Exposure Exhibition, Life of Reilly
5 Mr Roboto, 2007, Art Department promotional
6 The Void, 2004, Topman

RUI RICARDO

NAME Rui Ricardo
WEBSITE www.rui-ricardo.com
LOCATION Matosinhos, Portugal

AGENT Folio <www.folioart.co.uk>
TOOLS Pencil, digital coloring

CLIENTS The Times, Telegraph, Macmillan, Ambar, Unicef/APAG, Impala, Victory Records, Mushroom Pillow

1

"Rui Ricardo's illustrations have a distinctive oriental influence and a quirky appeal, with digitally colored, hand drawn images."

« Les illustrations de Rui Ricardo présentent une influence orientale originale et un charme étrange, avec des images dessinées à la main et coloriées sur ordinateur. »

„Rui Ricardos handgezeichnete und digital kolorierte Illustrationen sind voll skurrilen Charmes und zeigen deutlich einen orientalischen Einfluss."

2

1 Sumo Wrestlers, 2007, Jornal de Negocios
2 Old Tokyo, 2006, personal work
3 War Children, 2007, Unicef/APAG

EDEL RODRIGUEZ

NAME Edel Rodriguez
WEBSITE www.edelrodriguez.com
LOCATION Mount Tabor, NJ, USA

TOOLS Pastel, oil-based printing ink, spray paint, Adobe Photoshop, acrylic, paper

CLIENTS The New Yorker, Time Magazine, The New York Times, Rolling Stone, Nike, Pepsi, Texas Monthly, Playboy, Gentleman's Quarterly, Reader's Digest, National Geographic Traveler, University of Chicago Press

1

2

1 Rwanda, 2006, CM Magazine
2 The New China, 2005, Time Magazine
3 The Roots, 2004, Esquire Magazine

"Much of my illustration work evolves from my sketchbooks or personal work. They are drawings about loss, oppression, joy, death, or whatever happens to be in my head at the time. Growing up in Cuba, the stories, religions, customs and people of my home country regularly influence the direction of my artwork."

« La majeure partie de mon travail d'illustration provient de mes carnets de croquis ou de mes projets personnels. Les dessins portent sur la perte, l'oppression, la joie, la mort ou tout ce qui me passe par la tête. Ayant grandi à Cuba, les histoires, les religions, les coutumes et les personnes de mon pays influencent souvent mes choix artistiques. »

„Viele meiner Illustrationen entwickeln sich aus meinen Skizzenbüchern oder meiner persönlichen Arbeit. Es sind Zeichnungen über Verlust, Unterdrückung, Freude, Tod oder was immer mir gerade im Kopf herumschwirrt. Ich bin in Kuba aufgewachsen und die Geschichten, Religionen, Gebräuche und Menschen meiner Heimat beeinflussen meine Kunst."

Warrior, 2005, San Francisco Chronicle
Havana, 2007, The New York Times Book Review
Bath, 2005, The New Yorker Magazine
Bed of Nails, 2006, West Magazine, Los Angeles Times

JONATHON
ROSEN

NAME Jonathon Rosen
WEBSITE www.jrosen.org
LOCATION Brooklyn, NY, USA

TOOLS Compass, stethoscope, paper, pencil, ink, wood panel, gesso, tracing paper, paint, canvas, camera, Adobe After Effects

CLIENTS McSweeney's, New York Metropolitan Museum, The New York Times, Le Dernier Cri, Time, Esquire
AWARDS Society of Publication Designers, Art Directors Club

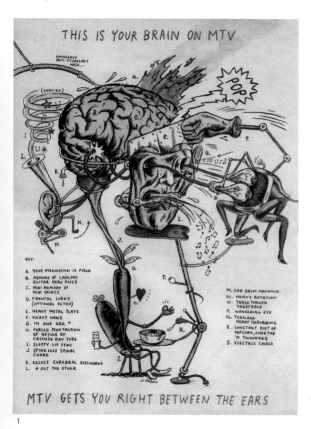

1 This is Your Brain on MTV, 1989, Warner Bros Records
2 "Free Will; Now You Have It, Now You Don't", 2007, The New York Times
3 Snake Eyes No. 2, cover, 1992, Snake Eyes, Fantagraphics

"Pictures, custom engineered to be applied directly onto the nervous system."

« Des images faites sur mesure pour être directement appliquées sur le système nerveux. »

„Bilder, die maßgeschneidert sind, um unmittelbar auf das Nervensystem zu wirken."

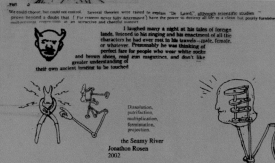

4 Seamy River, 2002, Blab! No. 13

ARNOLD ROTH

NAME Arnold Roth
WEBSITE www.arnoldroth.com
LOCATION New York, NY, USA

TOOLS Pen, watercolor
CLIENTS The New York Times, The New Yorker, Esquire, Sports Illustrated, Time, Playboy, Punch, City Journal, Alfred A. Knopf, Holiday

AWARDS National Cartoonists Society, Society of Illustrators, Art Directors Club (New York, Chicago & Philadelphia)

1 Rolling the Cradle, 1986, The New Yorker
2 Removing Fleas, 1986, Discovery Magazine
3 Bordeaux, 1997, Smoke Magazine

"A cartoon illustration must be graphically complete, legible, and relate to the subject matter of the text... with imagination and, above all, humour."

« Une illustration de bande dessinée doit être graphiquement complète, lisible et se rapporter au sujet du texte... avec imagination et, surtout, avec humour. »

„Eine Cartoonzeichnung muss grafisch vollständig und lesbar sein und mit Fantasie und vor allem Humor zum Thema des Textes in Beziehung stehen."

BRETT RYDER

NAME Brett Ryder
WEBSITE www.brettryder.co.uk
LOCATION London, United Kingdom
AGENT Heart <www.heartagency.com>

TOOLS 0.5 Pentel pencil, Adobe Photoshop, camera, reference books, collage
CLIENTS Dr. Stuart's, New Scientist, TIME, WPP, The Guardian, London Symphony Orchestra, BDO Stoy Hayward

AWARDS D&AD, American Illustration, Society of Publication Designers

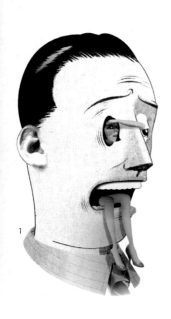

1 Living in a Man's World, 2007, The Telegraph
2 Cradle to the Grave, 2007, The Times
3 Mansfield Park, 2007, The Telegraph

"I've always had a fascination with bygone medical journals, dusty advertising boards and the Haynes BSA 650 manual. Such an assortment of taste in fine illustration combined with an ability to replace a four-cylinder manifold with only a few 'minor' screws left over was always destined to have a profound influence on my work."

« J'ai toujours été fasciné par les revues médicales d'autrefois, les planches publicitaires poussiéreuses et le manuel technique de la Haynes BSA 650. Cet assortiment de goûts, associé à la capacité de remplacer un collecteur à quatre cylindres avec seulement quelques ‹ petites › vis, devait forcément avoir une profonde influence sur mon travail. »

„Ich war schon immer fasziniert von alten Medizinzeitschriften, staubigen Reklametafeln und dem Handbuch der Haynes BSA 650. Ein so breitgefächerter Geschmack, gepaart mit der Fähigkeit, den Krümmer eines Vierzylindermotors so auszutauschen, dass nur ein paar ‚unwichtige' Schrauben übrig bleiben, musste unweigerlich einen entscheidenden Einfluss auf meine Arbeit haben."

MASAKI RYO

NAME Masaki Ryo
WEBSITE www.masakiryo.com
LOCATION Tokyo, Japan

AGENT CWC International <www.cwc-i.com>
TOOLS Adobe Photoshop

CLIENTS Caspari, Janovic, Penguin Putnam, Berkley Publishing, Transworld, Elle, UC Card, NTT Data, DESENTE, SEI

1 Walking in Fall, 2005, personal work
2 Dozing Off, 2006, personal work
3 Hotel Wonder, 2006, LaPerla

"Doing illustration is part of my life. I work on my illustration in the same manner as I wash my face in the morning, brush my teeth, and walk my dog. These are pleasures that I have in my daily life. In that way, I suppose 'I don't draw if I don't want to' would be my philosophy."

« Créer des illustrations fait partie de ma vie. Je travaille sur mes illustrations de la même façon que je me lave le visage le matin, que je me brosse les dents et que je promène mon chien. Ce sont des plaisirs qui remplissent mon quotidien. Je pourrais donc dire que ma philosophie est ‹ je ne dessine pas si je n'en ai pas envie ›. »

„Illustrieren ist Teil meines Alltags. Ich illustriere genauso, wie ich mir morgens das Gesicht wasche, die Zähne putze und mit dem Hund rausgehe. Das sind die Vergnügungen meines täglichen Lebens. Mein Motto lautet gewissermaßen: ‚Ich zeichne nicht, wenn ich es nicht möchte'."

4 Asian Bamboo, 2007, personal work
5 Passion, 2004, personal work

KUSTAA SAKSI

NAME Kustaa Saksi
WEBSITE www.kustaasaksi.com
LOCATION 1 Paris, France
LOCATION 2 Helsinki, Finland

AGENT 1 Dutch Uncle Agency, London, <www.DutchUncle.co.uk>
AGENT 2 Unit, Amsterdam, <www.unit.nl>

TOOLS Pen, pencil, watercolor, Adobe Photoshop, Adobe Freehand, Adobe Illustrator, Corel Painter
CLIENTS Levi's, The New York Times, Swarovski, Havaianas, Diesel, Mercedes-Benz, Issey Miyake, Lacoste, Samsung, Playboy

"Saksi's illustrations are a syrupy disarray of elements: playful, paradoxical, inviting, troubling, messy, and yet strangely clear. A Finnish born illustrator, living and working in Paris, Saksi combines organic touches and viscous shapes into a new world psychedelia. His unique imagination illustrates the wonderful world of surrealistic landscapes, strangely beautiful characters and strong atmospheres."

« Les illustrations de Saksi sont un ensemble sirupeux d'éléments disparates : elles sont espiègles, paradoxales, attirantes, troublantes, chaotiques et à la fois curieusement claires. Illustrateur finnois vivant et travaillant à Paris, Saksi mélange des touches organiques et des formes visqueuses dans un nouveau monde psychédélique. Son imagination originale dépeint un monde merveilleux de paysages surréalistes, de personnages d'une étrange beauté et d'atmosphères intenses. »

„Saksis Illustrationen bestehen aus einem siruphaften Durcheinander von Elementen: verspielt, paradox, einladend, beunruhigend, unordentlich, doch dabei seltsam klar. Der aus Finnland stammende und in Paris lebende Künstler verbindet organische und zähflüssige Formen zu einer psychedelischen neuen Welt. Seine einzigartige Fantasie erschafft surreale Landschaften, merkwürdig schöne Figuren und starke Atmosphären."

1

1 Mermaid, 2007, Catskills Records
2 Progressive, 2007, Swarovski, Crystallized Magazine
3 Glamour, 2007, Swarovski, Crystallized Magazine
4 Rollergirls, 2007, Sticky

SOUTHER SALAZAR

NAME Souther Salazar
WEBSITE www.southersalazar.net
LOCATION Los Angeles, CA, USA

TOOLS Pen, pencil, acrylic, collage, paper
CLIENTS Nickelodeon, Sony, Moviefone, Element, Roxy, Giant Robot, Bugaboo, Starbucks, Blue Q, Random House

AWARDS Society of Illustrators, Communication Arts, American Illustration

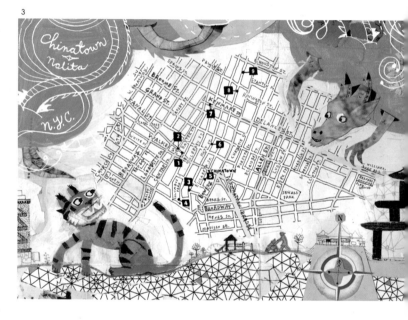

1 Shoe Designs, 2007, Dekline
2 Album cover for Built Like Alaska, 2005, Future Farmer Recordings
3 Walking Map for Bugaboo Strollers, 2005, 72 and Sunny
4 "The Amazing Life of Birds", book by Gary Paulsen, 2006, Random House

"I always try to leave the door open for chance and fun."

« J'essaie toujours de laisser la porte ouverte au hasard et au plaisir. »

„Ich versuche immer, die Tür für Zufall und Spaß offenzulassen."

AMITAI SANDY

NAME Amitai Sandy
WEBSITE www.amitaisandy.com
LOCATION Tel-Aviv, Israel

TOOLS Pencil, paper, acrylic, Adobe Photoshop, Adobe Illustrator, watercolor, mixed media

CLIENTS National Geographic, McCann-Erickson, Saatchi & Saatchi, BBDO, The Marker

"I don't want to talk about no big philosophy;
I just want to illustrate the joy of life!"

« Je ne veux pas faire de la grande philosophie, je veux juste illustrer la joie de vivre ! »

„Ich möchte nicht über große Philosophie reden. Ich möchte nur die Freude des Lebens illustrieren."

1 Love Spray, 2007, Haaretz Newspaper
2 A Sweet Happy New Year!, 2002, Dinamo Dvash Electronc Club
3 Oops!, 2005, Glendon & Isabella

ELISA SASSI

NAME Elisa Sassi
WEBSITE www.elisasassi.com
LOCATION Sao Paulo, Brazil

TOOLS Pen, pencil, acrylic, spray can, cardboard, canvas, Adobe Illustrator, Adobe Photoshop

CLIENTS Nike, Aiwa, O Boticário, Electrolux, Computer Arts magazine, Polenghi, Nova Schin
AWARDS Art Directors Club (Sao Paulo)

1

1 Moleskinho, 2006, personal work
2 Sarro, 2005, personal work
3 Pandamonium III, 2007, personal work

2

"From the bottom of my heart I can say that I do what I do with my soul, and when it touches any other soul, in any way, it keeps me going. I don't think much about what I do. I just breathe and live it."

« Du fond du cœur, je peux assurer que je fais ce que je fais de toute mon âme, et lorsque mon travail touche une autre âme de quelque façon que ce soit, ça me donne envie de continuer. Je ne réfléchis pas trop à ce que je fais. Je me contente de le respirer et de le vivre. »

„Ich kann aus tiefstem Herzen sagen, dass ich meine Seele in meine Arbeit lege. Wenn ich damit andere Seelen berühren kann, spornt mich das an. Ich denke nicht groß über meine Arbeit nach. Ich atme und lebe sie nur."

STEPHEN SAVAGE

NAME Stephen Savage
WEBSITE www.stephensavage.net
LOCATION Brooklyn, NY, USA

TOOLS Linocut, computer
CLIENTS The New York Times, The New Yorker, Entertainment Weekly, Scholastic Press, Newsweek, Time Magazine, BusinessWeek

AWARDS American Illustration, AIGA, Society of Illustrators, Communications Arts, The New York Times Best Illustrated Books

1 Polar Bear Night, 2004, Scholastic Press
2 Sleepy Seals, 2004, Scholastic Press
3 Baby Seal, 2000, The New York Times Book Review
4 Hugo Chavez and the Limits of Democracy, 2003, The New York Times

"Illustration is a 'pop art': its purpose is to amuse and entertain. And in that way, I think the field is closer to film and music than it is to painting and sculpture. I get more inspiration from a Gene Kelly musical than I do from looking at a Picasso canvas!"

« L'illustration est un ‹ art pop › : son but est d'amuser et de divertir. Je crois qu'elle est en ce sens plus près du cinéma et de la musique que de la peinture et de la sculpture. Une comédie musicale de Gene Kelly m'apporte plus d'inspiration qu'une toile de Picasso ! »

„Illustration ist eine ‚Popart'. Sie will amüsieren und unterhalten. In dieser Hinsicht ist sie näher an Film und Musik als an Malerei und Skulptur. Ich ziehe mehr Inspiration aus einem Gene-Kelly-Musical als aus einem Gemälde von Picasso."

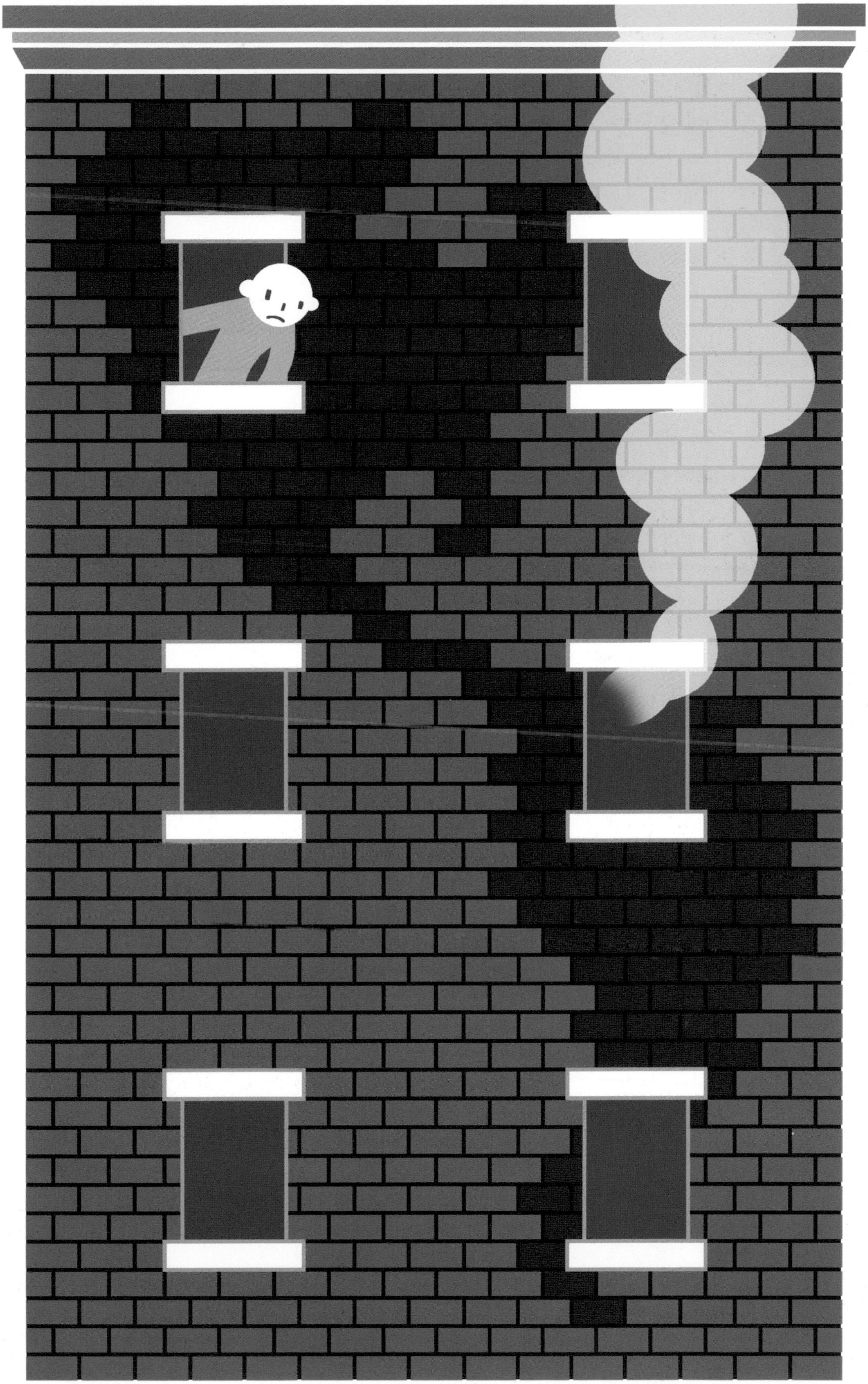

TOM SCHAMP

NAME Tom Schamp
WEBSITE www.tomschamp.com
LOCATION Wemmel, Belgium
AGENT Illustrissimo <www.illustrissimo.com>

TOOLS Acrylic, hardboard
CLIENTS Total, Philips Lighting, Bosch, Dexia, Humo, NRC Handelsblad, HP, De Tijd, Playboy, Telerama, Le Seuil, Actes Sud, Albin Michel, Milan, Lannoo, Djeco

AWARDS Society of illustrators, Prix des Incorruptibles, Prix Libbylit

1 Alcoholism, 2002, Humo
2 Mary Jolie, 2004, Editions Seuil Jeunesse

"My aim is to strive for beauty and at the same time to express an idea. The creation of an illustration to me is very often about finding the right balance between these two elements. Colours play a key role in order to obtain this balance. To me there is no such thing as a distinction between illustration and personal work as I approach both the same way: my way."

« Mon objectif est de rechercher la beauté, tout en exprimant aussi une idée. La création d'une illustration tient beaucoup pour moi à la recherche du juste équilibre entre ces deux éléments. Les couleurs jouent un rôle fondamental dans cet équilibre. À mon sens il n'y a pas de distinction entre projet d'illustration et travail personnel, puisque j'adopte dans les deux cas la même approche : la mienne. »

„Ich strebe nach Schönheit und möchte gleichzeitig eine Idee vermitteln. Wenn ich illustriere, geht es oft darum, die richtige Balance zwischen diesen zwei Elementen zu finden. Farben spielen dabei eine entscheidende Rolle. Ich mache keinen Unterschied zwischen Illustration und persönlicher Arbeit, denn ich gehe beide auf dieselbe Art an: auf meine Art."

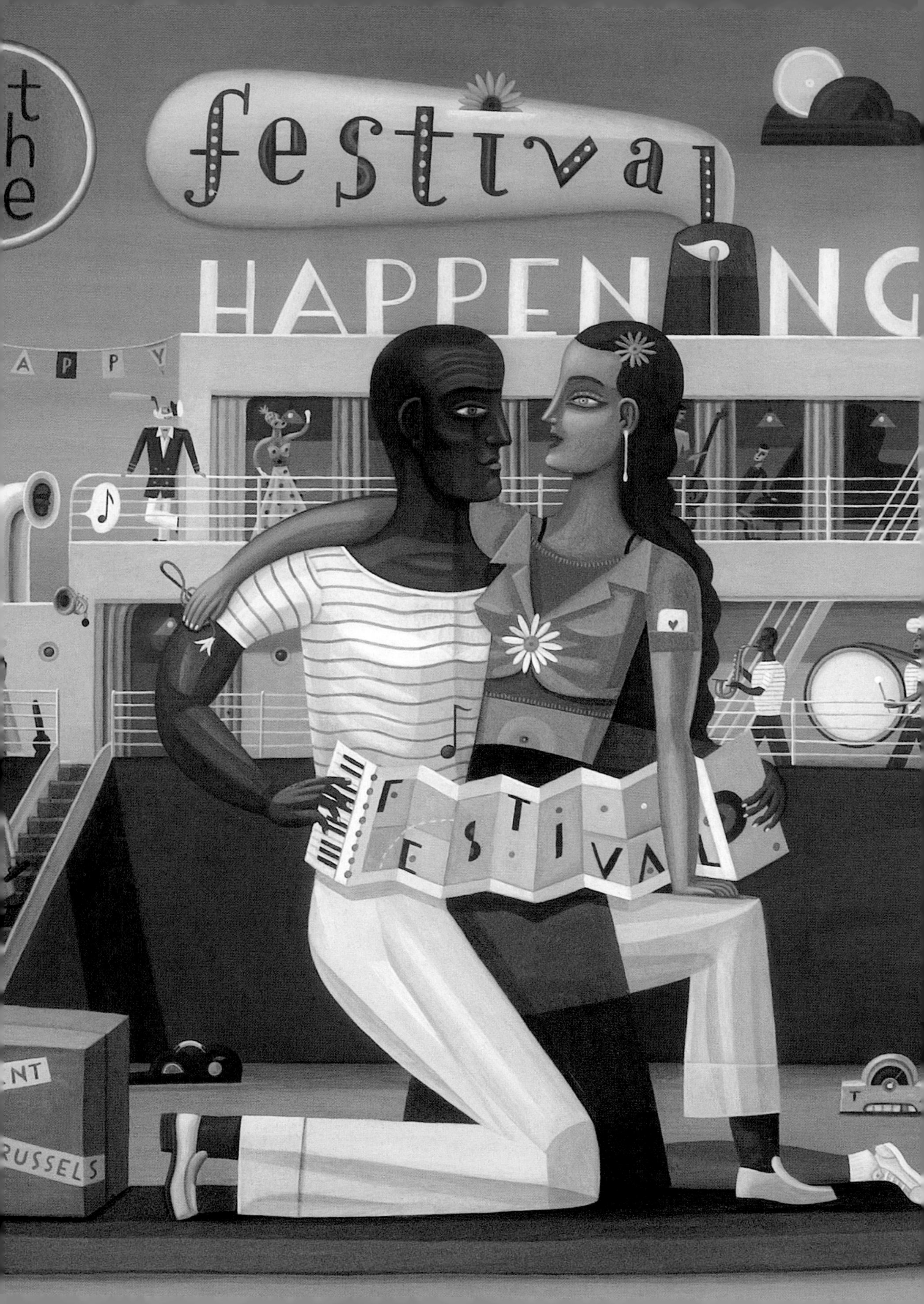
the
festival
HAPPEN
NG
APPY
FESTIVAL
NT
RUSSELS

4

5

6

3 The Festival Happening, 2001, Festival van Vlaanderen
4 Book Fair Antwerp, 2003, Boek.be
5 Rust, 1995, Blad
6 The Arab World Post 9/11, 2002, NRC Handelsblad Magazine

MIJN SCHATJE

NAME Mijn Schatje
WEBSITE www.mijnschatje.fr
LOCATION Paris, France

AGENT La Superette <www.lasuperette.com>
TOOLS Adobe Illustrator

CLIENTS Fornarina, Sony Entertainment, Reebok, Biba, Publicis Roma, WAD Magazine, Melody's Mercery, Nouvelles Images

1

2

1 Dance Me Until the End of the World, 2006, personal work
2 I Can't Stop Loving You, 2006, personal work
3 It's a Wonderful World, 2006, personal work

"I just want to share my imaginary world..."

« Je souhaite simplement partager mon monde imaginaire... »

„Ich möchte andere an meiner Fantasiewelt teilhaben lassen ..."

4 La Sirène, 2006, personal work
5 I Can Hear Wolves, 2006, personal work
6 Melancholia, 2006, personal work
7 The Girl and the Tiger, 2006, personal work

SHOUT

NAME Shout
LOCATION Milan, Italy
TOOLS Adobe Photoshop, Corel Painter, acrylic, ink, pencil

CLIENTS The New York Times, The Economist, Le Monde, LA Times, Wired, BusinessWeek, Penguin, Random House

AWARDS Society of Illustrators, Communications Arts, American Illustration, Print, 3x3 Magazine

1

1 Missing Saul Bellow, 2007, Internazionale
2 Diary, 2006, The New York Times, Steven Heller (Art Director)
3 Picking the Best, 2006, Plansponsor Magazine, SooJin Buzelli (Art Director)

2

"I try to eliminate as many details as possible
to get to an image's core essence."

« J'essaie d'éliminer autant de détails que possible pour obtenir l'essence d'une image. »

„Ich versuche, so viele Details wie möglich wegzulassen, um den Kern eines Bildes zu erfassen."

anger You Are Not Aware, 2006,
sponsor Magazine, SooJin Buzelli
Director)
e, 2006, Minimum Fax
ack Swan, 2007, The New York Times,
olas Blechman (Art Director)
ost, 2006
eautiful old world, 2006

MARIANA SILVA

NAME Mariana Silva
WEBSITE www.marianasilva.com.mx
LOCATION Mexico City, Mexico

TOOLS Adobe Photoshop, Adobe Illustrator, watercolour

CLIENTS Big Magazine (Mexico), Victoria's Secret, Verve Magazine (Germany), Curvy Magazine (Australia)

1

2

1 Make-up #2, 2007, personal work
2 Attraction, 2007, personal work
3 Make-up #1, 2006, personal work

"Frequently I like to do illustrations on the theme of nature. I think nature is very important so I like to represent a world where humans and nature coexist without damaging it. When I start an illustration I like to think that my characters are in a magic world. I really like the world of fashion so my characters evolve in that mood."

« Souvent, j'aime faire des illustrations sur le thème de la nature. Elle est tellement importante à mes yeux qu'il me plaît de représenter un monde dans lequel les hommes vivent sans lui porter préjudice. Lorsque je commence une illustration, j'aime penser que mes personnages se trouvent dans un monde magique. J'adore le monde de la mode et mes personnages évoluent dans cette atmosphère. »

„Ich mache gerne Illustrationen zum Thema Natur. Natur ist sehr wichtig und deshalb möchte ich eine Welt präsentieren, in der die Menschen mit der Natur leben, ohne sie zu zerstören. Wenn ich mit einer Illustration beginne, stelle ich mir gerne vor, dass meine Figuren eine Zauberwelt bewohnen. Ich mag die Modewelt und meine Figuren entwickeln sich aus dieser Stimmung heraus."

PETER SÍS

NAME Peter Sís
WEBSITE www.petersis.com
LOCATION New York, NY, USA

TOOLS Colored inks, watercolor, acrylic, gouache, oil pastel, mixed media

AWARDS MacArthur Fellowship

1 Galileo's Trial in the Pope's Court, book "Starry Messenger: Galileo Galilei", 1996
2 Jan Welzl Crossing the Frozen Bering Sea, book "A Small Tall Tale from the Far Far North: Jan Welzl", 1993
3 A Tree of Life, poster, 2003, Amnesty International USA

1

"I express most of myself through my art and hope that others may enjoy how I convey feelings and ideas through my work. I would like to enlighten people and show them how the world is fascinating, and complex and inspiring."

« J'exprime la plus grande partie de moi-même à travers mon art, et j'espère que ma façon de véhiculer des sentiments et des idées à travers mon travail plaira aux autres. J'aimerais arriver à éclairer les gens et à leur montrer à quel point le monde est fascinant, complexe et stimulant. »

„Ich drücke mich vorwiegend über Kunst aus und hoffe, dass es anderen gefällt, wie ich Gefühle und Ideen in meiner Arbeit vermittle. Ich würde Menschen gerne zeigen, wie faszinierend, komplex und inspirierend die Welt ist."

4 40 character studies for the animated short "You Gotta Serve Somebody" based on Bob Dylan's song, 1984, Fine Arts, Los Angeles

5 The Red Room, book "Tibet through the Red Box", 1998
6 Night After Night Galileo Gazed Through His Telescope,
book "Starry Messenger: Galileo Galilei", 1996
7 Diary page, book "Tibet through the Red Box", 1998

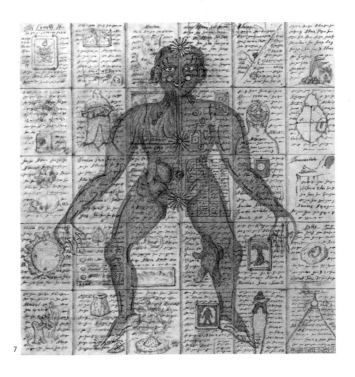

7

SIMON SPILSBURY

NAME Simon Spilsbury
WEBSITE www.spilsbury.co.uk
LOCATION Bath, United Kingdom
AGENT 1 Central Illustration Agency, London, <www.centralillustration.com>

AGENT 2 Bernstein & Andriulli, New York, <www.ba-reps.com>
AGENT 3 Hugo Weinberg, Paris, <www.centralillustration.com>
TOOLS Mixed media

CLIENTS The Independent, The Times, GQ, The Guardian, BBC, Channel 4, IBM, UBS, Virgin, Nike, BBH, Saatchi & Saatchi, eBay
AWARDS D&AD, Communication Arts, Creative Circle, Print

1

2

1 Carbon Fatprint #1, 2007, personal work
2 Carbon Fatprint #2, 2007, personal work
3 Mouse Surgery, 2005, personal work

"Spontaneous and investigative graphic image making. Solving visual problems via a drawing-based style that adapts to the individual demands of each brief, from a regular newspaper column to a 96 sheet."

« Création d'images spontanées et expérimentales. Résolution de problèmes visuels grâce à un style de dessin qui s'adapte aux besoins individuels de chaque projet, de la colonne de journal standard à un document de 96 pages. »

„Spontane und investigative grafische Bilder. Visuelle Probleme mit einem Zeichenstil zu lösen, der sich an die individuellen Erfordernisse eines jeden Briefings anpasst, egal, ob es sich um eine normale Zeitungsspalte handelt oder ein riesiges Werbebanner."

4 Drawn Porn, 2007, British Illustration Awards
5 Cityhell #2, 2001, exhibition
6 Cityhell #1, 2001, exhibition
7 USA Scape, 2007, personal work

MARK SUMMERS

NAME Mark Summers
LOCATION Waterdown, Canada
AGENT Richard Solomon, Artists Representative
<www.richardsolomon.com>

TOOLS Scratchboard, X-acto knife, oil, watercolor
CLIENTS Barnes & Noble, Rolling Stone, Time, American Express, Eddie Bauer, The Atlantic, Major League Baseball, Dupont

AWARDS Society of Illustrators, Print, Communication Arts, Step-by-Step Graphics

1 "Silent Film Star Anna May Wong", self-promotion, 2006
2 "Cougar", a promotional piece for Weyerhaeuser Company, 2006
3 Aviator Amelia Earhart, for the Creative Editions book "Versus: A Celebration of Outstanding Women", 2005

1

2

" 'Mark Summers takes the illustrator's art back a century by enlisting the wood engravers' craft to the scratchboard medium. He gives it a thoroughly contemporary flavor, however, in the power of his imagery.' *The Illustrator in America*, 1860-2000, by Walt Reed."

« ‹ Mark Summers fait remonter l'art de l'illustration un siècle en arrière en appliquant la technique de la gravure sur bois au support de la carte à gratter. Il lui donne cependant une allure tout à fait contemporaine, et c'est là toute la force de ses images. › *The Illustrator in America*, 1860-2000, de Walt Reed. »

„ ‚Mark Summers transportiert die Kunst des Illustrierens um ein Jahrhundert in die Vergangenheit zurück, indem er Holzschnitttechniken auf das Medium des Kupferstichs anwendet. Durch die Kraft seiner Fantasie erhält es jedoch eine durch und durch moderne Anmutung.' *The Illustrator in America*, 1860-2000, von Walt Reed."

El Greco walks into a bar. The bartender says, "Hey, why the long face?"

Picasso walks into a bar. Bartender asks, "Why so blue?"

Toulouse-Lautrec walks into a bar, asks for a beer, then adds, "Can I pay you tomorrow—I'm a little short today."

Henry Moore walks into a bar and asks for a drink. The bartender says, "You need another drink like you need a hole in the head."

Andy Warhol walks into a bar and asks, "Can I use the can?"

George Segal walks i a bar with one of hi sculptures. Bartender s "I'll serve you but n your friend—he alrea looks plastered."

4 "El Grego Walks Into a Bar...", Vanity Fair Magazine, 2006

Christo walks into a bar and starts draping everything in orange silk. Bartender says, "Hey, there's a $10 cover charge."

M. C. Escher walks into a bar and M. C. Escher walks into a bar and M. C. Escher walks into a bar and . . .

Van Gogh walks into a bar. Bartender asks what he wants. Van Gogh says, " . . . What?"

Jackson Pollock walks into a bar and says, "Give me a beer—oh yeah, and a mop."

Thomas Eakins walks into a bar with an oar over his shoulder. Bartender says, "Are you out of your skull?"

Edvard Munch walks into a bar and says, "CAN I GET A DRINK!"

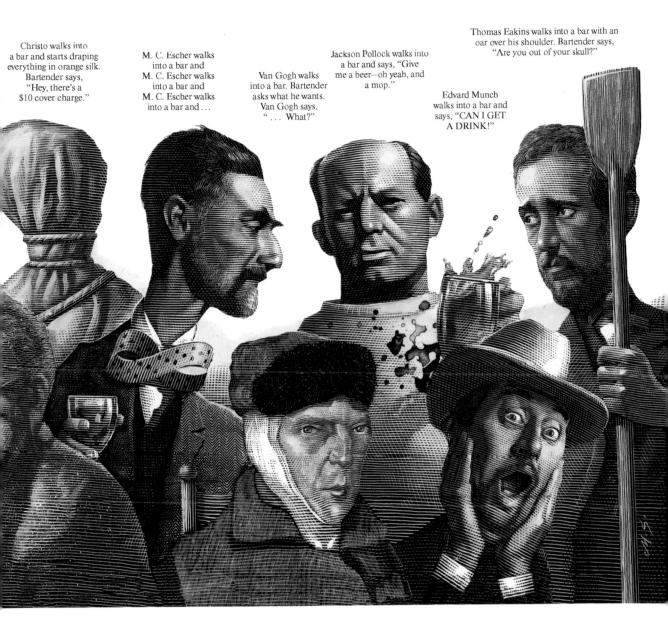

399

6

5 "Winter Reading: Leo Tolstoy", The Weekly Standard Magazine, 2004
6 "Summer Reading: Mark Twain", The Weekly Standard Magazine, 2004

MISS SWANNE

NAME Miss Swanne
WEBSITE www.folioart.co.uk
LOCATION London, United Kingdom

AGENT Folio <www.folioart.co.uk>
TOOLS Adobe Illustrator, Adobe Photoshop

CLIENTS Dotty Rhino, CHI, Ogilvy Healthworld, Marketing Solutions

1 Red Bobble Hat, 2007
2 Summer Sun, 2007
3 Tiger Tiger, 2007, personal work

"Miss Swanne is excited about colour and graphic compositions. Detail, pattern and ornamentation play a big part in her image making."

« Miss Swanne a le goût pour les compositions graphiques et de couleurs. Les détails, les motifs et les ornementations occupent une place de choix dans sa technique de création d'images. »

„Miss Swanne findet Farbe und grafische Komposition aufregend. Detail, Muster und Ornamentation spielen in ihren Bildern eine wichtige Rolle."

WILL SWEENEY

NAME Will Sweeney
WEBSITE www.alakazamlabel.com
LOCATION London, United Kingdom

AGENT Big Active <www.bigactive.com>
TOOLS Pencil, Rotring pens

CLIENTS Silas, Medicom Toy, Kramers Ergot, The Ganzfeld, Volkswagen, Der Spiegel

1 Tales From Greenfuzz, 2005, Amos Novelties
2 John Bonham Portrait, 2005, Dazed & Confused Magazine
3 Dazed Brotherhood Illustration, 2006, Dazed & Confused Magazine

"Involving, ever growing, like a fungus."

« Intervenir, toujours se développer, comme un champignon. »

„Aufsaugend, ständig wachsend, wie ein Schimmelpilz."

TADO

NAME Mike & Katie Tado
WEBSITE www.tado.co.uk
LOCATION Sheffield, United Kingdom

AGENT 1 Tiphaine Illustration, Paris,
<www.tiphaine-illustration.com>
AGENT 2 Debut Art, London, <www.debutart.com>

TOOLS Adobe Illustrator, Adobe Photoshop,
Adobe Flash, pen, pencil
CLIENTS Honda, Volkswagen, MTV International,
Smart Car, Nike, Adidas, Puma, British Airways,
Microsoft, WWF

1

1 Flowers, 2006, Sherbet
2 Lovestools, 2006, personal work

"We enjoy the diversity of our work and the different media that it crosses.
We have a lot of fun creating the artwork and hope this shows through the pieces!"

« Nous aimons la diversité de notre travail et les différents supports qui l'accueillent. Nous nous amusons
beaucoup à créer des illustrations et espérons que ce plaisir se retrouve dans nos œuvres ! »

„Uns gefällt die Vielfalt unserer Arbeit und die unterschiedlichen Medien, mit denen wir zu tun haben.
Wir haben viel Spaß beim Illustrieren und hoffen, dass dies auch in den Bildern sichtbar wird!"

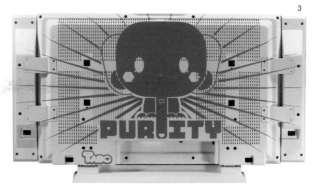

3 Purity, 2006, Sherbet
4 Mobility, 2007, Vodafone

HIROSHI TANABE

NAME Hiroshi Tanabe
LOCATION Japan
AGENT 1 Kate Larkworthy Artist Representation, New York, <www.larkworthy.com>
AGENT 2 A.K.A. Management, Tokyo, <www.akamg.com>

TOOLS Adobe Photoshop, mixed media, paper, pen
CLIENTS Anna Sui, Barneys, Bergdorf Goodman, Clinique, GQ, Issey Miyake, The New York Times, The New Yorker, Shiseido, Vogue

AWARDS American Illustration, Art Directors Club (New York & Tokyo), Communication Arts, Luerzer's Archive, Society of Illustrators

"Simple composition, straight colours, surrealist touch, distinctive flavour."

« Une composition simple, des couleurs franches, une touche de surréalisme et un parfum original. »

„Einfache Komposition, klare Farben, leicht surrealistische Anmutung und unverwechselbare Note."

1

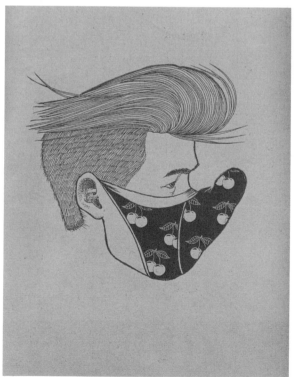

2

1 Ta Ta Face, 2007, S Magazine
2 Dick Head, 2007, S Magazine
3 Girls, 1997, Blue Mode book, Korinsha Press

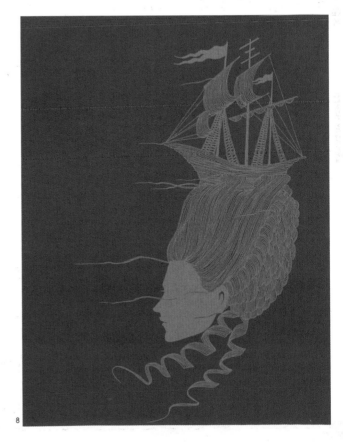

4 Marie Antoinette #1, 2006, Fumihiro Hayashi
5 Marie Antoinette #2, 2006, Fumihiro Hayashi
6 Deer, 2003, Graphic-sha Publishing Co., Ltd.
7 Untitled, 2003, Labrea, Japan
8 Marie Antoinette #3, 2006, Fumihiro Hayashi

TITI

NAME Titi
WEBSITE http://garden.party.free.fr
LOCATION Marseille, France

AGENT Agent 002 <www.agent002.com>
TOOLS Paper, pen, Adobe Illustrator

CLIENTS Nestlé, Delacre, Total, Tefal, Peugeot, Citroën, Seat, BNP, SFR, GDF, Editions Marabout, Fleuve Noir, Wilkinson, Jasmin

1 Le Mime Marceau, 2006, personal work
2 L'Age des Glaces, 2007, personal work
3 The Duke, 2006, personal work
4 Green Peace, 2006, personal work

"I like things that are aesthetic, simple, effective and fun. My main inspirations are the illustrations in adverts and record sleeves, film credits, starlets, the tea in Tati's films, Hanna-Barbera cartoons, North American soap operas, the designs and the colours of the 50's, 60's and 70's. I am a son of my time, but there has been nothing like that since then."

« J'aime ce qui est esthétique, simple, efficace et drôle. Mes inspirations principales sont les illustrations des publicités et des pochettes de disques, les génériques de films, les starlettes, l'ambiance des films de Tati, les cartoons d'Hanna Barbera, les feuilletons américains, le design, et les couleurs des années 50, 60 et 70. Je vis avec mon temps mais depuis cette époque, on n'a pas fait mieux. »

„Ich mag Dinge, die ästhetisch, einfach, effektiv und lustig sind. Ich werde hauptsächlich inspiriert von Illustrationen in der Werbung und auf Schallplattencovern, von Filmnachspannen, Starlets, der Stimmung in den Filmen von Tati, den Cartoons von Hanna-Barbera, amerikanischen Fernsehserien, Design und Farben der 50er, 60er und 70er Jahre. Ich lebe zwar in meiner Zeit, aber seither ist nichts Besseres entstanden."

CLARISSA TOSSIN

NAME Clarissa Tossin
WEBSITE www.a-linha.org
LOCATION 1 Sao Paulo, Brazil
LOCATION 2 Los Angeles, CA, USA

TOOLS Adobe Illustrator, Adobe Photoshop, scanner, handmade elements
CLIENTS Vogue, MTV, Avene, Adidas, Adobe, Custo Barcelona, Sao Paulo Fashion Week, Vermelho Gallery, Duran Duran

AWARDS Worldstudio, AIGA, Videfest Canada, Graphic Designers Association Brazil

1

1 Gold Drops, 2006, Clube Brahma, Resfest Brazil
2 Urban Wallpaper, 2004, Resfest Brazil

"My illustration work mainly consists of the exploration of the digital medium's poetics. As a counterpoint, I disrupt the notion of digital imagery as cold and remote by working with a vibrant and wide color palette in complex compositions."

« Mon travail d'illustration consiste principalement à explorer la poétique des supports numériques. En contrepoint, je bouleverse la perception des images numériques comme froides et distantes grâce à l'emploi d'une large palette de couleurs vives et de compositions élaborées. »

„Meine Arbeit besteht im Wesentlichen darin, die Poetik des digitalen Mediums zu erforschen. Ich zerstöre die Vorstellung von digitalen Bildern als kalt und unbeteiligt, indem ich innerhalb von komplexen Kompositionen mit einer umfangreichen Palette an lebendigen Farben arbeite."

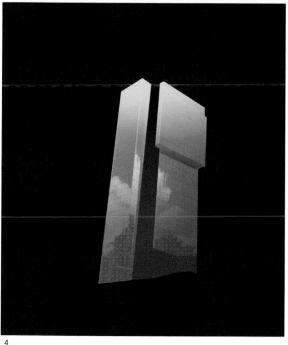

4

3 Symbiosis, 2004, Graphic Magazine #4
4 Sky Boxes, 2004, personal work

JEREMY TRAUM

NAME Jeremy Traum
WEBSITE www.jeremytraum.com

LOCATION Brooklyn, NY, USA
TOOLS Mixed media

CLIENTS The New York Times, The New Yorker, Harper's, Atlantic Monthly, The Progressive, The Walrus, Architecture, The Wall Street Journal, Village Voice, LA Weekly, The Washington Post

1 Saddam, 2004, personal work
2 Cowmachine, 2004, personal work
2 Progress, 2005, personal work

1

2

"I am a firm believer that content should always dictate style. Style is a periphera element in ones work that comes naturally from working hard. Content will always resonate with the viewer no matter what package it comes in."

« Je crois fermement que le contenu doit toujours commander le style. Le style est un élément périphérique qui arrive naturellemen lorsqu'on travaille dur. Le contenu trouve toujours un écho chez le public, quel que soit son emballage. »

„Ich glaube fest daran, dass der Inhalt immer den Stil bestimmen sollte. Stil ist ein nebensächliches Element, das sich automatisc ergibt, wenn man hart arbeitet. Der Inhalt wird immer auf den Betrachter wirken, egal wie er verpackt ist."

4 Street Art, 2005, personal work
5 Creation, 2007, personal work
6 China #1, 2006, personal work

ARISTEIDIS TSINAROGLOU

NAME Aristeidis Tsinaroglou
LOCATION Athens, Greece

AGENT Smart Magna <www.smartmagna.com>
TOOLS Plasticine, Adobe Photoshop

CLIENTS Mothercare, Castor Publishing House, Veterin

1-2 From Here Up To the Moon and Still Further, 1997, Castor Publishing House
3 The Black Sheep With White Sheeps, 2006, Smart Magna

"Plasticine is a malleable material that can be moulded and sculpted into so many forms. It is familiar to everybody, as we have all played with it during our childhood. Photography then gives the illusion of 3D, bringing the spectator into the scene."

« La pâte à modeler est un matériau malléable que l'on peut mouler et sculpter à l'infini. Tout le monde la connaît pour avoir joué avec dans l'enfance. La photographie crée une illusion 3D et fait pénétrer le public dans la scène. »

„Knetmasse ist ein formbares Material, aus dem unglaublich viele Formen modelliert werden können. Jeder kennt es aus seiner Kindheit. Durch Fotografie entsteht eine Illusion von Dreidimensionalität, die den Betrachter in die Szenerie hineinzieht."

LINA VILA

NAME Lina Vila
WEBSITE www.estudiolinavila.com
LOCATION Valencia, Spain

AGENT Agent 002 <www.agent002.com>
TOOLS Pencil, Freehand, Adobe Photoshop

CLIENTS Group Eroski, Swatch, Gandía Blasco

1 Welcome, Santa Claus, 2005, Hesperia Hotels
2 Festival Jazz-Flamenco, 2003, El Loco Mateo
3 Mambo Club, 2004, Formica

2

1

"Things such as the kitsch atmosphere, the yellow press, the Spanish cinema from the 60's and 70's are my endless sources. I like illustrating the anecdote, the flustered moment or a character's portrait with a few strokes and fun. I think my work has to make every little thing around us become joyful and bright."

« Pour moi, les atmosphères kitsch, la presse à scandales et le cinéma espagnol des années 60 et 70 sont des sources inépuisables d'inspiration. J'aime illustrer une anecdote, un moment de trouble ou le portrait d'un personnage en quelques traits et avec humour. Je pense que mon travail doit égayer tous les détails qui nous entourent. »

„Meine unerschöpflichen Quellen sind Kitsch-Atmosphäre, Klatschblätter und das spanische Kino der 60er und 70er Jahre. Ich illustriere eine Anekdote, einen Moment der Verwirrung oder das Porträt einer Figur gerne mit ein paar Strichen und Humor. Ich möchte, dass meine Arbeiten alle noch so kleinen Dinge um uns herum fröhlich und hell machen."

SALLY VITSKY

NAME Sally Vitsky
WEBSITE www.vitsky.com
LOCATION Richmond, VA, USA
AGENT Morgan Gaynin Inc.
<www.morgangaynin.com>

TOOLS X-acto blades, handmade papers, foam board, balsa wood, textured bristol, watercolor paper

CLIENTS American Forest & Paper Association, Newsweek, Standard & Poor's, Harcourt, Cartier, Mad Magazine, GE, IBM, Macmillan/McGraw-Hill, The Wall Street Journal, Bayer
AWARDS Society of Illustrators, Papercraft Champions (Tokyo TV)

1 Bench, 2005, American Forest & Paper Association
2 Window, 2002, personal work
3 Birds, 1999, personal work

"Although my professional title is 'Illustrator', I consider myself a creative thinker with strong conceptual abilities. There's nothing more fun for me than the 'aha' moment – the challenge of coming up with an idea! I'm drawn to the tactile and versatile qualities of paper. The possibilities inherent in a clean white sheet of Bristol are endless!"

« Même si ma carte de visite dit ‹ Illustratrice ›, je me considère plutôt comme une créative avec de bonnes capacités conceptuelles. Rien n'est plus amusant pour moi que le moment du ‹ ah, ah ! ›, le défi de trouver une idée ! Je suis attirée par les qualités tactiles et versatiles du papier. Les possibilités qu'offre une feuille blanche de Bristol sont infinies ! »

„Obwohl meine Berufsbezeichnung ‚Illustratorin' ist, sehe ich mich als kreative Denkerin mit starken konzeptionellen Fähigkeiten. Nichts bereitet mir mehr Freude als der ‚Aha-Moment', wenn einem eine zündende Idee eingefallen ist. Die fühlbaren und vielseitigen Merkmale von Papier ziehen mich an. Die Möglichkeiten, die in einem sauberen weißen Blatt Bristolpapier stecken, sind endlos!"

4 Wake-Up, 1996, personal work
5 BCBS, 1999, Blue Cross, Blue Shield Consortium
6 Cadmus, 1997, Cadmus Printing
7 Self Portrait, 2005, Morgan Gaynin Illustration

5

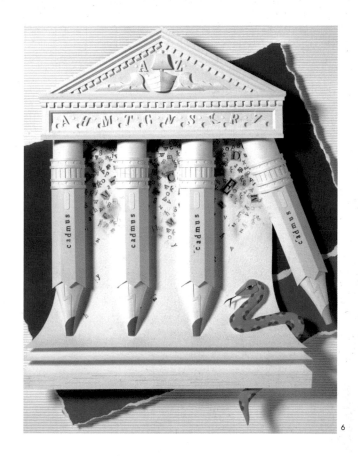

6

7

KONSTANTINOS VRAZIOTIS

NAME Konstantinos Vraziotis
LOCATION Athens, Greece

AGENT Smart Magna <www.smartmagna.com>
TOOLS Pencil, Adobe Illustrator, Adobe Photoshop

CLIENTS Toi & moi, Madame Figaro,
Elle, Votre Beauté, Maison Decoration
AWARDS Madame Figaro

1 Collage, 2007, personal work
2 Devon, 2006, personal work
3 Stella, 2006, personal work

"The dark shine of my 'it girls' reproduces 'my' surrealistic world of fashion. My inspiration comes from beauty campaigns, fashion magazines and Kate Moss as a prototype. The attitude of my work represents the sparkling world of fashion by showing the different aspects of my visual models."

« Le sombre éclat de mes ‹ filles à la mode › illustre ‹ mon › monde surréaliste de la mode. Je puise mon inspiration dans les campagnes de produits de beauté et les magazines de mode et Kate Moss est mon prototype. L'approche de mon travail montre le monde étincelant de la mode à travers les différents aspects de mes modèles visuels. »

„Der dunkle Glanz meiner ‚it girls' gibt ‚meine' surreale Welt der Mode wieder. Ich werde inspiriert von Kosmetikwerbung, Modezeitschriften und Kate Moss als Prototyp. Meine Arbeiten, in denen ich verschiedene Facetten meiner visuellen Modelle zeige, repräsentieren die schillernde Welt der Mode."

MARIO WAGNER

NAME Mario Wagner
WEBSITE www.mario-wagner.com
LOCATION Cologne, Germany

AGENT 1 2 Agenten, Berlin, <www.2agenten.com>
AGENT 2 Anna Goodson Management, <www.agoodson.com>

TOOLS Collage, acrylic, paper, canvas, letterset
CLIENTS Adidas, The New York Times, Nylon, The Boston Globe, Playboy, Die Zeit, Neon, Gruner+Jahr Verlag, BusinessWeek

1

1 Wolke, 2006, Rojo Magazine
2 Fest der Völker, Olympia, 2006, Booklet Magazine
3 First Contact, 2007, personal work

2

"A few keywords relevant to the subject are usually enough for me to create an illustration, leaving me sufficient space for my own interpretation. I search sixties magazines and old books for picture elements, bringing them together with acrylic paint on paper, canvas or cardboard, out of which form illustrations between past and fiction."

« Quelques mots clés résumant le thème me suffisent généralement à créer une illustration tout en me laissant assez de marge pour une interprétation personnelle. Je recherche des éléments d'image dans des magazines des années soixante et dans des vieux livres, et je les relie avec de la peinture acrylique sur du papier, une toile ou du carton. Le résultat est une illustration à mi-chemin entre passé et fiction. »

„Meist reichen mir ein paar stichworte des themas um eine illustration zu erstellen, dadurch erhalte ich mir dann genügend platz für meine eigene interpretation. Ich durchsuche magazine aus den 60ern und alte bücher nach bildelementen, bringe sie dann zumsammen mit acrylfarbe auf papier, leinwand oder karton und es entstehen illustrationen zwischen vergangenheit und fiktion."

BRIAN MICHAEL WEAVER

NAME Brian Michael Weaver
WEBSITE www.brianmichaelweaver.com
LOCATION New York, NY, USA

TOOLS Pencil, Adobe Photoshop, charcoal, ink, watercolor
CLIENTS The New York Times, Henry Holt, Radar Magazine

AWARDS Fumetto International Comics Competition, American Illustration

"I'm not a very big fan of 'art'. I like it when a piece serves a tangible purpose, like a joke or a story, as opposed to art for art's sake. There's another side to my work, inspired by the likes of Lenny Bruce or HBO's *Mr. Show with Bob and David*, where I try to mix very lewd, oftentimes inappropriate material with abstract and complex ideas. I sometimes feel like it's my own subconscious way of finding true, loyal fans."

« Je ne suis pas un inconditionnel de ‹ l'art ›. J'apprécie lorsqu'une œuvre remplit une mission tangible, comme raconter une blague ou une histoire, contrairement à l'art pour l'art. Mon travail possède une autre facette inspirée par Lenny Bruce ou le programme *Mr. Show with Bob and David* sur HBO : j'essaie de mélanger du matériel très obscène et souvent inapproprié à des idées abstraites et complexes. Parfois, je crois que c'est ma façon inconsciente de chercher des admirateurs authentiques et loyaux. »

„Ich bin kein großer ‚Kunst'-Fan. Ich ziehe ein Stück, das einem bestimmten Zweck dient, wie ein Witz oder eine Geschichte, einer Kunst um ihrer selbst willen vor. Eine andere Seite meiner Arbeit ist inspiriert von Leuten wie Lenny Bruce oder der Fernsehsendung *Mr. Show with Bob and David*. Ich versuche dabei, sehr schlüpfriges und anzügliches Material mit abstrakten und komplexen Ideen zu verbinden. Manchmal denke ich, das ist mein instinktiver Versuch, wahre loyale Fans zu finden."

1 Scientology On Broadway, 2006, Radar Magazine
2 Shitty Owl, 2005, Julie Klausner, Free To Be Friends
3 Enter the Blue Ghost, 2006, personal work

SAM WEBER

NAME Sam Weber
WEBSITE www.sampaints.com
LOCATION New York, NY, USA

TOOLS Acrylic, ink, watercolor, digital media
CLIENTS The New York Times, Time, Spin, ESPN, Sony BMG, The New Yorker, Herman Miller, Wired, Random House, Penguin, Scholastic

AWARDS Society of Publication Designers, Society of Illustrators, Communication Arts, American Illustration

"I'm interested in creating a sense of mystery in my pictures.
I hope to be able to continue to grow and develop as a storyteller,
something that continues to make illustration exciting."

« Je cherche à doter mes images d'une dimension mystérieuse. J'espère pouvoir continuer à progresser comme conteur d'histoires pour que mes illustrations restent intéressantes. »

„Ich möchte, dass meine Bilder etwas Rätselhaftes haben. Ich hoffe, dass ich mich als Geschichtenerzähler weiterentwickeln kann, denn das ist es, was Illustration aufregend macht."

1 Paper Soldier, 2005, personal work
2 Caliban, 2006, personal work
3 Healing Your Heart, 2007, Spirituality & Health

LEIGH WELLS

NAME Leigh Wells
WEBSITE www.leighwells.com
LOCATION San Francisco, CA, USA
TOOLS Collage, acrylic, mixed media, Adobe Photoshop

CLIENTS Absolut Vodka, Air New Zealand, American Express, Atlantic Records, BBDO West, Chronicle Books, Converse, Fujitsu, Goodby, Silverstein & Partners, Harper's, Levi Strauss, Landor & Associates, The New York Times

AWARDS American Illustration, Society of Illustrators, Communication Arts, Print, AIGA

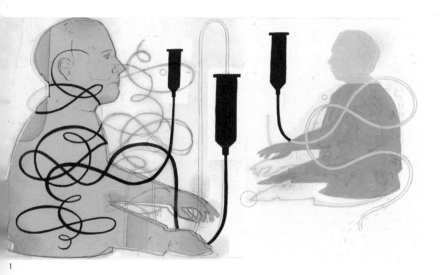

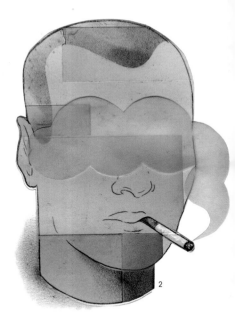

1 Dyalisis Ethics, 2006, New York Times, Science Times
2 Smoke Gets In Your Eyes, 2005, Time Magazine
3 The Brain: A User's Guide, 2007, Time Magazine

"Leigh Wells creates her astonishing images from her studio in San Francisco, strong concepts, matching colours and hand drawings."

« Leigh Wells crée des images étonnantes dans son studio de San Francisco, avec des concepts forts, des camaïeux de couleurs et des dessins à la main. »

„Leigh Wells erstaunliche Bilder entstehen in ihrem Studio in San Francisco. Starke Konzepte, aufeinander abgestimmte Farben und Handzeichnungen."

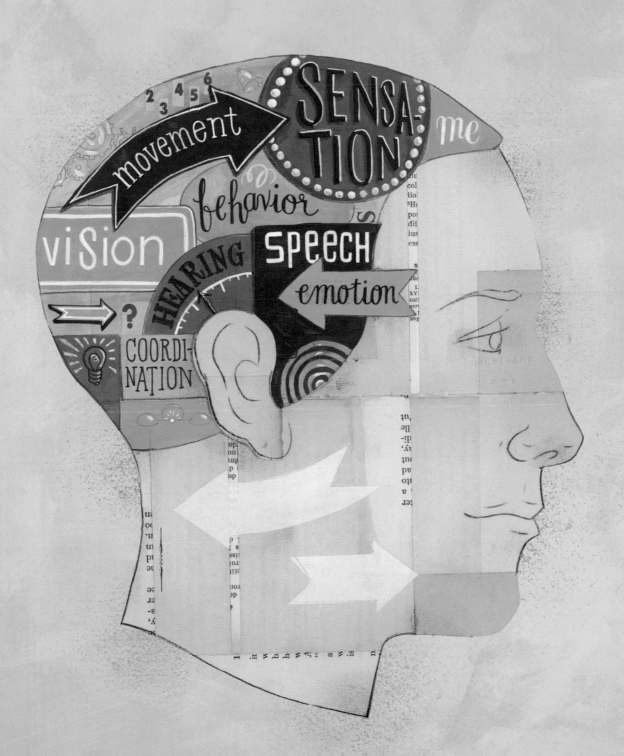

EDWINA WHITE

NAME Edwina White
WEBSITE www.edwinawhite.com
LOCATION 1 New York, NY, USA
LOCATION 2 Sydney, Australia

AGENT Kate Larkworthy Artist Representation
<www.larkworthy.com>
TOOLS Pen, ink, acrylic, collage, old paper

CLIENTS Merck, Flaunt, Vogue (Japan & Australia),
Random House, Viking, The Wall Street Journal,
The New York Times
AWARDS Art Directors Club, Folio Award, Print,
Creative Review United Kingdom

1 The Minimalist, 2006, EW
2 Last Wave, 2006, EW
3 A Game of Sardines, 2007, Kate Larkworthy
Artists Representation

2

1

"I use simple means to react to a brief, a fast pencil and wordplay. I think that illustration should encourage further reading and comprehension. I believe that gentle humor injected into artwork can allow for the sweet edge of ugliness to merge with that of beauty. As well as pinning down a subject it should allow room for a viewer's own eye to complete it."

« Pour réagir à un projet, j'utilise des moyens très simples : un crayon vif et un jeu de mots. Je pense que l'illustration doit encourager la lecture et la compréhension. Selon moi, un peu d'humour injecté dans une illustration peut être tout ce qu'il faut pour que le côté plaisant de la laideur émerge et s'associe à la beauté. À part la représentation de son sujet, l'illustration doit laisser une marge au regard du public pour qu'il la complète. »

„Ich antworte mit einfachen Mitteln auf ein Briefing: einem schnellen Stift und Wortspielen. Meiner Meinung nach sollten Illustrationen zum weiterführenden Lesen und Verstehen anregen. Wenn einem Kunstwerk sanfter Humor zugefügt wird, so können Häßlichkeit und Schönheit an den Rändern ineinanderlaufen. Eine Illustration sollte nicht nur ein Thema erfassen, sondern dem Auge des Betrachters Raum lassen, sie zu vollenden."

5

6

4 Faking Louis Vuitton, 2006, Bulletin Magazine
5 A Foodies Tour, 2006, Financial Review Magazine
6 Musical Chairs, 2006, Third Drawer Down

CHARLES WILKIN

NAME Charles Wilkin
WEBSITE www.automatic-iam.com
LOCATION Brooklyn, NY, USA

AGENT Magnet Reps <www.magnetreps.com>
TOOLS Paper, paint, glue, X-acto knives,
magazines, catalogs, Adobe Photoshop,
Adobe Illustrator, scanner

CLIENTS Arkitip, Maxim, Vanity Fair, AIGA,
Vogue (Australia), Coca-Cola, Showtime,
Urban Outfitters, Capitol Records, Sprint
AWARDS American Illustration, AIGA,
Communication Arts, Print Regional

1

1 Naughty or Nice, 2007, AIGA New York
2 Canary, 2007, World Access Insurance

"Charles Wilkin's multi-disciplinary background shines through in his signature mixed media and digitally assisted collage illustration work. His inventive combinations of handmade and creatively appropriated visual elements are simultaneously clean and messy, old and new, consciously communicative and beautifully abstract."

« La formation multidisciplinaire de Charles Wilkin transparaît dans son travail très personnel d'illustration par collage sur ordinateur et sur des supports variés. Ses compositions originales d'éléments visuels faites à la main et bien pensées sont à la fois nettes et désordonnées, semblent anciennes et nouvelles, parlent avec intention et affichent une beauté abstraite. »

„Der multidisziplinäre Hintergrund von Charles Wilkin zeigt sich in seinen digital bearbeiteten, gemischt-medialen Collage-Illustrationen. Seine originellen Kombinationen von handgezeichneten und kreativ angeeigneten visuellen Elementen sind gleichzeitig sauber und dreckig, alt und neu, bewusst kommunikativ und wundervoll abstrakt."

ASHLEY WOOD

NAME Ashley Wood
WEBSITE www.ashleywood.com
LOCATION 1 Hobart, Australia

LOCATION 2 San Diego, CA, USA
LOCATION 3 New York, NY, USA
TOOLS Oil, ink, marker, ziptone, Adobe Photoshop

CLIENTS Sony, Microsoft, DreamWorks, Lucasfilm, 55DSL, IDW Publishing, Hasbro, Bambaland
AWARDS Communication Arts, Spectrum Award

"… Interesting, fun, and sex."
« … Intéressant, drôle et avec une dose de sexe. »
„… Interessant, macht Spaß, sexy.“

1 Ouch!, 2006, IDW Publishing
2 Sneak, 2006, IDW Publishing
2 The Gang, 2006, IDW Publishing

CHANDLER WOOD

NAME Chandler Wood
WEBSITE www.chandlerwood.com

LOCATION Los Angeles, CA, USA
TOOLS Pen, ink, watercolor, Adobe Photoshop

CLIENTS LA Weekly

"Try to stay amused."

« Essayer de continuer à s'amuser. »

„Ich versuche, mich dabei gut zu amüsieren."

2

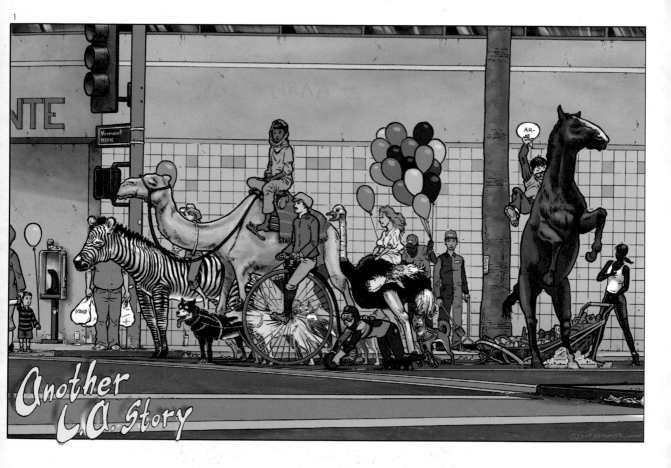

1 AAAFNRAA, 2007, LA Weekly
2 Downtown, 2007, Los Angeles Metro

3 Tryin', 2006, LA Weekly
4 Hot Dog, 2006, personal work
5 Promised Land, 2004, LA Weekly
6 Gentrification City, 2006, LA Weekly
7 The Chute, 2006, LA Weekly

5

6

YASSINE

NAME Yassine
LOCATION Paris, France

AGENT Lezilus <www.lezilus.com>
TOOLS Adobe Photoshop, Adobe Image Ready

CLIENTS Chocomix, Fluide glacial,
Lyonnaise des Eaux, Egis, Spirou, Condat

"Pixel power! The pixel should be the biggest possible!"

« Le pouvoir des pixels ! Les pixels doivent être les plus gros possible ! »

„Pixel power! Man sollte die größtmögliche Pixelzahl haben."

1

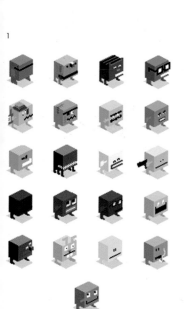

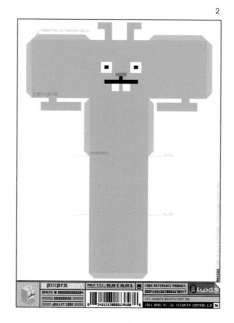

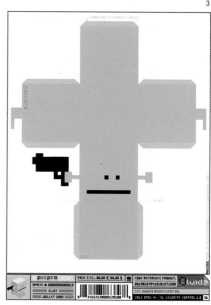

1 Personnages de Pixpro, 2003, Fluide Glacial
2 Boing Boing, 2003, Fluide Glacial
3 Clint, 2003, Fluide Glacial
4 La chaîne de fabrication du papier, 2006, Condat

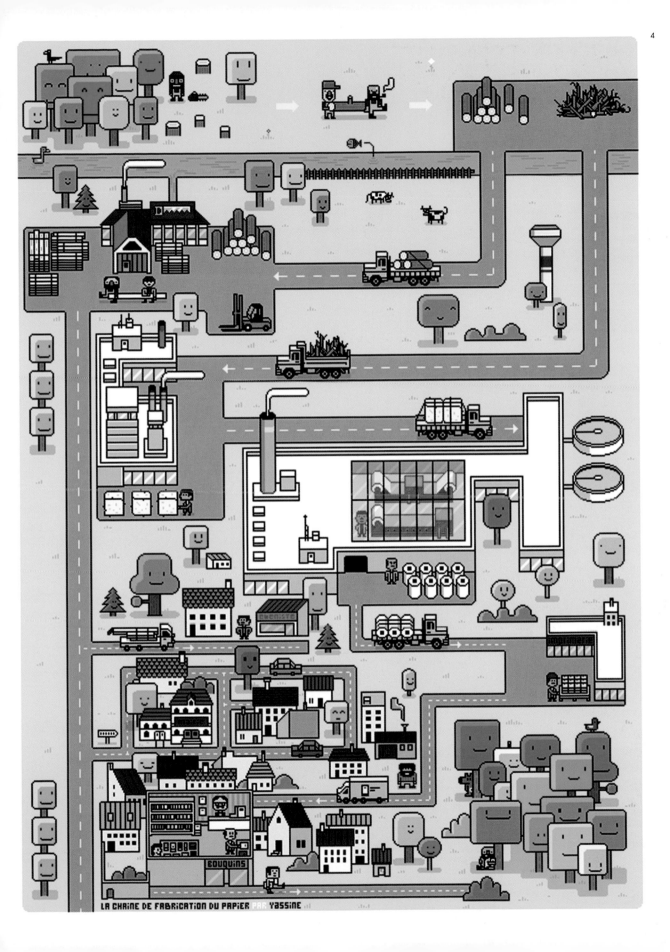

LA CHAINE DE FABRICATION DU PAPIER PAR YASSINE

BRAD YEO

NAME Brad Yeo
WEBSITE www.bradyeo.com
LOCATION Calgary, Canada
AGENT Gerald & Cullen Rapp <www.rappart.com>

TOOLS Acrylic, ink, mixed media
CLIENTS Warner Bros, American Airlines, Random House/Delacorte Press, Citigroup, Mercedes-Benz, Worth, Harper's, Paste

AWARDS Communication Arts, 3x3 ProShow, Society of Illustrators, American Illustration

1 The Board, 2006, Worth
2 Hikmat, 2007, Dartmouth College
3 Directional Sound, 2006, National Fire Protection Association

"Essentially, it's about finding or shaping meaning. The greater function of illustration is to communicate, no matter how one chooses to do this. I'll shift my illustrative approach accordingly, if I think this will better suit the premise or narrative. So in this sense, design becomes a part of style; some works read as pictorial scenes, others more like sign systems, or a combination thereof."

« L'idée est avant tout de trouver un message ou de lui donner forme. La grande fonction de l'illustration est la communication, quelle que soit la méthode adoptée. J'adapterai donc mon approche illustrative si je crois qu'elle peut mieux répondre au concept ou à l'histoire. C'est en cela que le design fait partie du style : certaines créations s'interprètent comme des scènes illustrées, d'autres davantage comme des systèmes de signes, ou une combinaison des deux. »

„Es geht im Wesentlichen um die Suche nach oder die Schaffung von Bedeutung. Das übergeordnete Ziel von Illustration ist es, zu kommunizieren, egal auf welche Weise. Ich passe meinen zeichnerischen Ansatz den gegebenen Voraussetzungen oder der Geschichte an. In diesem Sinn wird Design ein Teil des Stils. Einige Werke lesen sich wie Bildabfolgen, andere eher wie Zeichensysteme und wieder andere wie eine Kombination von beidem."

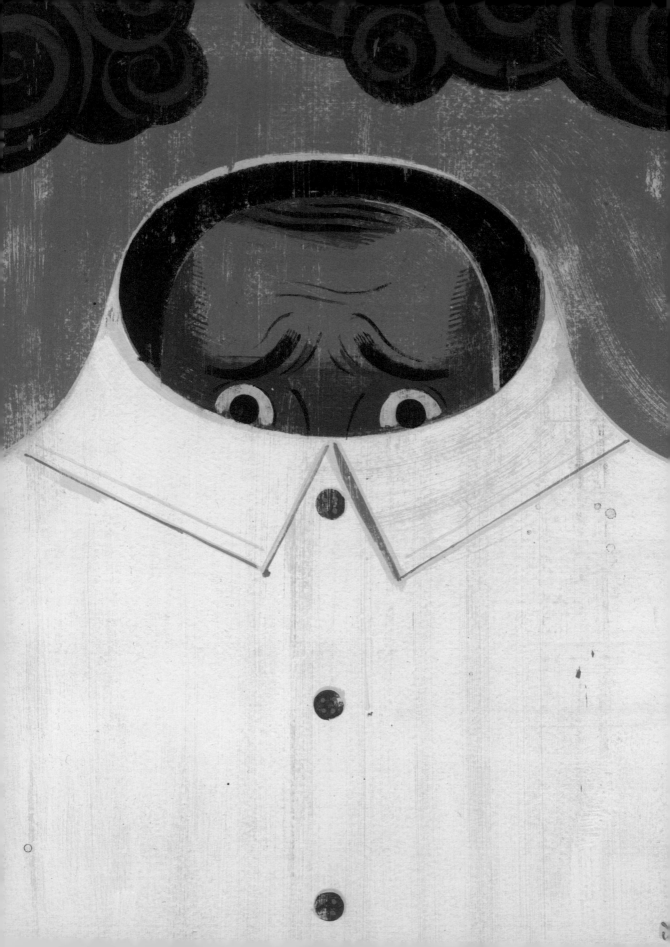

7

5

6

YOCO

NAME Yoco
LOCATION 1 London, United Kingdom
LOCATION 2 Osaka, Japan

AGENT 1 Dutch Uncle Agency, London,
<www.DutchUncle.co.uk>
AGENT 2 Pict, Tokyo/Osaka, <www.pict-web.com>

TOOLS Ink, pen, watercolor
CLIENTS Jo Malone, Moët & Chandon,
Shu Uemura, Max Factor, Penguin, Hodder,
Condé Nast Traveler, Time Warner

1 Karesansui, 2006, Shu Uemura
2 Beach, 2007, Moet & Chandon
3 Pool, 2007, Moet & Chandon

"I want to draw women who have a presence of beauty through well-trimmed simple lines."

« Je veux dessiner des femmes dégageant une idée de la beauté grâce à des lignes simples et nettes. »

„Ich möchte Frauen zeichnen, die mit einfachen klaren Linien Schönheit ausstrahlen."

STEVE YUEN

NAME Steve Yuen
WEBSITE www.workstation.com.hk
LOCATION Hong Kong, China

TOOLS Pencil, acrylic, Corel Painter,
Adobe Photoshop
CLIENTS HSBC, PCCW, Nike, Orange, Canon,
Volvo, Nokia, ICAC, Watson, Sony

AWARDS Pan Pacific Digital Artistry Competition
(Radius Award)

2

1 I Love Money, 2005, personal work
2 Trademark, 2007, personal work
3 I Still Have Feeling, 2006, personal work

"Hong Kong: a rapidly changing environment, the memory of things lost. These thoughts have given me the intention to paint this series. My ideas came entirely from my surroundings and my memories. It's a reflection of Hong Kong's living culture. Illustration is a good way to communicate and express myself to other people."

« Hong-Kong, environnement évoluant à toute vitesse, la mémoire des choses perdues. Ces pensées m'ont motivé à peindre cette série. Mes idées sont totalement inspirées par ce qui m'entoure et par mes souvenirs. Il s'agit d'une réflexion sur la culture vivante de Hong-Kong. L'illustration est pour moi un bon moyen pour communiquer et m'exprimer auprès des autres. »

„Hongkong: eine sich rasant verändernde Stadt, die Erinnerung an verlorene Dinge. Diese Gedanken brachten mich dazu, diese Reihe zu malen. Die Ideen kamen ausschließlich aus meiner Umgebung und meinen Erinnerungen. Die Bilder spiegeln die lebendige Kultur Hongkongs wieder. Durch Illustration kann ich mit anderen Menschen kommunizieren und mich ausdrücken."

4

5

6

7

4 Beancurd Shop, 2006, personal work
5 Midnight Playgound, 2003, personal work
6 Outside the Workshop, 2006, personal work
7 Smoking area, 2003, personal work

MONSIEUR Z

NAME Monsieur Z
WEBSITE www.monsieurz.com
LOCATION France

AGENT 1 Agent 002, Paris, <www.agent002.com>
AGENT 2 Traffic Creative Managment, New York, <www.trafficnyc.com>
AGENT 3 UA-NET, Tokyo, <www.ua-net.com>

TOOLS Pen, Pencil, Adobe Illustrator
CLIENTS Wallpaper, Vogue (Japan), Esquire, Elle, BMW, Evian, G by Guess, Bernardaud, McDonald's, Air France, UNICEF, Renault

1

2

1 Piscine, 2005, personal work
2 Steiner House, 2006, personal work

"Monsieur Z has a trend setting visual identity, with a sophistication that tries to reflect the aesthetic of high lifestyle design on the contemporary world."

« Monsieur Z affiche une identité visuelle innovatrice, dont la sophistication veut être le reflet de l'esthétique du mode de vie des classes privilégiées sur le monde actuel. »

„Monsieur Z besitzt eine trendsetzende visuelle Identität, die versucht, mit großer Ausgefeiltheit die Ästhetik von hochwertigem Lifestyle-Design wiederzuspiegeln."

3

3 BMW, 2005, BMW
4 Brasilia, 2006, personal work
5 Bernardaud, 2005, Bernardaud

5

4

MARCO ZAMORA

NAME Marco Zamora
WEBSITE www.rtystapparel.com
LOCATION Pomona, CA, USA

AGENT Munson Ind., Venice, CA
TOOLS Ink, gesso, wood, paper, Adobe Illustrator, Adobe Photoshop

CLIENTS Vans, Toyota

1 Dreamer, 2007, personal work
2 Searching For Love #1, 2007, personal work
3 Paletas, 2007, personal work
4 The Day Dreamer, 2007, Yaris / Toyota

3

1

2

"Using the paintbrush and pen to draw, Marco develops imagery about urban landscapes and the people that inhabit them. Producing a richly complex and experimental image, Marco goes into a neighbourhood and shoots a spot, recontextualizing and collaging figures to create each painting's identity."

« Muni d'un pinceau et d'un crayon, Marco crée des images sur les paysages urbains et les personnes qui les habitent. Auteur de créations très sophistiquées et expérimentales, il va dans un quartier et photographie un endroit, puis change le contexte et colle des personnages afin que chaque tableau ait sa propre identité. »

„Marco entwickelt mit Pinsel und Stift Bilder von urbanen Landschaften und den Menschen, die sie bewohnen. Marco fotografiert in bestimmten Stadtteilen und setzt die Figuren aus den Fotos dann neu zusammen, um die Identität eines Bildes zu schaffen. So entstehen sehr komplexe und experimentelle Bilder."

"commemorative sxsw 2007 poster, courtesy of yaris"

ZED

NAME Zed
WEBSITE www.zedonline.com.br
LOCATION Sao Paulo, Brazil

AGENT 1 Heflinreps, New York,
<www.heflinreps.com>
AGENT 2 Flair, Sao Paulo, <www.flairbr.com>
TOOLS Adobe Illustrator

CLIENTS Fast Company, People, Mixte, Plenty,
Self, Playboy, MTV, Pearson Longman, GE,
Snecma-Sagem, Coca-Cola
AWARDS HQMix

3

1 Animal Farm, 2005, Quatro Rodas Magazine
2 Tricky, 2002, Simples Magazine
3 Narciso De Janeiro, 2005, Mixt(e) Magazine

2

"A powerful illustration must hit the viewer in the guts and leave them not knowing what did it. Only many years of lustful devotion on drawing and an addictive relationship with the use of colors can bring along such ability. The highest goal for any illustrator should be to excite someone's senses to the point of causing a mental orgasm."

« Une illustration puissante doit remuer les tripes du public sans qu'il comprenne comment c'est arrivé. Seules de nombreuses années de dévotion avide passées à dessiner et un penchant très marqué pour les couleurs peuvent donner ce résultat. L'objectif suprême de tout illustrateur doit être d'éveiller les sens du public au point de lui provoquer un orgasme mental. »

„Eine starke Illustration muss den Betrachter in der Magengrube treffen. Das gelingt nur nach Jahren lustvoller Hingabe ans Zeichnen und einer süchtig machenden Beziehung zu Farben. Das höchste Ziel eines Illustrator sollte es sein, die Sinne des Betrachters an den Rand eines mentalen Orgasmus zu bringen."

ZELOOT

NAME Zeloot
WEBSITE www.zeloot.nl

LOCATION Den Haag, The Netherlands
TOOLS Pencil, pen, Adobe Photoshop, silkscreen

CLIENTS Sub Pop, Heineken, Holland Herald

"Colour and movement are two strong characteristics of Zeelot, taking illustration geometry to a new vision."

« La couleur et le mouvement sont deux grandes caractéristiques de Zeloot, qui donne à l'illustration et à la géométrie une nouvelle vision. »

„Farbe und Bewegung sind zwei Hauptmerkmale im Werk von Zeelot, die Illustration und Geometrie eine neue Vision geben."

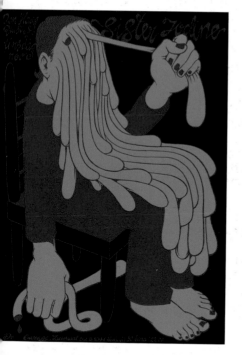

1 Untitled, 2005, poster, De Garage
2 Untitled, 2006, poster, De Garage
3 Untitled, 2007, poster, Size Records

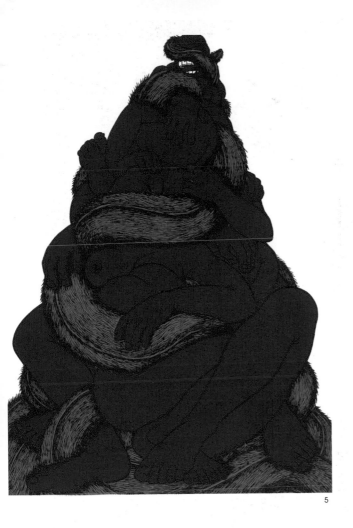

5

6

4-5 Untitled, 2006, poster, De Garage
6 Untitled, 2005, free work, Bongoût
7 Untitled, 2006, poster, Helbaard
8 Untitled, 2007, CD/LP cover, Textile Records

7

8

ACKNOWLEDGEMENTS   REMERCIEMENTS   DANKSAGUNG

First and foremost, my sincere thanks go to Daniel Siciliano Bretas. Daniel worked tirelessly on the design and layout, paying meticulous attention to detail and delivering the final proofs in record time. Huge thanks to you Daniel. My other big thanks, of course, go to all the illustrators for supplying the most astonishing work and for constantly feeding back with us in order to improve the end result. I would also like to express my deep gratitude to Steven Heller, who worked closely with us to select a truly diverse showcase of creative talent. Your vast knowledge of illustration is unsurpassed. Pairing up with Steven in our introduction is star illustrator Christoph Niemann, whose profound and insightful comments illuminate this subject. Big thanks to you both. On our production front, Stefan Klatte has done an amazing job from beginning to end. Through his valiant efforts we were, as always, able to optimize each step of the production process, improving the quality along the way. I would also like to acknowledge all the illustrators' agents, who were always on hand to lend us their support. Last but not least, thanks to Andy Disl and Birgit Reber for their expert touch on the overall design during the final weeks of production.

JULIUS WIEDEMANN

© 2007 TASCHEN GmbH
Hohenzollernring 53, D-50672 Köln
www.taschen.com

To stay informed about upcoming TASCHEN titles,
please request our magazine at www.taschen.com/magazine
or write to TASCHEN, Hohenzollernring 53, D-50672 Cologne,
Germany, contact@taschen.com, Fax: +49-221-254919.
We will be happy to send you a free copy of our magazine
which is filled with information about all of our books.

Page 4: "If you could do anything tomorrow,
I would spend more time with Suki", 2007 © Billie Jean
Pages 24-25: "Water", Avene Japan, 2005 © Clarissa Tossin
Page 478: "Meta", Beef Magazine, 2007 © Monika Aichele

Design: Sense/Net, Andy Disl and Birgit Reber, Cologne
& Daniel Siciliano Brêtas
Layout: Birgit Reber & Daniel Siciliano Brêtas
Production: Stefan Klatte

Editor: Julius Wiedemann
Editorial Coordination: Daniel Siciliano Brêtas

French Translation: Valérie Lavoyer & Aurélie Daniel
German Translation: Ronit Jariv

Printed in Italy
ISBN 978-3-8228-3016-1

All trademarks and images that appear or are related to the
artwork featured in this book belong to their respective artists
and/or companies that commissioned the work and/or feature
herein. TASCHEN is not responsible when a website has been
put offline, doesn't work anymore, or has any incompatibility
with the system accessing it.